TOPCIMA

Paper P10

Test of Professional Competence in Management Accounting

CIMA Study Text

KAPLAN PUBLISHING

British Library Cataloguing-in-Publication Data

A catalogue record for this book is available from the British Library.

Kaplan Publishing UK

Unit 2 The Business Centre

Molly Millars Lane,

Wokingham,

Berkshire,

RG41 2QZ

ISBN 978 1 84710 685 8

Printed and bound in Great Britain.

Acknowledgements

We are grateful to the Chartered Institute of Management Accounting for permission to reproduce past examination questions. The answers have been prepared by Kaplan Publishing.

We are grateful to the Chartered Institute of Management Accounting for permission to reproduce extracts from their ethical guidelines.

Introduction

The TOPCIMA (Test of Professional Competence in Management Accounting) is a new final assessment. It is based upon a case study and set within a simulated business context. TOPCIMA has no specific syllabus content (material from any part of the syllabus could be potentially relevant). The assessment format of this exam is unique too: pre-seen material is published in advance with the question and new unseen material provided in the exam.

This Study Text has been written to produce an interactive text that will help you to prepare successfully for your final CIMA examination.

Section A introduces the process and principles of the TOPCIMA case.

Section B is a detailed walkthrough, using the March 2007 exam for the Flyqual case, to illustrate the techniques involved.

Sections C and D have additional real exams for further practice.

Where sample solutions are provided, they must be viewed as just one interpretation of the case. Remember that there is no single 'correct' solution. Your own answer might reach different conclusions, and give greater emphasis to some issues and less emphasis to others.

Contents

Learning aims and rationale

Learning aims

The aim of the Test of Professional Competence in Management Accounting (TOPCIMA) is to test the capabilities and competence of students, to ensure that they:

A have a sound technical knowledge of the specific subjects within the curriculum

B can apply technical knowledge in an analytical and practical manner

C can extract, from various subjects, the knowledge required to solve many-sided or complex problems

D can solve a particular problem by distinguishing the relevant information from the irrelevant, in a given body of data

E can, in multi-problem situations, identify the problems and rank them in the order in which they need to be addressed

F appreciate that there can be alternative solutions and understand the role of judgement in dealing with them

G can integrate diverse areas of knowledge and skills

H can communicate effectively with users, by formulating realistic recommendations, in a concise and logical fashion

I can identify, advise on and/or resolve ethical dilemmas.

The Test of Professional Competence in Management Accounting (TOPCIMA) comprises a case study that requires students to primarily apply strategic management accounting techniques to make and support decisions within a simulated business context.

Rationale

The TOPCIMA will provide an integrated test of syllabus content that is mainly included within the three Strategic level papers. However, it will also draw upon content covered within the six Managerial level papers.

The TOPCIMA will require the student to deal with material in less structured situations than those encountered in previous Strategic level papers, and to integrate a variety of tools in arriving at a recommended solution. It is unlikely that there will be a single right answer to a complex business problem and students will be expected to recognise the possible alternatives in dealing with a problem.

The emphasis will be on assessing candidates' capabilities and competence in the practical use of appropriate, relevant knowledge, the ability to demonstrate the application of the higher level skills of synthesis, analysis and evaluation, and skill in effectively presenting and communicating information to users.

A – Preparatory to the TOPCIMA exam

- Analyse and identify the current position of the organisation.
- Analyse and identify the relevant problems facing the organisation

Note: Activities undertaken using published 'pre-seen' case study materials.

B – TOPCIMA exam

- Appraise possible feasible courses of action available.
- Evaluate and then choose specific proposals.
- Identify and evaluate priorities related to the proposals.
- Recommend a course of action.
- Prepare and present information in a format suitable for presentation to senior management.

The examination

Assessment strategy

The Test of Professional Competence provides a final test and can be taken only after all the Strategic level subjects have been successfully completed.

There will be a written TOPCIMA examination paper of three hours (and 20 minutes reading time), with a limited number of questions (requirements). They will normally be answered using the form of a report and/or presentation, with supporting documents, to a variety of users. The questions will be based upon a case study, which will be published on the CIMA website, at least six weeks in advance of the examination. This will provide sufficient time before the examination to allow the student to undertake preparatory analysis based upon the pre-seen material. Further information regarding the case will be added as part of the examination paper.

As a guide to the volume of material within the case, it is likely to be between 8 and 20 sides of A4, published in advance of the exam and up to six sides of A4 contained within the examination paper.

Questions will test the students' capabilities and competence in the application of appropriate knowledge and the processes undertaken in dealing with the problems identified in the examination, together with their ability to present and communicate information.

Maths tables and formulae

Present value of £1 i.e. $(1 + r)^{-n}$ where r = interest rate, n = number of periods until payment or receipt.

Periods (n)	Interest rates (r)									
	1%	2%	3%	4%	5%	6%	7%	8%	9%	10%
1	.990	.980	.971	.962	.962	.943	.935	.926	.917	.909
2	.980	.961	.943	.925	.907	.890	.873	.857	.842	.826
3	.971	.942	.915	.889	.864	.840	.816	.794	.772	.751
4	.961	.924	.888	.855	.823	.792	.763	.735	.708	.683
5	.951	.906	.863	.822	.784	.747	.713	.681	.650	.621
6	.942	.888	.837	.790	.746	.705	.666	.630	.596	.564
7	.933	.871	.813	.760	.711	.665	.623	.583	.547	.513
8	.923	.853	.789	.731	.677	.627	.582	.540	.502	.467
9	.914	.837	.766	.703	.645	.592	.544	.500	.460	.424
10	.905	.820	.744	.676	.614	.558	.508	.463	.422	.386
11	.896	.804	.722	.650	.585	.527	.475	.429	.388	.350
12	.887	.788	.701	.625	.557	.497	.444	.397	.356	.319
13	.879	.773	.681	.601	.530	.469	.415	.368	.326	.290
14	.870	.758	.661	.577	.505	.442	.388	.340	.299	.263
15	.861	.743	.642	.555	.481	.417	.362	.315	.275	.239
16	.853	.728	.623	.534	.458	.394	.339	.292	.252	.218
17	.844	.714	.605	.513	.436	.371	.317	.270	.231	.198
18	.836	.700	.587	.494	.416	.350	.296	.250	.212	.180
19	.828	.686	.570	.475	.396	.331	.277	.232	.194	.164
20	.820	.673	.554	.456	.377	.312	.258	.215	.178	.149

Periods (n)	Interest rates (r)									
	11%	12%	13%	14%	15%	16%	17%	18%	19%	20%
1	.901	.893	.885	.877	.870	.862	.855	.847	.840	.833
2	.812	.797	.783	.769	.756	.743	.731	.718	.706	.694
3	.731	.712	.693	.675	.658	.641	.624	.609	.593	.579
4	.659	.636	.613	.592	.572	.552	.534	.516	.499	.482
5	.593	.567	.543	.519	.497	.476	.456	.437	.419	.402
6	.535	.507	.480	.456	.432	.410	.390	.370	.352	.335
7	.482	.452	.425	.400	.376	.354	.333	.314	.296	.279
8	.434	.404	.376	.351	.327	.305	.285	.266	.249	.233
9	.391	.361	.333	.308	.284	.263	.243	.225	.209	.194
10	.352	.322	.295	.270	.247	.227	.208	.191	.176	.162
11	.317	.287	.261	.237	.215	.195	.178	.162	.148	.135
12	.286	.257	.231	.208	.187	.168	.152	.137	.124	.112
13	.258	.229	.204	.182	.163	.145	.130	.116	.104	.093
14	.232	.205	.181	.160	.141	.125	.111	.099	.088	.078
15	.209	.183	.160	.140	.123	.108	.095	.084	.074	.065
16	.188	.163	.141	.123	.107	.093	.081	.071	.062	.054
17	.170	.146	.125	.108	.093	.080	.069	.060	.052	.045
18	.153	.130	.111	.095	.081	.069	.059	.051	.044	.038
19	.138	.116	.098	.083	.070	.060	.051	.043	.037	.031
20	.124	.104	.087	.073	.061	.051	.043	.037	.031	.026

Cumulative present value of £1

This table shows the Present Value of £1 per annum, Receivable or Payable at the end of each year for n years $\frac{1-(1+r)^{-n}}{r}$

Periods (n)	Interest rates (r)									
	1%	2%	3%	4%	5%	6%	7%	8%	9%	10%
1	0.990	0.980	0.971	0.962	0.952	0.943	0.935	0.926	0.917	0.909
2	1.970	1.942	1.913	1.886	1.859	1.833	1.808	1.783	1.759	1.736
3	2.941	2.884	2.829	2.775	2.723	2.673	2.624	2.577	2.531	2.487
4	3.902	3.808	3.717	3.630	3.546	3.465	3.387	3.312	3.240	3.170
5	4.853	4.713	4.580	4.452	4.329	4.212	4.100	3.993	3.890	3.791
6	5.795	5.601	5.417	5.242	5.076	4.917	4.767	4.623	4.486	4.355
7	6.728	6.472	6.230	6.002	5.786	5.582	5.389	5.206	5.033	4.868
8	7.652	7.325	7.020	6.733	6.463	6.210	5.971	5.747	5.535	5.335
9	8.566	8.162	7.786	7.435	7.108	6.802	6.515	6.247	5.995	5.759
10	9.471	8.983	8.530	8.111	7.722	7.360	7.024	6.710	6.418	6.145
11	10.368	9.787	9.253	8.760	8.306	7.887	7.499	7.139	6.805	8.495
12	11.255	10.575	9.954	9.385	8.863	8.384	7.943	7.536	7.161	6.814
13	12.134	11.348	10.635	9.986	9.394	8.853	8.358	7.904	7.487	7.103
14	13.004	12.106	11.296	10.563	9.899	9.295	8.745	8.244	7.786	7.367
15	13.865	12.849	11.938	11.118	10.380	9.712	9.108	8.559	8.061	7.606
16	14.718	13.578	12.561	11.652	10.838	10.106	9.447	8.851	8.313	7.824
17	15.562	14.292	13.166	12.166	11.274	10.477	9.763	9.122	8.544	8.022
18	16.398	14.992	13.754	12.659	11.690	10.828	10.059	9.372	8.756	8.201
19	17.226	15.679	14.324	13.134	12.085	11.158	10.336	9.604	8.950	8.365
20	18.046	16.351	14.878	13.590	12.462	11.470	10.594	9.818	9.129	8.514

Periods (n)	Interest rates (r)									
	11%	12%	13%	14%	15%	16%	17%	18%	19%	20%
1	0.901	0.893	0.885	0.877	0.870	0.862	0.862	0.847	0.840	0.833
2	1.713	1.690	1.668	1.647	1.626	1.605	1.585	1.566	1.547	1.528
3	2.444	2.402	2.361	2.322	2.283	2.246	2.210	2.174	2.140	2.106
4	3.102	3.037	2.974	2.914	2.855	2.798	2.743	2.690	2.639	2.589
5	3.696	3.605	3.517	3.433	3.352	3.274	3.199	3.127	3.058	2.991
6	4.231	4.111	3.998	3.889	3.784	3.685	3.589	3.498	3.410	3.326
7	4.712	4.564	4.423	4.288	4.160	4.039	3.922	3.812	3.706	3.605
8	5.146	4.968	4.799	4.639	4.487	4.344	4.207	4.078	3.954	3.837
9	5.537	5.328	5.132	4.946	4.772	4.607	4.451	4.303	4.163	4.031
10	5.889	5.650	5.426	5.216	5.019	4.833	4.659	4.494	4.339	4.192
11	6.207	5.938	5.687	5.453	5.234	5.029	4.836	4.656	4.486	4.327
12	6.492	6.194	5.918	5.660	5.421	5.197	4.968	4.793	4.611	4.439
13	6.750	6.424	6.122	5.842	5.583	5.342	5.118	4.910	4.715	4.533
14	6.982	6.628	6.302	6.002	5.724	5.468	5.229	5.008	4.802	4.611
15	7.191	6.811	6.462	6.142	5.847	5.575	5.324	5.092	4.876	4.675
16	7.379	6.974	6.604	6.265	5.954	5.668	5.405	5.162	4.938	4.730
17	7.549	7.120	6.729	6.373	6.047	5.749	5.475	5.222	4.990	4.775
18	7.702	7.250	6.840	6.467	6.128	5.818	5.534	5.273	5.033	4.812
19	7.839	7.366	6.938	6.550	6.198	5.877	5.584	5.316	5.070	4.843
20	7.963	7.469	7.025	6.623	6.259	5.929	5.628	5.353	5.101	4.870

chapter

1

INTRODUCING THE CASE STUDY

Contents

1 Learning aims for TOPCIMA

The syllabus states that the Test of Professional Competence in Management Accounting (TOPCIMA) requires candidates to apply mainly strategic management accounting techniques to make and support decisions within a case study (a simulated business context). CIMA wishes to assess:

- your possession of the higher skills of synthesis, analysis and evaluation, in addition to
- your technical knowledge of management accounting, and
- your skill in presenting and communicating information to users.

The TOPCIMA case study is therefore an attempt to simulate workplace problem solving. This allows examiners to move one step closer to the assessment of competence than is possible with essay-style questions.

Since the examination tests your higher level skills, preparing for this examination needs to be different from studying for a 'traditional' examination paper. The purpose of this study text is to suggest how you might prepare for the examination by developing and practising your skills.

2 How the case study examination works

The TOPCIMA exam is a written examination paper of three hours. Candidates cannot take the examination until they have successfully completed all the 'strategic' level subjects: Risk and Control Strategy, Business Strategy and Financial Strategy.

The exam is based on:

- pre-seen material issued in advance of the exam day, supplemented by
- additional, previously unseen material given to you in the exam room.

There will be a limited number of questions or requirements relating to this material. You will probably be required to answer the questions by presenting a report (but possibly another form of document) to one or more users of the information.

For this purpose, you will be required to present your answer in the role of a professional adviser, such as a management consultant or a newly appointed management accountant.

The pre-seen material is an extended scenario consisting of 15 to 20 pages of information about a business organisation. It is made available at least six weeks before the examination, to give you the opportunity for familiarisation and analysis, and is published on the CIMA website. You therefore have at least six weeks to study the pre-seen material and you should spend as much time as you can doing this, taking notes, analysing the information, doing background reading and research, and revising any technical topics that you think might be relevant.

You cannot take your copy of the pre-seen material, nor any notes or calculations that you have made relating to the material into the examination. Similarly, you will not be allowed to take in any textbook. Normal 'closed book' examination conditions will apply.

In the examination room you will be supplied with a fresh booklet containing the pre-seen material and the unseen material. The unseen material will be up to six pages in length. The pre-seen material might also be altered, for example by including more up-to-date figures in an appendix. When this happens, the examination paper will indicate where the pre-seen material has been changed.

Tables, such as discount tables, will be provided where appropriate.

Typically, the questions in the examination will require you to demonstrate your ability to assess and evaluate the strategic and financial position of the organisation in the case study, and to recommend suitable courses of action to deal with the issues involved. There will not be a 'correct' or 'incorrect' answer, but you will be expected to identify the key issues from the material provided, and to use your judgement in making recommendations, with suitable reasons.

3 The pre-seen material

CIMA releases the pre-seen material at least six weeks before the examination. This is posted on the student area of the CIMA website (www.cimaglobal.com) and it is your responsibility to download it and to print off a copy. Candidates without access to download and printing facilities can ask CIMA to post them a copy.

The pre-seen material is an introductory scenario to set the scene for the case study, together with accounting and financial information. Much of the financial information will probably be in the form of appendices to the main text, but the main text of the pre-seen might include some figures too.

The purpose of giving you access to this information in advance of the exam is to enable you to study, analyse and become very familiar with the organisation(s) and industry described.

This should incorporate the following:

- researching the industry involved
- detailed paragraph-by-paragraph analysis
- overall position analysis, incorporating a SWOT
- ratio analysis of financial statements and financial plans
- additional business strategy analysis, including generation of strategic options
- additional financial strategy analysis, including how the business is financed, how future finance could be raised and valuation techniques
- risk and control analysis to identify key risk areas, presence and suitability of management controls and performance measures.

4 The unseen material

In the examination room, you will be provided with:

- a clean copy of the pre-seen material incorporating the further pages of the unseen material
- the questions or requirements
- two blank answer booklets.

You will be required to present your answers in the main answer booklet, and you may use the supplementary booklet for any appendices or workings, if you wish. If you use the supplementary answer booklet for presenting appendices, you should make sure that they are clearly labelled and neatly presented.

The unseen material will be a continuation of the pre-seen and will usually bring the scenario up to date.

In many cases there is a 'twist' in the unseen i.e. a development that most students would not have anticipated from the pre-seen.

A common mistake made by weaker students is that they place too much emphasis on their analysis of the pre-seen material and do not develop the information in the unseen material adequately. Both are important, but the unseen material usually gives the strongest lead on identifying key issues to discuss in your answer.

5 Feedback from CIMA lecturers' conferences

The main points of note for TOPCIMA that arose from CIMA lecturers' conferences are as follows:

Prioritisation

- Each of the last seven diets has contained a very similar question:
  - identify and prioritise key issues
  - discuss the key issues
  - make appropriate recommendations on the key issues.

  So identifying the key issues is thus the critical success factor.
- Key issues were described as those that 'could have a substantial effect on the company's future success or even its very survival'.
- It was also stressed that students need to justify their prioritisation more e.g. a cash shortfall in the November 2005 case should be one of the top two issues as Domusco could become bankrupt if it continues to spend as planned.
- All of the key issues should also be in the SWOT.
- Each of the top five issues should be 'thoroughly discussed'.

Pre-seen v unseen material

- One of the problems identified was that students rely too much on themes identified in the pre-seen material and do not spend enough time identifying themes in the unseen material. In particular students often seem unprepared/unwilling/unable to cope with the 'twist'.
- Too many students put in pre-prepared analysis whether useful or not.
- Students need to have the confidence to … be able to adapt (or discard) ideas and pre-prepared material if it is no longer relevant.

Calculations

- There will only be up to 10 marks maximum available for calculations. Some students are spending far too long on lengthy analysis. 'They can pass TOPCIMA with no numbers at all.'

Exam technique

- Students were advised to:
  - list the new topics, and then
  - identify which are the really critical key issues, and then
  - prioritise them,
  - discuss them, and
  - make justified recommendations on them.

  'Then they should pass.'
- Some students seem to forget that TOPCIMA is a strategy exam:

  The company needs a clear, focused report that has identified key, critical issues and makes appropriate well-justified recommendations on its future strategic direction.

chapter

2

ASSESSMENT AND KEY SKILLS

Contents

1 The assessment criteria and marking process

1.1 Recap of the strategic planning process

From your studies in P6 (Management Accounting – Business Strategy) you will recall the three stage planning model of Johnson, Scholes and Whittington ("JSW"):

Strategic analysis

- External analysis to identify opportunities and threats
- Internal analysis to identify strengths and weaknesses
- Stakeholder analysis to identify key objectives and to assess power and interest of different groups
- Gap analysis to identify the difference between desired and expected performance.

↓

Strategic choice

- Strategies are required to "close the gap"
- Choices need to be made with respect to
  - Competitive strategy – for each business unit
  - Directions for growth – which markets / products should be invested in / divested from
  - Whether expansion should be achieved by organic growth, acquisition or some joint arrangement.
- Strategies can be evaluated using suitability / feasibility / acceptability criteria

↓

Strategic implementation

- Formulation of detailed plans and budgets – both short term and long term
- Implications for functional strategies – e.g. HRM, IT
- Monitoring and control implications – e.g.Target setting for KPIs

This is a useful model for understanding the TOPCIMA exam and the marking process and criteria.

1.2. What CIMA expect from you in the exam

CIMA have given the following guidance on passing the TOPCIMA exam:

> In order to succeed in TOPCIMA, you, in your role as consultant to an organisation, need to:
>
> 1. Use analytical techniques to help you analyse the issues in the unseen with relevant reference to the pre-seen material and the industry setting as well as real life parallels of the issues; you will also need to apply your technical knowledge.
> 2. Prioritise the issues and discuss the impact these issues may have on the organisation; you will then need to suggest a range of alternative actions that the organisation could undertake to address the issues. You will need to discuss the impact these issues may have on the organisation. In doing this, you also need to recognise any relevant ethical implications of the issues.
> 3. Make recommendations to whoever has commissioned your report on your choice of action for each issue from the alternative actions discussed earlier.

Note that these three stages do not match exactly against the JSW three stage process but the similarities make the comparison useful.

1.3 Marking criteria

Marks are awarded for fulfilling each of the three stages according to the criteria shown below.

Analysis of issues (typically around 25 marks)

- Technical (5)
- Application (15)
- Diversity (5)

Strategic choices (typically around 40 marks)

- Focus (5)
- Prioritisation (10)
- Judgement (20)
- Ethics (5)

Recommendations (typically around 35 marks)

- Logic (20)
- Ethics (5)
- Integration (10)

These are discussed in more detail below.

2 Technical skills

The aim of this part of the assessment is to test whether you 'have a sound technical knowledge of the specific subjects of the curriculum'.

2.1 CIMA Guidance

Use relevant theoretical techniques and frameworks and perform relevant calculations to help you to analyse the case material and support your arguments.

2.2 Interpretation / exam technique

The way to score highly for technical skills is to use at least three, but preferably, five different techniques or models in your answer.

A typical report should thus contain the following:

- a SWOT analysis, summarising the strategic position of the firm
- key ratios calculated and discussed
- up to three other techniques, specially selected for their relevance to the case (see Chapter 4 for a revision of such techniques).

In practice you may not feel that it is appropriate to show a Porter's five forces analysis, say, explicitly and would rather put just the key issues identified through such a model into your report. However, in the TOPCIMA exam, it is vital that you show the marker that you are using a range of techniques, with their appropriate labels.

Assuming a total of 5 marks for technical skills in the matrix, you could expect to score a mark per technique for appropriate (i.e. relevant) use.

3 Application skills

The aim here is to test whether you have the ability to 'apply technical knowledge in an analytical and practical manner'.

Marks will be awarded for the way in which technical knowledge is used in application to the case study and the requirements of the question(s).

3.1 CIMA Guidance

Use the techniques, frameworks and calculations you have produced to support your analysis of the issues and your choices of actions.

3.2 Interpretation / exam technique

To some degree, the marks you earn here will be dictated by how many techniques and models you have used. If you have only used two techniques, say, then you are limited to only two techniques' worth of application.

Assuming a total of 15 marks, for application you should expect to be able to score up to 3 marks per technique for good application to the case.

To ensure that you get 3 marks rather than 1, ensure that you link the analysis to the key issues in the case. For example, you should interpret any ratios calculated rather than just leaving them as figures in an appendix.

If performing calculations, then try to keep them as simple as possible without trivialising them. While the marks they earn will impact other assessment criteria, it is unlikely they will be worth more than 10 marks in total.

4 Diversity

The aim here is to test whether you can bring in real-world commercial considerations into your discussion.

You will be awarded marks for the breadth of knowledge you demonstrate in your answer.

4.1 CIMA Guidance

Display knowledge of relevant real life situations within the same or similar context as that in which the case is set. Additionally, display knowledge of real life commercial or organisational issues relevant to the situation in the case. These may occur in the industry or organisational setting in which the case is set or in different industires or settings.

4.2 Interpretation / Exam technique

As well as including different technical areas, most students can earn extra diversity marks by incorporating two aspects in your answer:

- Incorporate three facts you have researched regarding the industry concerned. These could include the activities and strategies of real-life firms, recent trends and critical success factors.
- If the unseen material suggests a possible strategy, then bring in pre-learnt details of the practicalities of such strategies. For example, if a joint venture is put forward as a possible strategy for the firm, then you could suggest something along the lines of: 'In situations such as this, the key areas of negotiation are normally the sharing out of risks and rewards,...'

5 Focus skills

The aim of focus is to test whether you have the ability to 'solve a particular problem by distinguishing the relevant information from the irrelevant in a given body of knowledge'.

You will be rewarded for your ability to focus on the issues in the question, and use what is relevant but ignore what is not relevant.

5.1 CIMA Guidance

Select the issues you feel to be the most important and make sure that you properly address these issues in the report you produce.

5.2 Interpretation / exam technique

The main mistake students make with focus is to confuse it with prioritisation, below. Focus is not looking at which issues you have decided to put as major headings in your report. Rather it looks at whether you had addressed the main themes under these headings. For example, brand strength may be a key underlying theme that gets discussed under each of your prioritized "issues" but is not an issue as such in your report. If in doubt, use the headings given in the unseen to determine your "issues" but make sure key themes are brought in wherever appropriate. This should also allow some linking together of issues in your recommendations.

6 Prioritisation skills

The aim of prioritisation is to test whether you have the ability to 'in multi-problem situations, identify the problems and rank them in the order in which they need to be addressed'.

Rewarding candidates for their ability to prioritise the issues, and to recognise what problems are more important than others, was a regular feature of the case study under the 'old syllabus' and remains important.

6.1 CIMA Guidance

Rank the key issues, stating clearly and concisely your rationale to justify your ranking. Issues should be given high priority primarily because of their impact on the organisation in the case. Their urgency may also be a factor. Also, state the issues that you feel deserve a lower priority ranking and give your reasons.

6.2 Interpretation / exam technique

Prioritisation is possibly the most important skill within TOPCIMA, so ensure you spend sufficient time thinking about your answer.

- Start by identifying your top five issues. This should be based on a mixture of criteria including urgency, size and impact on the strategic goals of the organisation.
- With issue number 1 describe it as your 'top priority' and justify why it is the most important. Repeat with the rest of your top issues.
- Ensure that the order within each section of your report reflects your prioritisation.
- Ensure that you devote more time and space to your discussion of issue 1 than to issue 2 and so on.
- If you have done the prioritisation early enough or are sitting the computer-based case, then order your SWOT to reflect the order of prioritisation.

7 Judgement

The aim of the criterion is to test whether you have the ability to 'appreciate that there can be alternative solutions and understand the role of judgement in dealing with them'. Judgement' might be defined as 'informed common sense'.

7.1 CIMA Guidance

Exercise commercial and professional judgement to discuss the key issues. Discuss the impact the priority issues have on the organisation. Discuss alternative courses of action, with reasons, that the organisation could take to resolve these issues. Your analysis should include relevant supporting financial analysis.

7.2 Interpretation / exam technique

Judgement marks are likely to focus purely on the identified top five issues. For each of these your analysis should incorporate the following:

- The significance of the issue
- Alternatives to the suggested course of action and why they have been discounted
- Arguments for and against each option.

When doing this, try to incorporate any key figures and real-life business awareness points as well as points extracted from the material.

8 Ethics

To all strategic decisions there is an ethical dimension. Business is about compromise and, necessarily, someone must benefit at the expense of another. This criterion rewards you for recognising the ethical issues and, if appropriate, recommending action. Ethics is a broad topic, and you should consider whether the following different aspects are relevant to the case:

- Personal and professional ethics, as you will often be acting the role of a newly qualified Chartered Management Accountant and manager.
- Business ethics, as you will be acting as part of an organisation, or as an advisor to it.
- Corporate Governance, as strategic decisions have an impact on the stakeholders of the organisation.
- Social responsibility, as strategic decisions often impact on the world outside the organisation's boundary.

Although the Ethics criterion is shown under both the 'Strategic Choices' and 'Recommendations' section, it is not necessary for your discussion of ethical issues to be split in this way within your report. If you choose to do so, it is quite acceptable for the ethical issues contained in the case to be discussed within a single section of your report. You should take into account when you discuss ethical issues that some of them may impact on your discussion uner the Judgement and Logic criteria.

8.1 CIMA Guidance

Using your judgement, highlight and analyse the ethical issues in the case and state why you consider these issues to have ethical iplications. Discuss alternative courses of action that the organisation could take to resolve the issues.

Make clear, well justified recommendations for each of the ethical issues and ensure the reasoning for the recommended courses of action is clearly stated. The recommendations should follow on logically from the weight of the arguements you make in your report.

8.2 Interpretation / exam technique

Some students make the mistake of only discussing ethics if it is considered to be a key issue in the case. Rather ethical issues should be included for **all** cases.

To score high marks for ethics you should thus do the following:

- Identify at least three ethical issues using the types mentioned above – personal and professional ethics, business ethics, corporate governance and social responsibility.
- For each issue, explain why it has an ethical dimension. This could include highlighting the conflicts of interest involved.
- For each issue, suggest what could be done to resolve it.

Ethics now features in Paper P3 of the syllabus but, if you have not studied this area in depth, or have forgotten your earlier studies, a chapter on the CIMA Ethical Guidelines is provided in this text (Chapter 5).

9 Logic

The aim of this part of the assessment matrix is to test whether you have the ability to 'communicate effectively with users by formulating realistic recommendations in a concise and logical fashion'.

The ability to think logically is a prime quality in a management accountant, and you will be awarded marks for your ability to demonstrate logical thinking and a logical approach.

Throughout your answer, the content should be structured in such a way that the arguments you put forward lead logically to your conclusions and recommendations. Failure to provide recommendations really makes your answer a waste of time, and would not to gain much credit on this criterion.

9.1 CIMA Guidance

Make clear, well justified recommendations for each of the prioritised issues and ensure the reasoning for the recommended courses of action is clearly stated. The recommendations should follow on logically from the weight of the arguements and choices of actions given earlier in the report.

9.2 Interpretation / exam technique

There are two keys to scoring high logic marks:

- Ensure that clear, well-argued recommendations are made for each key issue.
- Where alternatives have not been recommended, give your justification why.

Note that the skills of judgement, integration and logic are very much linked and are essentially marks for your ability to reach a professional judgement and communicate your views in a realistic and logical manner.

You are also encouraged to communicate in a 'concise' manner. The marker will not give you credit for writing at unnecessary length. The suggested solutions provided later in this text are probably longer than most students would be able to manage in a three-hour examination.

10 Integration

The aim of this criterion is to test whether you have the ability to 'integrate diverse areas of knowledge and skills'. In order to produce a professional business report.

You should demonstrate good communication skills. This means that the language you use should be professional and appropriate, avoiding slang and being appropriately formal. You should also produce a business document, normally a report or a presentation, which has the appropriate format and content. This is a type of business communication criterion, and will reward you for preparing a report that follows all points logically through, from identification of a weakness to the selected and recommended course of action.

A CIMA spokesperson has said that 'this is about the "balance" in the script and how "holistic" the answer is'.

10.1 CIMA Guidance

Produce a well-structured report in an appropriate format and linguistic style. (3) These marks are awarded holistically according to the overall quality and functionality of your report. (7)

10.2 Interpretation / Exam technique

Many students struggle to understand what integration is really looking for. The marker will be looking at the report as a whole, rather than at just one section and will be concerned that:

- Final recommendations are consistent with the main body of analysis, which in turn is consistent with key prioritised issues, which in turn are consistent with the SWOT analysis. For example, if a key issue discussed later on is not in the SWOT then you will be marked down on integration.
- The report flows well.
- All key issues identified are discussed in sufficient detail and result in recommendations being made.

  For example, some students identify five key issues but only make clear recommendations on three of them. This is usually due to poor time allocation. It is better to discuss issues in less depth if it results in a better balanced report that is 'finished'.

The higher-skills aspect of integration is to look at each of the key issues and consider the overall balance and fit of the strategies concerned. For example, three strategies may be proposed, each of which has sufficient merit to recommend accepting them. However, the firm may be experiencing capital rationing and so could only undertake one. Identifying this problem and discussing how to proceed would score highly on integration.

Note that, due to the nature of this skill, markers' views will tend to be polarised so your script is either good or bad with few scripts earning middle marks.

11 Summary

The above comments can be summarised into the following generic grid. Note: the distribution of marks is variable.

Criterion (marks)	What you need to do
Technical (5)	Prepare appendices or use key techniques. A SWOT should be the starting point. Other examples: ratios, Ansoff, PEST, Porter's five forces, Porter's generic strategies, BCG, Product lifecycle, balanced scorecard, NPV calculation, suitability/feasibility/acceptability, etc.
Application (15)	Use/apply the above techniques / technical knowledge. Prepare relevant calculations.
Diversity (5)	Show business awareness for both the industry dealt with in the scenario and situations and events that impact a business in general e.g. franchising, acquisitions, etc.
Focus (5)	Select relevant key themes for discussion. These themes will be drawn from both the unseen and the preseen information.
Prioritisation (10)	Using your SWOT, identify five key issues. Following the approach: • Clearly identify the issue • Justify the prioritisation of the issue. You must ensure it is CLEAR that you have prioritised: 'The following key issues identified from the SWOT analysis identified in Appendix x have been prioritised in the following order.' 'The main priority is.....' These issues will mainly be from the unseen information.
Judgement (20)	Discussion of the five key areas in greater detail. Assess the significance of each of the issues

	Evaluate any options and consider alternative solutions or actions.
Ethics (5 + 5)	Identify an ethical issue. Explain/justify the issue. Offer advice. To highlight this area show ethics as a separate section of the report and do the recommendations here rather than in the recommendations section.
Logic (20)	Clear recommendations should be given for the five key areas first and then any other areas discussed in the report. Avoid recommendations without prior discussion.
Integration (10)	Does the report cover the main issues and flow from identification to recommendation? Prioritised Discussed Evaluated Recommendations Did you follow the guidelines on report structure?

chapter

3

REPORT WRITING

Contents

1 Report contents

The unseen information usually asks you to prepare a report that

- prioritises, and
- discusses the issues facing the company, and
- makes appropriate recommendations.

It is thus vital that your report is structured to clearly separate these three steps.

While many different report formats are used in practice, we recommend that you use the following format unless you have strong reasons to do otherwise.

1.1 Front sheet

All reports have a front sheet. Yours should contain the following information:

- The word 'report' large and clear on it somewhere
- The recipient of the report e.g. 'To the Directors of X'
- The producer of the report
- Date
- The title of the report
- The status of the report e.g. 'draft', 'confidential'.

1.2 Contents page

A contents page shows the marker how you have structured your report and should help towards integration and logic marks.

A typical report could have the following contents:

1.0 Introduction

2.0 Terms of reference

3.0 Key issues

4.0 – 8.0 Analysis of issues

9.0 Ethical considerations

10.0 Recommendations

11.0 Conclusion

Appendices 1, 2,...

1.3 Introduction

The introduction sets the scene for the report and, to some degree, reveals why the report has been requested. A good introduction can be constructed using three short paragraphs covering the following:

- performance to date, possibly incorporating a key ratio from the very start (e.g. declining margins)
- current position, again possibly incorporating key ratios (e.g. growth rates)
- key challenges and future prospects facing the firm, focussed on the unseen (note: evidence of prioritisation from the beginning).

1.4 Terms of reference (TOR)

The terms of reference section usually answers the 'who, what, why?' of report writing:

- **Who** has asked for the report and who are we?
- **What** have we been asked to do?
- **Why** have we been asked to do it? This looks at the strategic context of the case and has already been partly covered in the introduction

In the real world the terms of reference would also contain any disclaimers the writer wishes to make, for example:

- 'This report is for the sole use of the recipients and no liability is accepted for any losses incurred by any other persons acting upon any information contained herein.'
- 'We have relied on figures provided by the Board of X and our recommendations may have to be revised should any of the figures used prove to be materially inaccurate.'

In the exam these can be shortened to save time.

A typical terms of reference could thus be as follows:

"The purpose of this report is to provide the board of Directors of ======== with a clear picture of the company's position as at ============, in particular to identify and prioritise the main issues facing ========, respond to the issues, assess the opportunities currently available, and make appropriate recommendations.

This report has been prepared by ========= and relies upon information and explanations provided by the board to date and financial information at ===========".

1.5 Identification and prioritisation of key issues

In this section you identify the key issues and explain the basis of your prioritisation. You do not discuss the issues beyond that – detailed analysis and recommendations will be made elsewhere.

Some students get confused by the term 'issues'. This does not necessarily mean problems only but could equally refer to opportunities/proposals. These two types of issue are discussed in more detail below.

This section could begin with a statement linking the key issues to a SWOT analysis. For example:

'A detailed SWOT analysis of the firm has been carried out and is summarised in Appendix 1. Based on this analysis we have prioritised the key issues facing the firm as follows.'

For each key issue you should aim to do the following:

- Identify the issue and explain why it is an issue.
- Justify the basis of your prioritisation. As stated above, this assessment could include reference to the issue's urgency, size and impact on the strategic objectives of the firm.
- State the need for a management decision (in the case of a proposal being evaluated) or for management action to develop a plan (in the case of an identified problem).

Ensure that:

- issues are discussed in order of priority
- all key issues appear in the SWOT analysis in Appendix 1.

You should also include a brief section on other issues to show the examiner that you have thought about them. Such a section could be worded along the lines of

"There are a number of other issues that have not been prioritised as they are not considered to merit the strategic importance of the above priorities within the scope of this report. These are........." These can then be listed in a sentence.

1.6 Main body of the report – analysis of issues

Each of the prioritised issues should have a section of their own. For example:

4 Franchising

5 Loss of major customer

6 etc

Your approach to each section will depend on whether the issue is a proposal to evaluate or a problem to solve.

Problems

- The opening paragraph needs to explain the **extent** of the problem with reference to theory or real-world examples. Numbers should be used to substantiate the extent where applicable.
- Subsequent paragraphs should then deal with what **could** be done i.e. provide alternative solutions, starting with 'do nothing' (used sparingly) and then moving onto other possibilities. No recommendations should be made at this stage.

Proposals

- With proposals the opening paragraph should explain the theoretical backdrop to the proposal – e.g. market development within Ansoff's matrix – and how it applies.
- In addition you could include an explanation of what the proposal is e.g. what franchising involves.
- Numerical references (e.g. possible valuations) can also be included here.
- Subsequent paragraphs could include the advantages and disadvantages of the proposal or an analysis using the suitability/feasibility/acceptability model.
- Again, no recommendations should be made at this stage.

1.7 Ethical issues

One approach for dealing with ethical issues is to discuss them within the context of contrasting stakeholder views (e.g. higher profits may be at the expense of poor working conditions, in which case there is a conflict between shareholders and employees).

The ethics section should thus contain the following:

- An opening paragraph explaining ethics in the context of stakeholders.
- For each ethical issue identify the nature of the issue, explain why it is an ethical issue, highlighting the specific nature of contrasting stakeholder views and make reasonable recommendations.

You should aim to discuss two ethical issues well and a third briefly.

1.8 Recommendations

As with the main body of the report, each of the prioritised issues should have a subsection of their own here.

For each key issue you should aim to address the following:

- What you actually recommend the firm does – don't sit on the fence here! For problems you need to recommend a solution. For proposals you need to recommend whether to accept it or not and, if the latter, suggest alternative courses of action.
- At least two key issues supporting your recommendation.
- Short-term specific actions and longer-term general recommendations.

Remember to incorporate bigger issues at this stage.

For example, preliminary conclusions may be that all proposals are attractive, but you could then bring in issues of capital rationing and suggest which strategy should be undertaken.

According to the examiner: "Business awareness will prevent you from making unrealistic comments and will enhance the commercial and professional judgement that you display throughout the report. The Judgement criterion is the main area of weakness for many candidates. What is required to gain marks is realistic clear discussions and recommendations that are commercially viable and professionally assessed."

1.9 Conclusion

The conclusion is really just finishing off the report in a professional manner in no more than five lines. One approach is as follows:

- Start by restating the key issue(s) facing the firm, as outlined in the introduction.
- Briefly summarise the main recommendations.
- Make a brief comment on the future.

For example:

'In conclusion, the main issues facing X are dealing with competitive rivalry and managing growth. Once the publicity and HR issues are resolved, X should again have a platform for high future growth.'

The conclusion could also be a useful place to mention any further information required and possible further work.

1.10 Appendices

Appendices should be at the back of the report and clearly labelled.

Typically:

- Appendix 1 will be a position analysis using a SWOT.
- Appendix 2 will give key ratios.
- Appendices 3 to 5 will cover other techniques used / calculations.

With calculations you should comment on the method used and any assumptions / limitations of your analysis.

2 Writing style

2.1 Introduction

Writing style is something that develops over time. It is influenced by your education and experiences. To some it comes easily, they enjoy words – but you are not looking to win any prizes in literature.

It's about putting facts, ideas and opinions in a clear, concise, logical fashion.

Some students get very worried about their writing styles. As a general rule you try to write as you would talk.

2.2 Logical flow

A typical point starts with a statement of fact, either given in the case or derived from analysis – 'what?'

This can then be followed by an interpretation – 'so what?'

This can then lead to an implication – 'now what?', or 'what next?'

For example:

1 What? – The NPV is positive.

2 So what? – Suggesting we should go ahead with the project.

3 Now what? – Arrange board meeting to discuss strategic implications .

A similar structure can be obtained using the Socratic approach – what, why, how?

- So what?
- Why should we use it?
- How does it work?

2.3 Who is reading the report?

Failure to pitch the level correctly will inevitably result in failure to communicate your ideas effectively, since the reader will either be swamped with complexity, or bored with blandness.

The recipients of the report should also dictate the level of tact required.

Tactless	Tactful
The directors have clearly made errors	There were other options open to the board that, with hindsight, would have been beneficial
The marketing director is responsible for this disastrous change in strategy	The board should consider where this went wrong? It would appear that the marketing department may have made some mistakes

2.4 Making your report easy to read

To ensure that the marker finds your report accessible and easy to read, you should try to do the following:

- Use short words, short sentences, short phrases and short paragraphs. If you are adopting the 'what, so what, what now' approach, then you could have a paragraph containing three sentences. The next point can then be a new paragraph, also containing three sentences.
- Use the correct words to explain what you mean! For example, students often get confused between:
  - recommendations (what they should do – actions) and options (what they could do – possibilities)
  - objectives (what we want to achieve – the destination) and strategies (how we intend to achieve them – the route).
- Avoid unnecessary repetition. Some students fall into the trap of thinking that writing a professional report means simply writing more words to say the same thing! The issue is quality not quantity.

For example, compare the following:

'I, myself, personally'	OR	'I'
'export overseas'	OR	'export'
'green in colour'	OR	'green'

- Spelling – this may seem a small and unimportant point, but poor spelling makes a document seem sloppy and may convey an impression that the content is as loose as the general appearance! Poor spelling interrupts the marker as they read your report, so there is the danger that they conclude that it did not have a logical flow.

chapter

4

TOOLS FOR TECHNICAL ANALYSIS

Contents

1 Why a detailed analysis is important

It is extremely important that you should have studied the pre-seen material thoroughly before you go into the examination. There are two main reasons for this:

- It will save time in the examination itself if you are already familiar with the pre-seen material.
- It enables you to develop a view of the situation facing the organisation in the case study, and in particular its strategic and financial position and prospects.

You will not be able to answer the examination question itself from the pre-seen material alone, and the unseen material given to you in the examination will present significant new information that will alter the situation substantially. Even so, a major step towards success in the examination is a careful study and exploration of the pre-seen material.

2 Our recommended approach – outline

It would be wrong to suggest that there is a unique method of analysing the pre-seen material. However, it is important that you should have an organised approach to the analysis. The approach described and illustrated in this text is as follows:

- **Read the pre-seen material from beginning to end without making any notes**, simply to familiarise yourself with the scenario. Read the material again, as many times as you think necessary, without making notes. You can do this over a period of several days, if you wish. When you think you are reasonably familiar with the situation described by the material, you should start to make notes.
- **Start to make notes.** By making notes, you will become more familiar with the detail of the scenario. We recommend that you make notes on each paragraph (or each group of short paragraphs) in the pre-seen material. Think about what the paragraph is telling you, and consider how this information might be of interest or relevance.
- **Do some simple calculations.** You will almost certainly be given some figures in the pre-seen material. These might relate to the company's profits or losses, or product profitability. There might be income statements and balance sheets for previous years, future business plans, cash flow statements, capital expenditure plans, EPS and share price information and so on. Do some simple calculations, such as financial ratio calculations or a cash flow analysis. These might give you a picture of changes in profitability, liquidity, working capital management, returns on capital, financial structure or cash flows over time.

- **Revise any 'technical' topics that might be relevant.** The pre-seen material might make a reference to a particular 'technical' issue, such as the balanced scorecard approach, corporate governance requirements, internal controls, the use of derivative instruments, company valuations, and so on. If you have forgotten about any topic that might be relevant, go back to your previous study materials and revise it.
- **Find out what you can about the industry in which the case study organisation operates.** Carry out some research into the industry in which the organisation described in the case study operates. You can use a search engine such as *Google* or *Yahoo* to find information on the Internet. If you can identify the name of one or more companies that actually operate in the industry, visit their websites and find out what you can about them. Occasionally, the case study might relate to an industry that has been in the financial news, and you might therefore find useful articles in the newspapers, such as the *Financial Times.*

  You might think that the case study is describing an actual company (under a different name). However, this will not be the examiner's intention. Although it will help you to be familiar with what is happening in the industry, the case study should avoid 'real-world' examples.
- **Use 'formal' techniques to analyse the pre-seen material**, using your notes and your background understanding of the industry. A number of formal techniques are suggested later in this chapter. The aim of this analysis is to identify, if possible, the strategic and financial position and prospects of the organisation in the case study.
- **Summarise your analysis.**
- **Give yourself more time to think.** You should now spend some time thinking about the case study, as much as you can. You don't have to be sitting at a desk or table to do this. You can think about the case study when you travel to work or in any spare time that you have for thinking.
  - When new ideas come to you, jot them down.
  - If you think of a new approach to financial analysis, carry out any calculations you think might be useful.

3 Techniques for analysis

You can use any techniques for analysis with which you are familiar. The aim of analysing the pre-seen material, however, should be to identify any strategic or financial issues, or possibly operational and management issues or ethical issues, that could be of relevance.

You might be familiar with the following techniques:

- 7-S framework analysis
- value chain and supply chain analysis
- McFarlan's grid analysis for IT systems
- a resources audit (5 M audit)
- Porter's five forces model analysis
- PESTEL analysis
- Porter diamond analysis
- identifying critical success factors
- financial analysis
- SWOT analysis.

We recommend in particular that you use at least one technique for strategic position analysis (such as SWOT analysis) and that you carry out some financial analysis of the figures in the pre-seen material.

4 Operations and management

The pre-seen material is likely to give you a lot of information about the management and the operations of the organisation in the case study. Some of this information might seem unimportant (or of doubtful importance). You can use a number of techniques to consider what issues seem important, and what issues seem more significant than others.

4.1 7-S framework analysis

This approach was developed by McKinsey and others to help understand the factors that determine the effectiveness of an organisation. You should consider each of the '7 Ss' and make a note of any factor that could be of some importance.

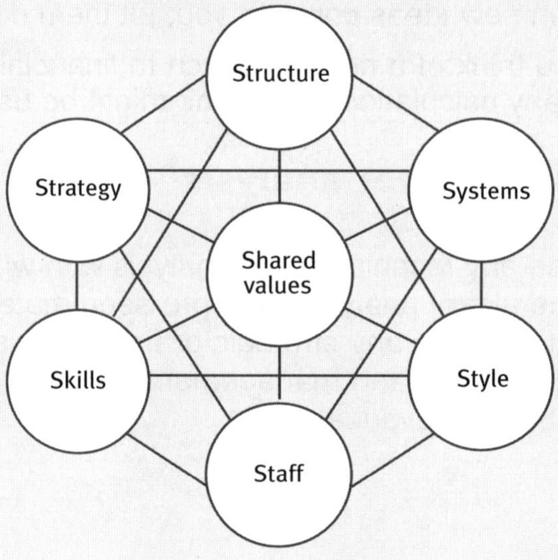

Systems. Systems are the formal and informal procedures that govern day-to-day operational activity. Do these appear to operate effectively, or have there been problems? For example:

- a company might have experienced problems with the procurement of key materials from suppliers, thus suggesting difficulties with its procurement systems
- there might be problems with the IT systems
- there might be problems with the fulfilment of orders (despatch to customers).

Style. This refers to how management spends its time and presents itself to staff. Does management style help to create greater efficiency, or is there a problem with management style that has created some resentment amongst employees?

Shared values. These are the fundamental values and aims that guide an organisation. They can be particularly strong in a small company, but might be difficult to sustain as a company grows bigger. When there is a strong sense of shared values, there is often a strong motivation for achieving success.

Skills. What are the distinctive capabilities or competences of the organisation? Are these being fully exploited? Is a lack of skills affecting the efficiency of the organisation?

Staff. Staff can contribute to the efficiency of an organisation, or can be inefficient. In some cases, there might be a shortage of staff. In a case study scenario, you might be given a short description of the experience and personality of several key members of staff, such as divisional managers. Are there any key individuals? Are they easily replaceable? Does the pre-seen material suggest that there is a problem (or potential problem) with any individual? Are there bad personal relationships between any key individuals?

Structure. Structure refers to how the firm is organised. What is the management and organisation structure of the company? Do there appear to be any strengths or weaknesses in this structure? Who makes the decisions? Who should be making the decisions?

Strategy. Strategy can be defined simply as the route chosen by the firm to achieve success. Your analysis of the pre-seen material will almost certainly need to include a detailed analysis of strategy.

4.2 The value chain and the supply chain

The value chain

It might be helpful to look at what the pre-seen material tells you about the value chain within the organisation. The concept of the value chain was developed by Porter. He argued that management should see the operations within their organisation as sequences of activities delivering value to the customer. Management should consider how each activity can be made to provide greater value.

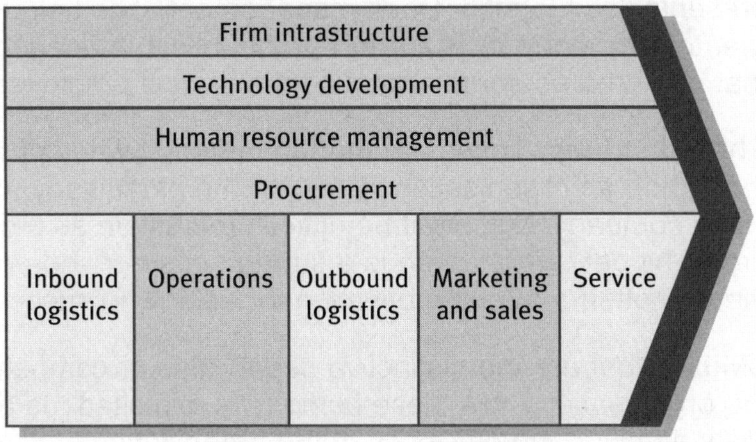

Each activity in the value chain is a source of:

- costs to the firm: these reduce profits and render it vulnerable to competitive attack by lower cost rivals. Value can be increased by reducing costs
- benefit to the customer: these generate revenue and, if superior, can justify higher prices. Value is increased by creating more benefits in excess of the costs of providing them
- benchmark comparison: if the firm performs an activity less well than a rival, it will suffer adverse comparison to rivals and excessive costs.

The supply chain

The supply chain describes the links from the production of raw materials for a product or service to the delivery of the final product to the end-consumer. An organisation has a position in the overall supply chain. Value delivered to the end-consumer can be increased by making improvements at any point in the supply chain, and an organisation often relies on its suppliers to add value.

Procurement policy and the management of supplier relationships can be a key operational issue. You might find it useful to think about the supply chain of the company in the case study, and the effectiveness of the company's relationships with its suppliers.

4.3 McFarlan's grid

The pre-seen material might give you data about the IT systems or management information systems currently used by the organisation. McFarlan's grid is a simple technique for identifying the way a firm uses its information systems and the likely scale of future investment needed.

		Future strategic value	
		Low	High
Current strategic value	Low	Support	Turnaround
	High	Factory	Strategic

It might be useful to consider the following issues:

- Does the IS adequately support current operations?
- Are there internal changes (such as new working practices, production techniques or competitive strategies) that demand a change in IS provision?
- Are there external changes (such as e-commerce, IT/IS innovations or adoption of new methods by rivals) that demand changes to the firm's IS?
- What is management's support for IS and is it likely that the necessary changes will get approval and funding?

5 Resources audit

Another approach to analysing the strategic, financial and operational position of a company is to carry out a resources audit, also called a '5 M audit' because the main categories of resources are men, money, machinery, markets and materials. The matters identified by a resources audit might duplicate many of those that would be revealed by a 7-S analysis. It is therefore unlikely that you will benefit from doing both a 7-S analysis and a resources audit. Select the approach that you prefer.

To carry out a resources audit for the purpose of analysing the pre-seen material, you should go through the pre-seen material, making a note of any information that might seem relevant in relation to that category of resources.

The table overleaf suggests the type of information you might be able to extract.

Resource	Matters covered	Things to look out for
Men	• Characteristics of work force (age, skill) • Characteristics of managers (age, experience, track record) • Costs of labour • Staffing levels and labour turnover • Organisation culture • Organisation structure	Details of named individuals. They could feature in the unseen material in scenarios such as: • being available for a new project or promotion • precipitating a crisis by leaving • being the person you write your report to. People whose opinions or agendas are detailed as: • a source of conflict • a progressive force for change • resisting change.
Money	• Profitability of business • Liquidity and solvency of the business • Availability of capital for expansion • Relationship with shareholders: shareholder returns/dividends • Value of the business in event of sale or merger	If the company has falling profits, a strategy might be required to halt the decline and turn the company round. If the company has too little capital to fund its expansion, you might need to consider whether additional funding is possible. If not, the company will have to restrict its expansion plans.

Machinery	• Quality of capital assets (premises, machines, vehicles) • Methods of operations • Quality of IT • Quality control; process quality	Are some assets in need of replacement and can the company afford to replace some/all of them? Opportunities to improve financial returns by improvements to assets, technology or operating methods.
Markets	• Competitive positioning and market share • Brand recognition, strength and values • Quality and position of product(s) in product life cycle • Customers served and their potential profitability • Route to market (e.g. relationship with sellers; use of e-commerce)	Assess whether sales of the product are likely to grow or contract in the future. Vulnerability to competition. Power exercised by buyer/customer could depress profits. Products reaching the decline stage or late maturity stage of their life cycle will need replacement. Does brand/reputation limit the business?
Materials	• Relations with suppliers • Costs of materials • Quality of inputs • Purchasing policy and methods • Security of supplies of key inputs • Extent of collaboration or reliance on suppliers	Check cost of sales and gross margins for evidence of supplier power. Consider ways to reduce input costs by: • greater supplier choice • collaboration in JIT arrangements/ strategic supplier relationships.

6 Environmental assessment

Environmental assessment is the evaluation of factors in the environment of an organisation that could have a significant influence or effect on its future. Techniques of assessment that can be used are:

- Porter's five competitive forces analysis or five forces model
- PESTEL
- Porter diamond.

6.1 Porter's five forces model

Porter has argued that the long-term profitability of companies within an industry is reduced by the presence of one or more strong competitive forces. The profitability and survival of any company in the industry will depend on countering these five forces.

For the purpose of analysing the pre-seen material, you can assess the apparent strength of any of these five factors and whether they might be relevant to the future strategic direction that the organisation should be taking.

Force	**This force is strong if:**
Buyer power This is the power of buyers in the industry – the organisation's customers. Strong buyer power: • forces down prices • exerts pressure for expensive quality improvements and service improvements.	The industry or company depends on a small number of buyers/customers. The company's product is unbranded or undifferentiated, so that buyers have no particular reason to select the company for its supplies. The company has excess capacity or the industry is in recession. There are no costs or few costs involved for buyers in switching from one source of supply to another. The buyers have information on prices of alternative producers in the industry.

Supplier power This is the power of suppliers to firms in the industry. Strong supplier power: • reduces profits by raising prices • reduces the pressure on suppliers to provide a high quality product and service • increases the risk of unreliability in supply.	The product/service provided by the supplier is unique or differentiated, and buyers have no alternative choice of supply. There are few suppliers in the industry, and possibly a monopoly supplier. The cost of switching from the current supplier to a new supplier would be high.
Threat of entry This is the threat that new competitors will enter the market and increase the competition. When the threat from new entrants is strong: • long-run profitability in the industry will be low • companies in the industry may reduce prices to deter entry by new competitors, forcing down short-term profitability.	The industry has good long-run market potential, giving new entrants opportunities to enter and gain a competitive position. There are low set-up costs. New entrants can enter the industry without incurring high costs. A company in the industry has a good market share but poor financial position, making it a potential takeover target for a more powerful new entrant.
Substitute technologies When there are substitute technologies, customers in the industry have the option of switching from buying one product to buying the substitute/alternative. The existence of a substitute technology: • reduces demand for the product • forces manufacturers of the product to keep their prices low.	The substitute technology or product can perform the same function just as well or even better. The substitute technology is reasonably priced. It is easy for customers to transfer to the substitute technology and the costs of transferring would be low.

Competitive rivalry The strength of rival firms in the industry is clearly a major competitive force. Strong competition: • forces down prices • forces firms to make costly quality improvements to be competitive • creates a risk of takeovers in the industry.	Competitive forces can be particularly strong when: • the rate of growth in the industry is slowing down • customers are prepared to change to a lower price supplier • companies in the industry have high fixed costs that must be absorbed and covered by sales income.

6.2 PESTEL analysis

PESTEL analysis is an extension of PEST analysis. It involves the analysis of environmental influences on a company or an industry, within the six categories: political, economic, social, technological, ecological/ethical and legal. These are regarded as six categories of environmental influence that might be significant.

Factor	**Examples to look for**
Political	Government policy affecting the industry or firm Stability of government in firm's main countries of operations Potential trade wars Change of government and possibility of change in taxation or attitudes to industry and the economy
Economic	Whether the economy is wealthy or poor Growth rate of the economy and potential for recession Level and trends in interest rates and effects of firm's markets and costs of borrowing Exchange rates and the risk of a rise or fall in key exchange rates

Social	Trends in buying behaviour Demographic changes (location, age of customers) Distribution of income between social groups Lifestyle changes
Technological	Changes in the technologies of consumption (e.g. buying methods) Changes in the technology of production Changes in the technology of organisations (e.g. applications of IT to improve efficiency and effectiveness)
Ecological/ethical	Impact of the industry on natural environment: pollution, waste, sustainability issues Impact of the firm's activities on the community
Legal	Competition policy Regulation of wages and prices Regulation of employment (e.g. rules on discrimination)

6.3 Porter diamond

The purpose of the Porter diamond model is to assess to what extent the firm (or its potential foreign rival) gains world-class advantages as a consequence of having operated in its home country. This model might be useful for analysis in a case study where:

- the firm is considering developing businesses outside its home country, or
- the firm is likely to be subject to competition from outside its home country.

Factor	What to look for	Implications
Demand conditions	Are home demand patterns for the firm's goods/services in advance or behind foreign demand patterns? How similar are home customers' demands to those of foreign customers? Will high levels of home demand confer cost advantages in the foreign market?	Where home demand is broadly similar but ahead of foreign countries, the firm will have an advantage over foreign rivals. If economies of scale can be exported, it will provide the competitive advantage of lower costs.
Factor conditions	Does the firm have access to resources not generally available to foreign rivals? Will the resources in the foreign market be similar to those of which the firm has experience?	These advantages apply better to manufacturing than services. If resources are not similar, the firm may have problems transferring its competitive strategy to the foreign market.
Related and supporting industries	Does the firm depend on particular key suppliers or partners for success in the home market? Will these be available in the foreign market? Is demand generated by the existence of a particular industry in the home country and will this be present in the foreign country?	Firm will not be competitive without establishing similar partnership arrangements in the foreign country.

Competitive rivalry	How strong is the competition likely to be? Does the firm have experience of beating similar competition at home?	Apply the five forces model analysis to the foreign market to assess this.
Culture and chance conditions	Does the current success of the firm depend on factors peculiar and unique to its home country?	These are unlikely to be available in the foreign country.

7 Product portfolio analysis

7.1 BCG matrix analysis

The BCG matrix is an all-in-one strategic planning tool that not only performs position analysis but also generates strategies.

The matrix simplistically considers market share to assess competitive strength and market growth to assess market attractiveness. Once classified, products can be managed as follows:

Market share	*Market growth: Low*	*Market growth: High*
High	**Cash cow** • Strong position in a low growth market • Little threat from rivals • Just keep the product ticking over and collect the cash	**Star** • Attractive market so have to reinvest heavily to defend market share and grow • Little cash surplus
Low	**Dog** • Too small to benefit from economies of scale • Market does not justify further investment • Divest	**Problem child** • Attractive market but too small to capitalise on it • Either invest heavily to gain market share or get out • 'Double or quit'

NB: Less useful for service industries where economies of scale may not exist

NB: Measurement problems e.g. which market are we looking at?

If using the matrix, try to comment on whether the firm has a balanced portfolio as far as cash flow is concerned.

7.2 Product lifecycle (PLC) analysis

Products are classified according to their position in the lifecycle:

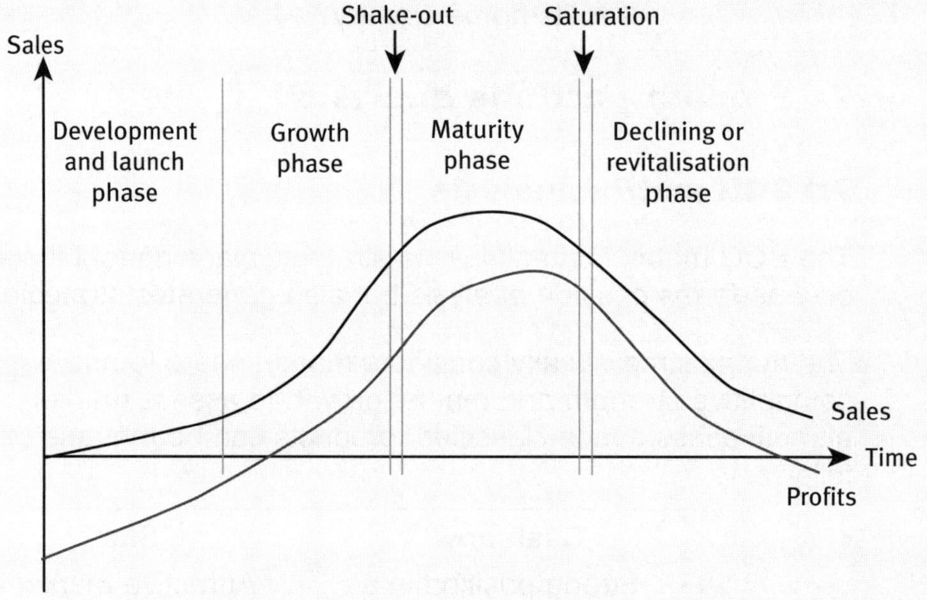

The key use of PLC analysis is to assess whether the firm has a balanced portfolio:

- Does it have new products coming through to replace older ones?
- Does it have cash-generating products to finance products that need investment?
- Does it have safe low risk products to complement high risk ones?

8 Critical success factors and performance appraisal

8.1 Critical success factors

Critical success factors (CSFs) are the factors that will determine whether a firm will be a success in its industry. CSFs vary from industry to industry.

CSFs can often be identified by answering four questions:

- What factors drive costs in the industry?
- What factors influence the revenues the firm can generate?
- What drives asset investment?
- What poses risks for the firm?

The following table expands on these by indicating what to look for.

Critical success factor	**Things to look for**
What factors drive costs in the industry?	• If fixed costs are high, this means that gaining sales volume is critical. • If product complexity is being used to gain orders (e.g. special customisation of products or width of product range), this will increase costs. Firms must understand and allow for this. • If economies of scale (volume) or economies of scope (breadth of product range) are available, this makes relative size and market share a critical success factor. • If a firm must incur high spending on advertising, research and development or asset refurbishment in order to compete, the firm must be able to afford it. • Where costs can be reduced by merger/acquisition, the firm needs to gain size and look for a merger partner or a takeover target. • If costs are affected by exchange rates or the availability of cheaper supplies from abroad, the firm might need cross-border supply chains.
What factors influence the revenues the firm can generate?	• If the firm's product commands a premium price, this means that sales promotion, brand image, meeting customer needs and technical quality are critical. • If the product competes by low prices it is critical that this market segment continues to include a substantial number of buyers willing to buy on price.

	• If revenue growth has been gained by accessing new customers and wider locations, the marketing and logistic skills of the firm are critical. • If revenue growth has been accomplished by new products and exploiting the early stages of product life cycles, it means that innovation and launch marketing are critical. • Competitors and new entrants will put pressure on revenues and so it is critical that competitive advantages are sustained and enforced.
What drives asset investment?	The CSFs in industries subject to high ongoing asset investment are: • ability to afford the costs of investment • ability to project manage and implement investment swiftly and successfully. Ensure that the firm's management (and you) appreciate that asset investment includes intangibles such as human resources and brands. • In consumer industries their rising expectations will necessitate continuous improvement and updating of premises, customer service and facilities. • In technological industries there will be need for continuous investment in R&D and production technology. • Sales growth drives asset investment if it needs extra production or distribution capacity. • Industries utilising IT strategically will need to ensure systems are kept up to date. The progress of IT applications is swift and continuous.
What poses risks for the firm?	These are events that could close the business down or severely restrict its space to operate and its earnings. **Asset risk:** factors that could result in loss of productive assets or their earning power

	(e.g. theft, destruction, legal challenges to their use). **Commercial risk:** reduction of earnings below forecast due to loss of customers, failure of new products, successful competition by rivals. **Operational risk:** breakdown in ability to provide the product or service, leading to loss of earnings and potential costs of legal claims by customer, suppliers and staff. **Financial risk:** loss of value of investments due to volatility of markets, adverse foreign exchange movements or adverse interest rate movements.

8.2 Key performance indicators

Each of the CSFs identified above should be measured by a number of key performance indicators (KPIs). If not, there is the risk that the issue concerned will not be monitored and controlled sufficiently.

A useful way of incorporating these is to use the balanced scorecard, which looks at a range of issues / factors relevant to different stakeholders:

Financial perspective	**How do we look to shareholders?**
Customer perspective	**How do customers see us?**
Innovation and learning	**Can we continue to improve and create value?**
Internal business processes	**What must we excel at?**

9 Financial analysis

To answer the questions in the case study examination, you will have to do much more than calculate and analyse some commonly used financial ratios. However, financial ratio analysis is a very useful approach to finding out about the financial position of an organisation, and its financial strengths and weaknesses. Depending on the information provided in the pre-seen material, you might be able to carry out some simple ratio analyses on historical data or on the data in a financial plan or business plan.

Here is a brief checklist of ratios and other calculations you might find useful. You should be familiar with all of them.

9.1 Analysing trends and magnitudes

Financial indicator	Things to look for
Sales turnover • Absolute figure shows the size of the company • % change per annum shows growth rate	• The company's stage in the product or industry life cycle. • Healthy companies have annual growth rate in sales in excess of the rate of inflation.
Group operating profit • Absolute figure shows the amount of profits • Annual growth in annual profit shows rate of increase	• If the company is unprofitable, or profits are falling, then the case study is probably about a profitability crisis and finding a turnaround strategy. • A high % increase in profit in comparison to % increase in sales turnover indicates a high fixed cost base. Look for increases in sales turnover that do not generate a large increase in profit. Does this indicate a problem?
Divisional sales revenue and operating profit • Absolute figure for divisional profit • % change per annum in divisional profit	• Assess the relative size and importance of the divisions. • Loss-making divisions need to be dealt with urgently. • Compare growth rates of each division to assess where strategic investment should perhaps take place.
Borrowings (loans and overdraft)	• High or rising borrowings might suggest high financial risk. • Consider why finance is debt and not equity.

Share price • The change in price through time • P/E ratio compared to rival companies	• An upward trend in share price is healthy. • A low or falling share price shows loss of investor confidence.

9.2 Ratios

Profitability ratios

You might find useful information from an analysis of profit/sales ratios, for:

- the company as a whole
- each division, or
- each product or service.

Profit margins can be measured as a net profit percentage and as a gross profit percentage. You can then look at trends in the ratios over time, or consider whether the margins are good or disappointing.

Analysing the ratio of certain expenses to sales might also be useful, such as the ratio of administration costs to sales, sales and marketing costs to sales or R&D costs to sales. Have there been any noticeable changes in these ratios over time and, if so, is it clear why the changes have happened?

Liquidity ratios

The two main measures of liquidity are:

- the current ratio (= ratio of current assets: current liabilities)
- the quick ratio or acid test ratio (= ratio of current assets excluding inventory: current liabilities).

The purpose of a liquidity ratio is to assess whether the organisation is likely to be able to pay its liabilities, when they fall due for payment, out of its operational cash flows.

The current ratio is probably more useful when inventory is fairly liquid and inventory turnover is fast. The quick ratio or acid test ratio is a better measure of liquidity when inventory turnover is slow.

Check these ratios for any significant change over time, or for the possibility of poor liquidity. As a very rough guide, a current ratio below 2:1 and a quick ratio below 1:1 might be low. However, the liquidity ratios are only likely to be of significance for the case study when the ratios get very low, or the deterioration in the ratios is very large. For example, if a company has current liabilities in excess of its current assets, a liquidity problem would seem likely.

Working capital ratios

Working capital ratios can be calculated to assess the efficiency of working capital management (= management of inventory, trade receivables and trade payables). They can also be useful for assessing liquidity, because excessive investment in working capital ties up cash and slows the receipt of cash.

The main working capital ratios are:

- average turnover period for inventory: slow turnover might indicate poor inventory management
- 'receivables days' or the average time that customers take to pay: the industry average might be 30 or 60 days
- average time to pay suppliers: again, the industry average might be 30 or 60 days.

You should be familiar with these ratios and how to calculate the length of the cash cycle or operating cycle.

Financial structure ratios

You might be required to consider methods of funding in your case study examination. If a company plans to expand in the future, where will the funds come from?

- Additional debt finance might only be possible if the current debt levels are not high, and financial gearing is fairly low. (The interest cover ratio is also a useful measure of debt capacity. It is the ratio of profit before interest and tax to interest costs. When the ratio is low, possibly less than 3, this could indicate that the company already has as much debt capital as it can safely afford.)
- If a company will need additional equity finding, will internally generated profits be a sufficient source of funds or will a new share issue be necessary?

9.3 Cash flow analysis or funding analysis

If the main objective of a company is to maximise the wealth of its shareholders, the most important financial issues will be profitability and returns to shareholders. However, other significant issues in financial strategy are often:

- cash flows and liquidity, and
- funding.

If the pre-seen material gives you enough data, you might be able to carry out a rough assessment of the company's cash flows, by constructing a cash flow statement. The purpose of such an analysis should be to get an idea of where the company has been getting its cash, and how it has been using the cash. A possible cash flow problem occurs whenever the cash flows from operations do not appear to be sufficient to cover all the non-operational cash payments that the company has to make, such as spending on capital expenditure items.

An analysis of future funding can be carried out by looking at the history of changes in the balance sheet. It is a relatively simple task to look at the growth in the company's assets over time, and at how the asset growth has been funded – by equity, long-term debt or shorter-term liabilities. If equity has funded much of the growth in assets, it might be possible to see how much of the new equity as been provided by retained profits, and how much has come from new issues of shares (indicated by an increase in the allotted share capital and share premium reserve).

10 Strategic position analysis: SWOT analysis

Many of the techniques of assessment described above should give you ideas about the future problems and potential of the firm in the case study. A final step in your analysis should be to draw up a SWOT analysis.

The analysis might change when you get the unseen material in the examination, but SWOT analysis is a simple technique that enables you to present a wide range of issues clearly and effectively.

You should include a SWOT analysis in your examination answer, particularly when the question asks you to present a report that discusses the issues facing the case study organisation. A SWOT analysis could be presented as an appendix to your report.

If you prepare a SWOT analysis from the pre-seen material in advance of the examination, you will find it much easier and quicker to prepare a similar analysis in the examination itself.

A SWOT analysis of an organisation is simply a listing of the following:

- The STRENGTHS of the organisation. These are internal factors that give the organisation a distinct advantage.
- The WEAKNESSES of the organisation. These are internal factors that affect performance adversely, and so might put the organisation at a disadvantage.

- The OPPORTUNITIES available. These are circumstances or developments in the environment that the organisation might be in a position to exploit to its advantage.
- The THREATS or potential threats. These are factors in the environment that present risks or potential risks to the organisation and its competitive position.

Strengths and weaknesses are internal to the organisation, whereas opportunities and threats are external factors.

A SWOT analysis can be presented simply as a list of strengths, followed by weaknesses, then opportunities and finally threats. It would be useful to indicate within each category which factors seem more significant than others, perhaps by listing them in descending order of priority.

Alternatively a SWOT analysis, if it is not too long and excludes minor factors, can be presented in the form of a 2 x 2 table, as follows:

Strengths	**Weaknesses**
Opportunities	**Threats**

With this method of presentation, the positive factors (strengths and opportunities) are listed on the left and the negative factors (weaknesses and threats) are on the right.

The analysis is improved if:

- the factors within each category are listed in descending order of priority, and
- minor factors are excluded entirely.

You should not forget that you will be assessed on your ability to prioritise the problems and issues facing the organisation in the case study, and preparing a SWOT analysis will help you to organise your thoughts.

11 Strategic options

Having completed a position analysis you can start to consider the strategic options facing the firm by answering three questions:

1 How are we going to compete – what should our competitive advantage be based on?

2 Where are we going to compete – what are the directions for growth?

3 How do we get there – organic growth, acquisition or a joint arrangement of some sort?

11.1 Porter's generic strategies

Porter argues that there are three ways to gain a sustainable competitive advantage.

Overall cost leadership

- Based on achieving the position of lowest cost producer in the industry for **standard** products and services – not necessarily inferior ones.
- The company can operate in even the most marginal segments of the market and undercut rival's prices at any time. (Price usually becomes the main weapon in competing.)
- Cost advantages come from economies of scale, large production runs, automation, learning effects, etc – use the value chain if you need more detail.

Differentiation

- Based on offering a **better** quality product than competitors.
- Customers are willing to pay extra for this differentiation.
- The difference must be valued by customers and may be real or created via advertising.

Focus/niche

- A company may find it difficult to gain a cost or quality advantage across the whole industry but can do so by focusing on a particular buyer group, market segment or a section of the product range.

'Stuck in the middle?'

- Porter argues that firms must choose between cost leadership and differentiation. Any attempt to do both will result in the firm having neither – a recipe for disaster.

Porter's generic strategies can be used in a number of ways:

- Position analysis – competitive advantage is a key part of a SWOT analysis e.g. being stuck in the middle is a major weakness.
- Prioritisation – maintaining a competitive advantage in a competitive marketplace would be considered important in most scenario.
- Strategy evaluation – competitive advantage is a useful issue to include when assessing potential strategies.

11.2 Ansoff's matrix

Ansoff's matrix analyses current and proposed strategies into four classifications:

	Existing products	**New products**
Existing markets	*Market penetration* • Price cuts? • Spend more on advertising? • Small improvements to products? • Buy rivals? • Competitive strategy?	*Product development* • R&D could be critical • Acquire rights to make other firms' products • Buy in products and re-badge • Joint developments • Can use existing distribution channels
New markets	*Market development* • New customer segments • Industrial v consumer markets • New regions of the country • Foreign markets • Barriers to entry?	*Diversification* • Related diversification (e.g. vertical integration) • Unrelated diversification (conglomerate diversification)

Ansoff's matrix is very easy to use and hence score technical skills marks. As well as classifying current strategies it is particularly useful at identifying possible directions for growth.

12 Strategic choice

The pre-seen analysis may contain details of the firm's future plans, which should be evaluated. The suitability/acceptability/feasibility model developed by Tilles is particularly useful here:

Suitability – is the strategy consistent, both externally and internally?

- Does it give the firm a better fit with the environment?
- Portfolio analysis – how do new products fit with existing ones?
- Are their synergies with other parts of the business?
- Resource deployment analysis – how does the strategy match against strengths and weaknesses?

Acceptability – look at risk and return.

- Is the risk acceptable?
- Does the strategy meet the criteria for 'success' for different stakeholder groups?
- Techniques could include NPV, IRR, expected present value.
- Problems dealing with multiple objectives and non-quantifiable objectives.
- Could involve sensitivity analysis to assess risks.

Feasibility – is the strategy within the resources and capability of the organisation?

- Is the time-scale achievable?
- Do we have the critical success factors necessary to implement the strategy?

13 Thinking about the pre-seen material

When you have completed your analysis of the pre-seen material, you should still have some time before the examination to think about the case study and to re-assess the analysis you have made so far.

The examination will test your ability to appraise a situation, identify critical issues, evaluate problems and recommend a way forward. In effect, the examination is testing your ability to contribute to decision-making at a senior level within an organisation.

Thinking about the case study should give you an opportunity to exercise your potential talent. If you were a senior manager in the organisation in the case study, what would be concerning you most of all? Are there any decisions that might have to be made?

- **Strategic issues.** What do you think the company should be trying to achieve? What about the strategic direction the organisation is taking? What do you think the organisation's strategy ought to be? (But remember, the unseen material in the examination will introduce an unexpected 'twist'.)

- **Financial issues.** What is the financial position of the company, and what are its future financial prospects? What do you think about the balance sheet, profitability, sales, growth, working capital management, cash flow management and liquidity, capital investment and funding?
- **Management issues.** If you were a director of the organisation, working with the individuals in the case study, would you be aware of any problems of management? Are there any individuals who are not doing their job as well as they should? Is the organisation over-reliant on any particular individual? Is authority being delegated in the most appropriate way?
- **Ethical issues.** Do there appear to be any ethical problems? How would you want to resolve them? (The pre-seen material might hint at possible ethical problems, but you are more likely to find problems of this kind introduced on the examination day in the unseen material.)
- **Objectives.** Never forget what the objectives of the organisation ought to be. Is the current management team giving proper consideration to the organisation's objectives (probably increasing shareholder value)? How would you be expecting to increase earnings, dividends and, if the company's shares are quoted on a stock market, the share price? If the company is a private company, how might shareholders be expecting to 'realise their investment' – through an eventual listing and stock market launch, or a trade sale of the business to a competitor?

Never forget that this examination is not really testing what you have learned. It is testing your ability to analyse, assess, evaluate and apply judgement to 'realistic' business problems. Thinking about the case study allows you to exercise these abilities. We therefore recommend very strongly that you allow yourself as much time as possible for the thinking process.

Just before the examination, you should go over the pre-seen material, and your notes, again. Compare your earlier thoughts about the case study with your current thinking, which may well have changed. Make sure that your ideas are still consistent with the information in the pre-seen material.

You should now be ready to take the examination.

chapter

5

CIMA'S ETHICAL GUIDELINES

Contents

1 Ethics and the TOPCIMA examination

One criterion on which you will be assessed in the TOPCIMA examination is your ability to advise on or resolve ethical dilemmas. These could relate to any of the following areas:

- corporate social responsibility

- corporate governance issues

- personal ethical behaviour of individuals in the case

You should therefore be aware of CIMA's Guidelines on ethical conduct. You can download a copy of the Ethical Guidelines from CIMA's website, if you want to read the full text.

The Ethical Guidelines are included in the syllabus for Paper P3 *Management Accounting: Risk and Control Strategy*. However, if you have not studied the Guidelines before, this chapter gives you a summary. There are lengthy quotations from the Guidelines themselves, which are reproduced by kind permission of CIMA.

The case study might present ethical issues in a different way, and you might need to apply judgement in deciding how to apply the Guidelines to the particular circumstances presented in the case study. The Guidelines state: 'It is not practical or possible to establish ethical requirements which apply to all situations and circumstances members may encounter. The objectives as well as the fundamental principles of the Guidelines are of a general nature and are not intended to be used to solve a member's ethical problems in a specific case. Members should consider the principles set out in the Guidelines as the basic principles which they should follow when performing their work.'

2 The requirement to act professionally

The Guidelines stress the point that CIMA members and students are professional accountants, and must behave professionally.

- 'As members of a profession, CIMA's members have a duty to observe the highest standard of conduct and integrity.'
- 'The Guidelines assume that, unless a limitation is specifically stated, the objectives and fundamental principles are equally valid for all members, whether they be in industry, commerce, the public sector, public practice or education.'

'A profession is distinguished by certain characteristics including:

- mastery of a particular intellectual skill, acquired by training and education
- acceptance of duties to society as a whole in addition to duties to the client or employer
- an outlook which is essentially objective
- rendering personal services to a high standard of conduct and performance.'

3 The public interest

'A distinguishing mark of a profession is acceptance of its responsibility to the public.' For a professional accountant, the public consists of:

- employers
- creditors
- clients
- governments
- employees
- investors
- the business and financial community, and
- others who rely on the objectivity and integrity of professional accountants to maintain the orderly functioning of commerce.

This reliance imposes a public interest responsibility on the accountancy profession. The public interest is defined as the collective well-being of the community of people and institutions the professional accountant serves.'

The Guidelines go on to make the crucial point that the responsibility of a professional accountant is not exclusively to an employer or client, because a public interest consideration might also apply. In other words, a conflict of interest could arise.

'A professional accountant's responsibility is not exclusively to satisfy the needs of an individual client or employer. The standards of the accountancy profession are heavily determined by the public interest, for example:

- financial managers serve in various financial management capacities in organisations and contribute to the efficient and effective use of the organisation's resources
- internal auditors provide assurance about a sound internal control system which enhances the reliability of the external financial information of the employer

- independent auditors help to maintain the integrity and efficiency of the financial statements presented to financial institutions in partial support for loans and to shareholders for obtaining capital
- tax experts help to establish confidence and efficiency in, and the fair application of, the tax system
- management consultants have a responsibility toward the public interest in advocating sound management decision making
- professional accountants have an important role in society.

Investors, creditors, employers and other sectors of the business community, as well as the government and the public at large, rely on professional accountants for sound financial accounting and reporting, effective financial management and competent advice on a variety of business and taxation matters. The attitude and behaviour of professional accountants in providing such services have an impact on the economic well-being of their community and country.'

4 Objectives of the accountancy profession

The objectives of the accountancy profession are to work to the highest standards of professionalism and also to meet the public interest requirement. The Guidelines state that, to meet these objectives, four basic requirements must be met:

- **Credibility.** There must be credibility in information and information systems.
- **Professionalism.** Employers, clients and other interested parties must recognise that accountants are professionals.
- **Quality of services.** There must be assurance that all services obtained from a professional accountant are carried out to the highest standards of performance.
- **Confidence.** 'Users of the services of professional accountants should be able to feel confident that there is a framework of professional ethics to govern the provision of services.'

5 Fundamental principles

Having stressed the need for accountants to act professionally, and for others to recognise that accountants are professionals, the Guidelines go on to list a number of fundamental principles that accountants must observe. These are:

- **Integrity.** The accountant should be straightforward and honest in performing professional services. Significantly perhaps, for the purposes of the case study examination, the Guidelines state that 'accountants should not be party to the falsification of any record or knowingly or recklessly supply any information or make any statement which is misleading, false or deceptive in a material particular'. So what should you do if your chief executive officer suggests that the financial statements should be altered to make the company's position look better, and that the external auditors should be persuaded to agree to the changes?

- **Objectivity.** 'A professional accountant should be fair and should not allow prejudice or bias or the influence of others to override objectivity.' Objectivity is considered in more detail below.
- **Professional competence and due care.** It is worth studying this principle in full. The Guidelines state that: 'In agreeing to provide professional services, a professional accountant implies that there is a level of competence necessary to perform those services and that his or her knowledge, skill and experience will be applied with reasonable care and diligence. Professional accountants must therefore refrain from performing any services which they are not competent to carry out unless appropriate advice and assistance is obtained to ensure that the services are performed satisfactorily. A professional accountant should perform professional services with due care, competence and diligence. There is a continuing duty to maintain professional knowledge and skill at a level required to ensure that a client or employer receives the advantage of competent professional service based on up-to-date developments in practice, legislation and techniques.'
- **Confidentiality.** 'A professional accountant should respect the confidentiality of information acquired during the course of performing professional services and should not use or disclose any such information without proper and specific authority or unless there is a legal or professional right or duty to disclose.'
- **Professional behaviour.** Accountants should behave in a professional way, and should not act in any way that brings discredit to the profession or CIMA. An interesting additional comment inserted in the Guidelines is that: 'A professional accountant, particularly one having authority over others, should give due weight to the need for others to develop and hold their own judgements in accounting matters, and should deal with differences of opinion in a professional way.'
- **Professional and technical standards.** The fundamental requirement that professional accountants must apply professional and technical standards to the work that they do could have some relevance to a case study examination. Again, it is worth reading the Guidelines in full on this point. 'A professional accountant is expected to present financial information fully, honestly and professionally, so that it will be understood in its context. S/he also knows, understands and follows professional standards; a professional accountant should carry out professional services in

accordance with relevant technical and professional standards. They have a duty to carry out, with care and skill, the instructions of the client or employer insofar as they are compatible with the requirements of integrity, objectivity and, in the case of public practice, independence.'

6 Specific guidelines

Having stated the fundamental principles on which ethical conduct must be based, the Guidelines consider a variety of more specific issues. It is useful to look at a number of these, since the situations they envisage could easily feature in a case study.

6.1 Objectivity

The fundamental principle of objectivity imposes the obligation on accountants to be fair, intellectually honest and free of conflicts of interest. This requirement applies both to accountants in public practice and accountants who are not in public practice, who 'prepare financial statements as a subordinate of others, perform internal auditing services, and serve in financial management capacities in industry, commerce, the public sector and education'. The Guidelines state that 'all members should protect the integrity of their professional services, maintain objectivity, and avoid any subordination of their judgement by others'.

The Guidelines state that matters concerning objectivity could arise in the following circumstances:

- An accountant could be exposed to a situation in which pressure might be brought to bear on him or her, which could damage his or her objectivity.
- Reasonableness should be applied when identifying relationships that are likely to impair an accountant's objectivity.
- Relationships should be avoided that allow prejudice, bias or the influences of other individuals to override objectivity.

6.2 Resolution of ethical conflicts of interest

Conflicts of interest can arise in a variety of different ways. When a conflict of interest arises, there is a conflict between:

- the professional responsibilities of the accountant, and
- either internal or external pressure on the individual to do something different that is not consistent with professional requirements.

For example:

- There might be a danger of pressure from an overbearing supervisor, manager, director or partner.
- There might be family or personal relationships which can give rise to the possibility of pressures being exerted on the accountant.
- An accountant should not mislead his employer as to the degree of expertise or experience he possesses and, where appropriate, should obtain expert advice and assistance.
- An accountant might be asked to act contrary to technical or professional standards.
- There could be a problem of divided loyalty, between loyalty to an employer or superior and loyalty or duty to the profession.
- 'Conflict could arise when misleading information is published which may be to the advantage of the employer or client and which may or may not benefit the member as a result of such publication.'

When an accountant in employment is faced with a significant ethical issue, his first step should be to take up the matter through the established grievance procedure or similar appropriate procedure of the organisation. The procedures recommended by the Guidelines are worth noting:

- 'If following these policies does not resolve the problem or the member is unable to use such procedures, the member should consider discussing the problem with his or her immediate superior, unless that person is involved, in which case the issue should be submitted to the next higher level of management.'
- 'At higher levels of management the acceptable reviewing authority may be some or all of the board of directors, or the auditors, but contact with levels above the immediate superior should only be initiated with the superior's knowledge, assuming non-involvement.
- 'Prior to or following any of these stages, discussion with an objective adviser or the member's professional accountancy body may be useful. Such discussion should be concerned to clarify the issues involved and to identify possible courses of action without breaching the duty of confidentiality to the other parties involved.'
- If the ethical conflict still exists after fully exhausting all levels of internal review, the last resort with a significant matter such as fraud might have to be to resign and submit an information memorandum to an appropriate representative of his or her employing organisation.

6.3 Professional competence

Accountants 'should refrain from agreeing to perform professional services which they are not competent to carry out unless competent advice and assistance is obtained to enable them to satisfactorily perform such services'.

6.4 Confidentiality

A professional accountant has an obligation to respect the confidentiality of information about an employer's or a client's affairs acquired in the course of his work. This duty of confidentiality continues even after the end of the relationship with the employer or client.

- 'Confidentiality should always be observed unless specific authority has been given to disclose information or there is a legal or professional duty to disclose.'
- 'Confidentiality is not only a matter of disclosure of information. It also requires that anyone acquiring information in the course of performing his or her work will not use that information for personal advantage or for the advantage of a third party.'

7 Conclusion

This chapter has not covered the Ethical Guidelines in full, but has drawn attention to ethical issues that could arise in the TOPCIMA examination. It is quite possible that a case study will introduce a different ethical issue. If you think that an ethical issue does arise, and these notes do not seem to cover the situation, you might wish to read the Guidelines in full on the CIMA website (www.cimaglobal.com and key 'ethics' or 'ethical guidelines' into the search function).

chapter

6

FLYQUAL: ANALYSING THE PRE-SEEN MATERIAL

Contents

Scenario – Pre-seen material

Flyqual was the TOPCIMA case for both the March and May 2007 examination papers. When analysing this material and answering the examination question, you should assume that 'now' is early 2007.

What follows is the detailed paragraph by paragraph analysis that was carried out in the 'knowledge' publication for Flyqual.

You could try answering each of the questions before looking at the suggested answers to aid your understanding of the case.

1 Case and commentary – Flyqual

1.1 Introduction

Flyqual Airlines (FQA) is a member of N, an aviation alliance which includes another seven airlines based in different regions of the world. The purpose of the alliance is to extend a large range of travel opportunities to passengers of each constituent airline and FQA is now able to provide travel to over 500 destinations throughout the world by using alliance partners' routes. The benefits include more choices of flights to suit the passengers' travel requirements, easier transfers between member airlines and access to their passenger lounges, priority check-in at airport terminals and enhancement of frequent flyer programmes. Greater frequency of flights is provided by the various codeshare agreements which FQA has entered into with various airlines which operate both within and outside the N alliance. A codeshare agreement is where flights to a particular destination are operated by an airline which accepts passengers who have purchased tickets from other airlines.

As its name implies, FQA prides itself on providing a first rate passenger service and enjoys a strong reputation for quality service to passengers. As a consequence, FQA does not need to apply a low pricing policy for airline travel in response to sensitivity of market demand and is able to charge premium prices. Established just after the Second World War, FQA itself now flies to over 100 destinations worldwide from its home base in Asia and employs over 20,000 people around the world as aircrew, cabin attendants, maintenance staff, airport check-in operatives and ground staff.

Two large listed companies together hold the majority of the shares of FQA and the company is listed on its home stock exchange. These two companies are not themselves engaged in the airline industry although one of them does have subsidiaries whose business is in the export of goods.

FQA holds a 45% shareholding in a smaller airline. This smaller airline is not a member of the N alliance and engages mainly in short-haul scheduled and cargo flights around the Asia-Pacific region. FQA does undertake some short-haul schedules in the Asia-Pacific region but its principal business is in long-haul intercontinental flights to the USA and Europe.

Questions and comments on Section 1.1 – Inroduction	Response
What are the benefits and costs for FQA of belonging to N?	Benefits • Greater range of destinations • Easier transfers between member airlines • Access to other firms' passenger lounges • Priority check-ins • Enhancement of frequent flyer schemes (e.g. 'air miles') • 'Codeshare' agreement These effectively give customers the services of a larger firm and so should increase demand. Problems • FQA's quality image could be compromised by other member firms' behaviour. Customers may see FQA as providing the whole package and blame them for other members' mistakes.
Are there any areas in which larger rivals still have a competitive advantage, despite FQA's membership of N?	Larger rivals may still have some advantages over an alliance like N: • Greater buyer power over aircraft suppliers allowing them to achieve lower costs. • Greater power over airports allowing them to win more routes and get lower charges. • Possible economies of scale when buying fuel. Also, most large airlines are also members of such alliances.
What type of competitive strategy is being adopted by FQA?	FQA is stated as competing on quality rather than cost, so would be classed as a differentiator.

1.2 Future demand for passenger air travel

Some airlines offer services at both the high quality and the basic 'with no extras', so called 'low-priced' or 'no frills' end of the market. FQA has chosen to offer services at the high quality end of the market only.

The largest consumer markets over the next two decades are likely to be China and India. This is expected to result in large growth in air travel to and from, and within these countries. This is likely to be generated by increasing wealth within the economies of these two countries in particular and continued inward investment from other parts of the world.

It is normal for increased air travel in emerging economies to begin with increases in domestic demand followed by international demand as income levels rise and greater inward investment takes place. Major centres of population and business tend to generate strong development of air traffic. It is estimated that 80% of air traffic between Europe and Asia is carried between only 17 major cities.

It is estimated that by the mid 2020's three-quarters of the entire world fleet of very large aircraft will be used on flights from the largest airports in the world and 60% of these airports are situated in the Asia-Pacific region.

Questions and comments on Section 1.2 - future demand for passenger travel	Response
What are the main determinants of demand for passenger air travel?	• Disposable incomes, which in turn are determined by the state of the economy in the countries concerned. (High systematic risk) • Perceived risk – e.g. threats from terrorism, health scares • Price – cheaper airfares will boost demand
What are the implications for FQA of increasing demand in China and India?	• Increasing demand in China and India present new opportunities for FQA, especially given its base in Asia. • However, this may involve having to win slots at new airports and a review of the type of aircraft needed.

What is the significance of the statement that 80% of air traffic between Europe and Asia is carried between only 17 cities?	• Stresses the importance of winning slots at these airports and hence the high power airport operators have over airlines.
What is the significance of the statement concerning 'very large aircraft'?	• One forecast industry trend is towards larger aircraft (see later and industry awareness). The predicted demand for such aircraft will be a factor for FQA to consider when deciding upon their replacement policy.

1.3 Future demand for air cargo

Demand for international cargo services is also expected to increase in areas of high population and industrial growth.

Demand for air cargo is influenced by the nature of the goods being transported, for example the need to transport perishable foods quickly. However, high value goods which are demanded in very quick time, such as high technology equipment have also grown and represent about 75% of the financial value of exports from Asia but only 40% of exports in terms of weight. This has resulted in significant growth in demand for air cargo. For example, about 25% of high technology equipment by value was transported by air from China to Europe in the mid 1990's. A decade later, this had risen to 60%.

Questions and comments on Section 1.3 – future demand for cargo	Response
What are the determinants of demand for air cargo?	• How quickly manufacturers need to get their products to market, e.g. if perishable or high tech goods • Cost – mainly determined by weight (in contrast to shipping where cost is determined mainly by volume) • Profitability of client firms – linked to state of economies concerned (high systematic risk)

What does the growth in business to/from Asia and China mean for FQA?	• Demand for shipping from China will continue to grow and be an opportunity for FQA. • As the economies of China and Asia grow, there will also be greater demand for cargo to these destinations.

1.4 Aircraft replacement within the industry

Traditionally, replacement of aircraft has been a result of economic cycles and developments of aircraft technology. Fuel prices have also had a major influence on aircraft replacement. Aircraft retirements on a large scale began to take place in 2002 following a slow-down in global demand. Many airlines replace passenger aircraft before the end of their economic life in order to take advantage of new technology. Market conditions, legislation on noise and exhaust emissions and strengthening competition have resulted in an increasing demand by airlines for more fuel efficient and quieter aircraft. Some forecasts state that by the mid 2020's only about 15% of the fleet which currently exists will still be operated by airlines across the world.

Questions and comments on Section 1.4 – aircraft replacement	Response
What are the main factors to consider when deciding aircraft replacement policies?	• Demand will influence the number and size of aircraft needed • Capital cost • Maintenance costs • Reliability • Maintenance time as this affects turn around times. • Fuel efficiency and fuel cost • Estimated economic life • Flexibility • Size / capacity • Implications for staffing levels • Pollution / exhaust emissions • Noise • Safety records • Required infrastructure at airports (e.g. length of runways)

1.5 FQA's fleet of aircraft

The aircraft which FQA operate are all manufactured by either F (based in the USA) or C (based in Europe). The fleet of 170 aircraft is as follows:

	Leased	Owned	Seating capacity pre aircraft
F 858	27	36	500
F 888	9	22	270
C 440	14	30	320
C 450	10	22	450

Of the 27 leased F 858 aircraft, seven are employed entirely for carrying cargo. The F 888 can be converted to fly long-haul, although it is normally used on short-haul routes. For conversion to long-haul, the F 888 would reduce the passenger capacity by 100 seats. The C 440 is used exclusively on short-haul routes. There are a number of aircraft whose leases are due to expire over the next two years.

Questions and comments on Section 1.5 – FQA's fleet	Response
What are the main differences between buying and leasing aircraft?	• With leasing the initial capital outlay is avoided. However, a similar cash flow can be achieved by borrowing to buy. • Under leases ownership does not pass so FQA would not benefit from any disposal values. • With operating lease maintenance would be done by the lessor. • There is little difference between buying and a finance lease.
Estimate FQA's total seating capacity	As stated: • Capacity = (27-7+36)×500 + 31×270 + 44×320 + 32×450 = 64,850 If F888s are converted to long-haul • Capacity = (27-7+36)×500 + 31×(270 – 100) + 44×320 + 32×450 = 61,750

1.6 Replacement of some of the fleet

A major dilemma faced by FQA, as well as other airlines, is which aircraft should it now procure in order to replace the ageing aircraft in its fleet. FQA could acquire newer models of the same type of aircraft which it currently has in service or obtain replacements from the next generation of aircraft which are being developed. In considering this matter, the directors of FQA need to take into account the way the airline industry is moving and the increasing trend for larger aircraft carrying more passengers and having a greater range capability. F and C are the leading manufacturers of passenger aircraft and are bitter rivals. Both F and C have produced prototypes of the next generation of passenger aircraft. The F 898 has a smaller capacity in terms of passengers carried than the C 491 but, in general terms, has greater flexibility. This is due to the F 898 being capable of reaching more destinations than its C rival as it is smaller and makes less demand on airports in terms of the infrastructure that is required to accommodate it. On the other hand, the C 491 can carry 600 passengers which is double the number which the F 898 can seat. Both aircraft have a similar range.

The C 491 will operate on a 'hub' system whereby the aircraft will land at a central location in each country or region which then permits passengers to transfer to other flights to reach their final destinations. However, the C 491 is a major double-decked aircraft which requires considerable investment in airport infrastructure to operate. In addition to the requirement for longer runways for take off and landing, the C 491 will not be able to use the existing airport gates for embarkation and disembarkation from the aircraft because it is too far off the ground. On the other hand, the F 898 may take off and land on the conventional length of runway which will accommodate the current aircraft in FQA's fleet. As it is a single-decked aircraft it will also be able to use the gates which are currently available in airports.

The Board of FQA must decide whether it should:

- invest in the C 491 and be able to transport more passengers in a single flight but which may result in a degree of inconvenience to passengers as they will need to transfer to other flights for onward travel; or
- obtain the F 898 with the smaller passenger capacity, which has the same range as the C 491, but is able to land at more destinations.

The directors of FQA must consider the economies of scale associated with the larger passenger aircraft and the consequent loss of flexibility. In addition, with regard to the F 898, FQA needs to take account of the increased costs of paying more in landing charges for operating at a larger number of final destinations. This is a major item of cost bearing in mind that some countries offer landing slots to airlines on a bid system. Some landing slots at major airports in the world, which are located in popular destinations, are extremely expensive.

Other issues which need to be considered by FQA include:

- expected levels of passenger demand over the period of the life of whichever aircraft it procures;
- the impact of competition over that period within the airline industry;
- the cost of manpower;
- re-training and operational costs such as fuel.

A further consideration is how other competitor airlines are likely to respond to the dilemma, as they all face the same issue of replacement of their fleets at some time or another. If the trend of the world's airlines favours one aircraft over the other, then FQA does not want to be committed to obtaining the aircraft which are less favoured by other airlines. This may cause spare parts to be less available and at a higher cost. However, FQA is itself an influencer given its market position and other airlines are likely to take account of the decision made by the FQA Board in making their own choices.

Questions and comments on Section 1.6 – Possible replacement aircraft	**Response**
Summarise the pros and cons of each aircraft mentioned.	
C491	Pros • Greater capacity fitting with predicted trend in industry • Hub system should increase usage efficiency. • Economies of scale re landing fees – could be very important given bid-ding system for slots

	Cons • Airports need to invest in infrastructure and runways to accommodate them. Many airports may not be ready. • Hub system requires customers to make more transfers
F898	Pros • Greater flexibility as can use smaller airports • Able to use existing airports • In periods of low demand firms % utilization would be higher. Cons • Smaller capacity • Higher landing fees per passenger

1.7 FQA Board members

Chairman:

Appointed Company Secretary in 1990, then a director in 1994 after relinquishing Company Secretary role. Appointed Chief Executive in 1998 and Chairman in 2005. Lawyer by profession and was a barrister specialising in aviation law until becoming Company Secretary in 1990. Holds 3 million shares in FQA.

Chief Executive:

Joined group in 1975 and has been a director since 1995. Holds 5 million shares in FQA.

Chief Operating Officer:

Was a pilot until 1993 and has worked with FQA in operational matters since then. Was sponsored by FQA to take a post graduate degree in Operational Management at an 'Ivy League' University in the USA in 1993/4.

Finance Director:

Joined the group in 1998 and is a qualified CIMA accountant. Previously she held posts in the airline industry in Europe where she had good contacts in respect of obtaining investment capital. While working for a European airline, she successfully established a subsidiary low-priced airline but returned to her roots in the Far East for domestic reasons.

Engineering Director:

Previously employed by the International Civil Aviation Organisation and joined the group in 1992. He is an Aeronautical Engineer by profession. Holds 3 million shares in FQA.

Director of Sales and Marketing:

Held a variety of posts with FQA since 1988 and is a member of a recognised professional body in marketing having been senior sales manager for a rival airline until her appointment to FQA.

Director of HRM:

Appointed in 1996 from the board of a multi national conglomerate and is a member of a recognised professional body in the field of personnel management.

Director of Corporate Development:

Joined FQA as a management trainee in 1982 and is responsible for corporate planning. Holds 5 million shares in FQA. He has held a number of senior management roles in FQA and worked his way up the organisation culminating in being appointed to the Board in 2003.

Director of Service Delivery:

Has dual role as manager of Corporate Communication and also responsible for Information management. Her academic background is that she holds a PhD in software development and joined FQA in 1999.

Director of Quality Management:

Joined the group in 1984 and has no formal qualifications. Currently has responsibility for quality assurance and catering contracts. Holds 2 million shares in FQA.

All executive directors of FQA have share options.

There are also 12 non-executive directors on the FQA Board.

Questions and comments on Section 1.7 – Board	Response
Comment on the information given about the Board members.	Overall less information than with other cases.
Chairman	• Good experience regarding aviation law.
Chief Executive	• Insufficient detail given
Chief operating officer	• Good experience as a pilot and operational management.
Finance Director	• Good experience in low-cost airlines and raising capital
Engineering Director	• Good experience in ICAO
Director of Sales and Marketing	• Qualified
Director of HRM	• Experience in a multi-national • Qualified
Director of Corporate Development	• Little experience outside FQA
Director of Service Delivery	• Expertise in communications and software development, but little information given regarding customer service.
Director of Quality Management	• No formal qualifications
Comment on the overall balance of the board	• 12 NEDs should indicate a commitment to good corporate governance • The Board lacks experience in some critical areas – customer service and quality. • There does not appear to be a director of IT • Share ownership should enhance board motivation. However, only four directors hold shares whereas one might expect all directors to participate in share bonus schemes of some type.

1.8 New terminal

One area of which the Board is particularly proud is FQA's reputation for being one of the most punctual and safest airlines in the world. This in turn has given rise to national pride and the government has provided financial support in terms of grants and loans particularly in regard to a new terminal development at the airport in the capital city in FQA's home country. This airport is owned and operated by an airport authority which is independent of FQA.

In 2008, the airport in the capital city of FQA's home country plans to open a new passenger terminal which would be dedicated for the use of the airline. This will permit rationalisation of staff resources to take place, enabling FQA's ground passenger service staffing levels to be reduced. However, no negotiations on the required staffing levels have yet been undertaken with the trade unions (which are organisations established to negotiate pay agreements and improvements in working conditions on behalf of their members). Airline staff, however, have heard rumours of the likely rationalisation and this has resulted in enquiries to the Board being made by the trade unions. There has been no official response by the Board to this, but it is taking seriously the threat of strike action resulting from rationalisation. The threat of strike action has been reported in daily newspapers. The newspapers have attributed their source of information to the trade unions.

Questions and comments on Section 1.8 – New Terminal	**Response**
Comment on the proposed expansion to the airport in FQA's home country.	• The new terminal should enable FQA to increase its domestic capacity but does the demand exist or is the expansion politically motivated? • How are fees between FQA and the domestic airport calculated? • Is there a risk that the new slots will be given to competitors?

Assess the causes and implications of the threat of possible strike action.	Causes • Low staff morale (see section 1.9 below) • A lack of communication • Rumours of redundancies. Implications • Reduced customer service quality • Damage to FQA's reputation

1.9 Managerial Style of FQA

FQA always prides itself on having staff who are dedicated to providing a high quality service. The Director of HRM regularly reviews FQA's human resource and remuneration policy taking account of legislation, industry practice and market conditions. The Board has been under increasing pressure to reduce costs. This has resulted in much more emphasis being placed by the Board on individual and company performance than previously in determining human resource and remuneration policy. This has caused considerable staff discomfort over the last two years.

FQA faced difficult employee relations issues through the summer period of the last financial year. It encountered demands for higher pay from ground staff, for improved working conditions and reduced working hours from both air crew (pilots and flight engineers) and cabin staff. These demands led to hard negotiations with the trade unions. All operational staff at FQA, including flight crew and cabin staff, are members of trade unions.

These negotiations resulted in some improvements in pay for the baggage handlers and reduced working hours for air crew and cabin staff. However, the demands made by the trade unions were not met in full. The agreement made between FQA and the trade unions was on condition that targets in productivity increases were achieved. This has resulted in some voluntary redundancies being made in order to meet the productivity targets and a general reduction in the cabin staff on the payroll. The strong tactics employed by the directors of FQA have resulted in many cabin staff feeling that they have been mistreated by the company. They also feel let down by their trade union representatives, which has led to poor morale among the staff.

In addition, FQA has faced many difficulties with suppliers, particularly its outsourced catering service at its home based airport in the capital city. The issue has been that the main catering service supplier (CG) has complained that the hard bargaining stance by FQA management has reduced its margin to such an extent that it is barely making any profit.

At the same time, the Director of Quality Management has made serious complaints regarding the reduced level of quality in the catering service itself following an increasing level of complaints from passengers over recent months. CG's management has responded by threatening to withdraw the service altogether unless FQA agrees to re-negotiate the price for the service which is supplied. In reply, FQA has stated that it will only renegotiate on price when the quality of the service has shown improvement over a sustained period and has threatened legal action for breach of contract if the service is withdrawn.

Questions and comments on Section 1.9 – Managerial style	**Response**
Given that FQA tries to compete on the basis of higher quality, why do you think the board has been under pressure to reduce costs?	• Pressure from major shareholders (see section 1.10 below) • Intense competitive rivalry is forcing all operators to review their cost base.
How important do you think staff are to FQA?	• Good customer service is part of FQA's competitive strategy, so having motivated staff will be a key part of this. • However, cost cutting may be more important given market conditions, so attempts to reduce staff costs and improve efficiency are justified.

Comment on the recent negotiations with trade unions.	• Management style seems very aggressive. • Management appear to have achieved a good deal in the short term for the company. However, the resulting low staff morale will compromise quality. • It also increases the risk of more militant union representatives being elected with the increased possibility of future strikes
Assess the problems with the catering supplier in FQA's home airport.	• As with internal disputes, the management of FQA may be fighting too hard to get a good deal for the company with poor quality the result. • FQA should view suppliers as partners rather than adversaries. • If the catering firm goes bust, then there will be major disruption to change to a new supplier. (**Note:** British Airways had a dispute with its Heathrow caterers Gate Gourmet in 2005. Gate Gourmet claimed that low prices had forced them to the edge of bankruptcy. BA originally sold its catering operations to Gate Gourmet in 1997 and then pressed for cheaper contracts.)

Summary: it may be that FQA are chasing cost savings too aggressively and at the expense of quality.

1.10 Pressure from shareholders

The Chairmen of the two largest shareholders of FQA have held discussions with FQA's Chairman and Chief Executive in an attempt to find ways to increase shareholder value. They have made it clear that they believe the running costs of the airline are too high and must be reduced to enable the airline to become a leaner and fitter organisation. This, they argue, will enable FQA to be better able to increase market share in the increasingly competitive airline industry by being able to pass on cost reductions to passengers.

The Chairman and Chief Executive of FQA, advised by the Board, have replied to the two Chairmen of the largest shareholders that any significant impact on lowering costs can only be achieved by reducing the staffing levels which will in turn impact negatively on quality. They also point out that there has been a wave of voluntary redundancies in order to satisfy the increased pay levels and improved working conditions. The Chairman and Chief Executive have warned that further reductions in the staffing levels in the existing operations will erode staff morale even more and may be counter productive in terms of achieving greater market share. At the same time as making this point, the Chairman has instructed the Director of HRM to give serious thought to how further staff reductions could be achieved.

Questions and comments on Section 1.10 – Shareholders	Response
Comment in the relationship between FQA and its shareholders.	• FQA's shareholders seem to be much more aggressive in putting their views across than with many firms. • While putting forward counter arguments, the directors seem to comply anyway. • The directors are paid to run the company to maximise the wealth of all shareholders. It would be useful to canvass the views of other shareholders to see if they agree with the ones given.

Assess the arguments given by the chairman and Chief Executive of FQA	• The concerns of the FQA directors are well founded as quality does appear to be being compromised. • However, the market is becoming increasingly price driven so the share-holders views are also well founded.

1.11 Financial Results for the previous two years

Extracts from the financial results for the previous two financial years for FQA are presented at Appendix A.

Questions and comments on Section 1.11	Response
Go to Appendix A and analyse the figures using the proformas given.	See Appendix A below

1.12 Competition data

The following information provides a short statistical comparison between FQA and two competitors in the last financial year:

	FQA	Competitor 1	Competitor 2
Revenue (in$ million)	10,895	17,784	8,632
Profit attributable to shareholders ($million)	371	546	286
Share price at year end ($)	9.0	6.0	4.5
Shares in issue at year end (million)	520	1,100	600
Long-term liabilities ($ million)	4,220	6,400	3,330
Fleet size (number of aircraft)	170	290	165
Kilometres flown (million)	560	920	480
Aircraft departures (thousand)	152	250	130
Passenger load factor (overall % of capacity used)	80	75	73
Passengers carried (million)	27	42	22
Ontime departures *(within 15 minutes) %	93	76	75

Questions and comments on Section 1.12 – Competition data	Response
Assess FQA using the following categories:	
Average length of flight (km)	FQA 3,684 C1 3,680 C2 3,692 All 3 companies have a similar mix of short and long haul flights
Revenue passenger kilometres (RPK) = total no of passengers × average length of flight (Billion kilometres)	FQA 99.5 C1 154.6 C2 81.2 C1 is larger than FQA, so should benefit from economies of scale (the margin info would suggest otherwise, however – see below)
Revenue per passenger = average fare ($)	FQA 403.5 C1 423.4 C2 392.4 FQA's average fare is lower than C1 –this is not due to flight distances. It could be a pricing decision by FQA (e.g. last minute price cuts to ensure higher loading), but it may be that C1 has a better reputation or is targeting more lucrative routes.
Load factor (%)	FQA has the best load factor – a critical success factor in the industry. This could be due to lower fares and/or better punctuality.
On time departures (%)	FQA's punctuality is much higher than competitors, implying better quality for customers. This could be a critical issue for frequent flyers.

Profit margins (using profit attributable to shareholders)	FQA 3.4% C1 3.1% C2 3.3% FQA has the best margins. This is not due to being able to charge higher prices (C1's fares are higher) so must be due to FQA having a more efficient cost base and/or its better load factors.
Revenue per RPK ($)	FQA 0.110 C1 0.115 C2 0.106 C1 has higher revenue per RPK, mainly due to the higher fares it achieves.
P/E ratios = (share price × no of shares)/ profit attributable to shareholders	FQA 12.6 C1 12.1 C2 9.4 FQA has a higher P/E suggesting that the market perceives FQA as having lower risk and/or better growth prospects. This bodes well for raising finance.
Revenue per aircraft ($ million)	FQA 64.1 C1 61.3 C2 52.3 Despite lower prices than C1, FQA is achieving more revenue per aircraft, a result of higher load factors and better asset utilisation.
Kilometres flown per aircraft (millions)	FQA 3.29 C1 3.17 C2 2.91 FQA has the highest distances flown per aircraft, implying better asset utilisation
Departures per aircraft	FQA 894 C1 862 C2 788 FQA has the highest departures per aircraft, implying quicker turnarounds and /or more efficient scheduling.
Gearing using market values (debt/equity)	FQA 0.90 C1 0.97 C2 1.23 All 3 firms have high gearing, a typical feature of the industry. FQA has the lowest of the three indicating that it would be able to raise debt finance without having excessive gearing.

Summary: FQA has the best P/E ratio, the highest margins, the best load factors, the best reliability, the best asset utilisation and the lowest gearing. The only area where there may be scope for improvement is whether it could command higher prices.

1.13 Cost structures

The constant challenge faced by all airlines is the increasing cost of fuel. Airlines are able to counter increased fuel charges in a number of ways. These include being able to make surcharges to the customer on fuel cost increases and by seeking ways of increasing efficiency in the fuel consumption of their fleets.

The following table shows the proportions of FQA's total costs which are accounted for by particular expense types:

Expense type:	% of total Operating Costs in the financial year ended: 30 September 2006	% of total Operating Costs in the financial year ended: 30 September 2005
Staff and employment verheads	21	21
Fuel	31	29
Landing and parking	10	9
Other (including maintenance, engineering and equiptment)	39	41

FQA managed to reduce its exposure to increased fuel costs by using hedging techniques in the year to 30 September 2006 which was a year when fuel prices increased significantly.

Questions and comments on Section 1.13	Response
Comment on the cost structures given.	• Fuel is the largest single cost, emphasising how sensitive airline profits are to oil price fluctuations. Other than switching aircraft it is difficult for operators to reduce this cost. • The second highest cost is labour, which is why this area is the main focus for cost cutting. • The main change from 2005 to 2006 is the larger % of fuel reflecting higher oil prices. • The increase in landing fees could indicate problems with airport supplier power. • Most costs are unaffected by achieving higher load factors indicating how important this is (high operating gearing)
How could FQA reduce its exposure to oil price movements?	• Fuel price increases can be passed on to customers as surcharges but further information is needed as to whether customers would be willing to accept these unless all airlines adopted the same policy. • Hedging products can be used to fix oil prices but (with the exception of options, which are likely to be too expensive) prevent FQA from benefiting if prices fall. Hedging is advisable to reduce risk. • However, given high prices in 2005/2006 and predicted falls in 2007 it is debatable whether hedging products will be wanted as firms may prefer to be open to benefit from price falls.

1.14 New Aircraft

F 898

F expects to manufacture and sell over 1,800 of its F 898 aircraft by the mid-2020's in aiming to accommodate a market demand which it estimates will be for about 3,500 aircraft of this type and size. It expects the first delivery to a customer to be in 2008 with production and delivery at full capacity two years after that. Currently it has 200 firm orders from all over the world, with about one quarter of these from China. Its seating capacity varies depending on its configuration and customer requirements but it is designed to have 300 seats. It will fly at around 600 miles per hour, which is below the sound barrier.

The construction of the aircraft uses an advanced lightweight composite material and a greatly reduced amount of aluminium compared with older style aircraft. This provides a more robust airframe which is less prone to corrosion as well as significantly reducing the aircraft's weight. This means that it is about 18 tonnes lighter in weight than its nearest competitor aircraft of similar size and seating capacity.

F claims that its 898 aircraft is 20% more efficient in terms of fuel consumption and produces 20% fewer emissions than similar-sized existing aircraft. This is partly due to improved engine technology. The company claims this will have a significant impact in reducing emissions of carbon dioxide and nitrogen oxides thus keeping the air cleaner. In terms of noise pollution, F has designed the aircraft to be quieter on take off and landing than those currently in service. Therefore, F believes that its 898 aircraft will improve the lives of people living and working near airports and of its passengers. It is expected to achieve a 35% reduction in maintenance costs in comparison with similar sized aircraft.

With regard to customer facilities, F intends that the 898 aircraft will have a window size which is 40% larger than other aircraft. In addition, it provides more comfortable levels of humidity in the cabin, improved lighting, wider seats and aisles and larger luggage space above the passengers. This all contributes to making the 898 a more environmentally friendly and customer focused aircraft according to F. It is intended to fly between cities which are up to 16,000 km apart without passengers needing to make connecting flights. The F 898 provides passengers with access to in flight web-mail and the facility to use mobile telephones in the air.

C 491

C has stated that its C 491 aircraft is the first in the world to have a full upper and lower deck for passenger transport, with two aisles running in between the banks of seats. It has a range of 16,000 km which it can fly non-stop. C is implementing internationally accepted quality standards and aims to put this into practice in every aspect of its organisation. New technologies have been introduced enabling the C 491 aircraft to significantly reduce noise on take off, landing and in the air.

Improved technology has enabled the C 491 aircraft to achieve lower fuel consumption per seat making it more environmentally friendly than previous aircraft. The structure of the C 491 aircraft uses very hard wearing composite materials which are strongly resistant to fatigue. It uses lighter but durable materials and thus reduces its overall weight.

With regard to customer health and safety, in addition to improvements in cabin air supply and humidity, C has introduced a medical site on board the C 491 aircraft. The site is a seating configuration which can be varied into a table for patients and has storage for medical equipment such as a respirator, oxygen and electrocardiogram. The cabin crew will be trained in the use of the equipment.

The seating configuration can be modified to suit customer requirements and doors on the main deck and upper deck can be used simultaneously to allow embarkation and disembarkation of passengers. With two loading belts, the aircraft can more speedily achieve transfer of luggage onto and off the aircraft. The turnaround time taking account of refuelling, passenger disembarkation, cleaning, re-stocking and embarkation of the next group of passengers takes about 100 minutes which is considerably less than the time taken on current aircraft in FQA's fleet.

The C 491 will permit the ratio of cabin staff to passengers to be reduced on each aircraft compared with the F 898.

Questions and comments on Section 1.14 – New aircraft	Response
List the advantages given for the F898 given in this section.	• Lighter • Less prone to corrosion • Fuel efficiency • Fewer emissions • Quieter • Lower maintenance costs • Larger windows • Better environment (humidity control, lighting) • Better seating (wider seats, wider aisles) • More luggage space • In flight web-mail, mobile phone usage
List the advantages given for the C491 given in this section.	• Quieter • Lower fuel consumption per seat so less emis-sions • Lighter • Less prone to fatigue • Better environment (improved air supply and humidity) • On board medical site • Quicker turnaround • Fewer staff needed

Summary: both claim to be lighter, quieter, more fuel efficient, less prone to fatigue and to offer passengers an improved environment. Any discussion should thus focus on other aspects (e.g. size, turnaround time)

1.15 Forecast comparative costs and revenues generated by each aircraft

The following information gives the forecast comparative costs and revenues for one aircraft supplied by each manufacturer operating at FQA's normal capacity of 80% passenger load factor. The normal operating life of an aircraft is in excess of 20 years but the Board of FQA has decided to review the comparative information over a period of 10 years as technology is developing at such a rapid pace. It can be assumed that there is no re-sale value of the aircraft at the end of the 10 years. In producing this information, it has been assumed that either aircraft, once selected, will be available to come into service on 1 January 2008.

All revenues and costs can be assumed to be stated at 1 January 2008 price levels:

Cash inflows	Per aircraft C491 $ million	Per aircraft F898 $ million
Annual		
Income from passengers	115	70
Income from cargo	35	18
Income from other revenue generating services	4	2

The following inflation allowances are made for each income heading and apply to both aircraft. These apply from 1 January 2008:

- Income from passengers, and other services is expected to increase by an average compound rate of 5% per year.
- Income from cargo is expected to increase by an average compound rate of 10% per year.

Cash inflows	Per aircraft C491 $ million	Per aircraft F898 $ million
Annual		
Staff costs	12	9
Landing and parking costs	22	12
Fuel costs	30	26
Maintenance costs	12	4
Contribution to airport development	16	0
Other costs	4	3
Capital cost of each aircraft	250	150

Notes

(a) Staff costs take full account of estimated employment taxes.

(b) Revenue generated by FQA from carriage of cargo in the financial year ended 30 September 2006 represented about 5% of total revenue. Both the C491 and F898 have much greater carrying space available enabling a higher share of revenue per aircraft to be earned by carriage of cargo. The revenue earned by other activities besides that from passengers and cargo in the financial year ended 30 September 2006 was 2.6% of total revenue.

(c) FQA will be required to make a contribution to the development of the airports around the world servicing the C 491. This is a charge which will apply to each C 491 aircraft using the airports in order to provide facilities for handling it.

(d) Annual inflation allowances applying to both aircraft for each outflow heading are:

- Staff, maintenance and other costs are expected to increase by 3%.
- Landing and parking costs are expected to increase by 5%.
- Fuel costs are expected to increase by 15%.
- Contribution to airport developments is expected to increase by 4%.

(e) Depreciation is charged on a straight line basis over 10 years. Taxation depreciation allowances can be assumed to be calculated over a 10 year period also on a straight line basis.

(f) Corporate taxation in FQA's home country is at the rate of 25% per annum payable one year in arrears and it is not envisaged that this rate will change over the working life of each aircraft.

(g) A finance lease with a rental cost of $45 million (gross) per annum for the C491 and $30 million (gross) per annum for the F 898 can be obtained. The lease payments will be made annually over 10 years and can be assumed to start on 1 January 2008. Alternatively, FQA has the opportunity to purchase the aircraft using a term loan over 10 years at the annual fixed rate of interest of 8% pre-tax.

(h) The Finance Director considers a suitable risk adjusted money cost of capital rate to be 10% post tax.

Questions and comments on Section 1.15	Response
Calculate the NPV of operating each aircraft for ten years by preparing a spreadsheet package and comment.	F898: NPV = +$26 million C491: NPV = +$97 million (Workings below) Both aircraft appear to be viable, though the C491 gives the larger increase to shareholder value. This is partly due to the larger size but NPVs would suggest that a C491 is worth more than three F898s. However, other non financial factors such as pollution, noise, safety, etc also need to be considered. The assumptions underlying the figures also need to be challenged. Will hub-to-hub routes with larger aircraft be required (C491) or more aircraft that can use existing airport infrastructure (F898)? The C491 may have a higher NPV but could be the riskier option.
Evaluate the lease v buy decision for each aircraft	F898: Lease NPV = -$182 million Buy NPV = -$122 million C491: Lease NPV = -$273 million Buy NPV = -$208.3 million (Workings below) For both aircraft there appears to be a significant advantage in buying rather than leasing. This is partly due to FQA being able to borrow at a post-tax cost of 6%.

NPV - C491

£ millions	t = 0	t = 1	t = 2	t = 3	t = 4	t = 5	t = 6	t = 7	t = 8	t = 9	t = 10	t = 11
Income												
Passengers and other		125	131	138	145	152	159	167	176	185	194	
Cargo		39	42	47	51	56	62	68	75	83	91	
Costs												
Staff maintenance and other		-29	-30	-31	-32	-32	-33	-34	-35	-37	-38	
Landing and parking		-23	-24	-25	-27	-28	-29	-31	-33	-34	-36	
Fuel		-35	-40	-46	-52	-60	-69	-80	-92	-106	-121	
Contribution to airport development		-17	-17	-18	-19	-19	-20	-21	-22	-23	-24	
Net operating income		**60**	**63**	**65**	**66**	**68**	**69**	**69**	**69**	**68**	**66**	
Tax on operating income @ 25%			-15	-16	-16	-17	-17	-17	-17	-17	-17	-17
Capital cost	-250											
Tax re writing down allowances			6	6	6	6	6	6	6	6	6	6
Net cash flow	**-250**	**60**	**54**	**55**	**57**	**58**	**58**	**58**	**58**	**57**	**55**	**-10**
Discount factor @ 10%	1.000	0.909	0.826	0.751	0.683	0.621	0.564	0.513	0.467	0.424	0.386	0.350
Present value	**-250**	**55**	**44**	**42**	**39**	**36**	**33**	**30**	**27**	**24**	**21**	**-4**
Net present value	**97**											

C491 - Lease v Buy

Narrative	CF	Timing	DF@6%	PV
Lease				
Lease payments	-45	0-9	7.802	-351.1
Tax	11	2-11	6.943	78.1
NPV of lease				**-273.0**
Buy				
Capital cost	-250	0	1.000	-250.0
Tax	6	2-11	6.943	41.7
NPV of buying				**-208.3**

NPV - F898

£ millions	t = 0	t = 1	t = 2	t = 3	t = 4	t = 5	t = 6	t = 7	t = 8	t = 9	t = 10	t = 11
Income												
Passengers and other		76	79	83	88	92	96	101	106	112	117	
Cargo		20	22	24	26	29	32	35	39	42	47	
Costs												
Staff maintenance and other		-16	-17	-17	-18	-19	-19	-20	- 20	-21	-22	
Landing and parking		-13	-13	-14	-15	-15	-16	-17	-18	-19	-20	
Fuel		-30	-34	-40	-45	-52	-60	-69	-80	-91	-105	
Contribution to airport development		0	0	0	0	0	0	0	0	0	0	
Net operating income		**36**	**37**	**36**	**36**	**35**	**33**	**31**	**27**	**23**	**18**	
Tax on operating income @ 25%			-9	-9	-9	-9	-9	-8	-8	-7	-6	-4
Capital cost	-150											
Tax re writing down allowances			4	4	4	4	4	4	4	4	4	4
Net cash flow	**-150**	**36**	**31**	**31**	**30**	**30**	**28**	**26**	**24**	**20**	**16**	**-1**
Discount factor @ 10%	1.000	0.909	0.826	0.751	0.683	0.621	0.564	0.513	0.467	0.424	0.386	0.350
Present value	**-150**	**33**	**26**	**23**	**21**	**18**	**16**	**13**	**11**	**9**	**6**	**0**
Net present value	**26**											

F898 - Lease v Buy

Narrative	CF	Timing	DF@6%	PV
Lease				
Lease payments	-30	0-9	7.802	-234.1
Tax	8	2-11	6.943	52-1
NPV of lease				**-182.0**
Buy				
Capital cost	-150	0	1.000	-150.0
Tax	4	2-11	6.943	27.8
NPV of buying				**-122.2**

1.16 Appendix A – Extracts from the accounts of FQA

Balance Sheet

	As at 30 September 2006		As at 30 September 2005	
	$m	$m	$m	$m
Non-current assets (net)		8,408		7,918
Intangible assets		246		224
Total non-current assets		8,654		8,142
Current assets		2,669		2,469
Toal assets		11,323		10,611
Equity and reserves		3,948		3,759
Long-term liabilities				
Bank loans				
(repayable 2008)	1,000		1,000	
(repayable 2009)	1,000		1,000	
(repayable 2008)	720		420	
Other long-term liabilities				
(including leases)	1,500	4,200	1,450	3,870
Current liabilities		3,155		2,982
Total equity and liabilities		11,323		10,611

Note: Paid in share capital represents 520 million shares at $0.50 each at 30 September 2006.

Income statement

	Year ended 30 September 2006	Year ended 30 September 2005
	$m	$m
Revenue	10,895	10,190
Total operating costs	10,135	9,745
Operating profit	760	445
Finance costs	-265	-235
Tax expense	-124	-53
Profit for period	371	157

Statement of changes in equity

	Share capital $m	Share premium $m	Retained earnings $m	Total $m
Balance at 30 September 2005	26	1,714	1,785	3,759
Profit for the period			371	371
Dividends paid			-182	-182
Balance at 30 September 2006	260	1,714	1,974	3,948

Note: It can be assumed that the accounts for the year ended 30 September 2006 are final and have been audited.

Questions and comments on Appendix A	Response
Analyse the financial statements using ratio analysis:	See below

Your response

	2006	2005	2006 Workings	2005 Workings
Profitabiliy				
Growth in revenue	6.9%	-	(10,895/10,190) -1	-
Growth in operating profit	70.8%	-	(760/445) -1	-
Growth in net profit	136.3%	-	(371/157) -1	
Capital employed	8,168	7,629	3,948 + 4,220	3,759 + 3,870
ROCE	9.3%	5.8%	760/8,168	445/7,629
Return on equity	9.4%	4.2%	371/3,948	157/3,759
Operating profit margin	7.0%	4.4%	760/10,895	445/10,190
Net profit margin	3.4%	1.5%	371/10,895	157/10,190
Asset turnover	1.33x	1.34x	10,895/8,168	10,190/7,629
Liquidity				
Current ratio	0.85	0.83	2,669/3,155	2,469/2,982
Investor ratios				
Gearing - Debt/Equity - using book value	1.07	1.03	4,220/3,948	3,870/3,759
Interest cover	2.87	1.89	760/265	445/265
Dividend cover	2.04	-	371/182	-
E.p.s	0.71	0.30	371/520	157/520

Your comments

Improving financials in pretty much every respect and many quotable figures!

Together these should be viewed very positively by markets making finance easier to raise. Growth in profits, margins and ROCE are particularly impressive given high oil prices and intense competition.

Despite being higher than competitors, net margins are still very low at 3.4%. Also the return to equity of 9.4% would ideally be higher, given that bank loans are currently quoting an interest rate of 8% pre-tax.

Another area of concern could be the low current ratio. It is also noticeable that we are given no information regarding cash flow (or even the cash balance) and do not have sufficient detail to construct a cash flow statement. The unseen information may (will!) contain more on this.

chapter

7

FLYQUAL: INDUSTRY AWARENESS

Contents

1 Introduction

The case concerns a global airline so students were expected to research the industry. What follows is an example of the type of analysis that could have been done.

2 Market overview

Change within the aviation industry has been driven by three main factors:

- **Deregulation**

  Before the 1980s the industry was highly regulated, so it was very difficult for operators to access new markets and routes. Many national airlines were also state funded and supported, further enhancing barriers to entry. From the mid 1980s to the present the industry has been characterised by deregulation of markets and increasing liberalisation.

  While regulation still exists, many international markets now have 'open skies' policies. This freer access has resulted in greater intensity of competition.

- **Aircraft capabilities**

  Before 1985 operators were given a very narrow choice of aircraft by manufacturers. Since then the choice of aircraft offered has increased dramatically – a trend that is predicted to continue.

- **Operator strategies**

  As with many markets, operators must choose between quality and cost based approaches to competition. However, in the air travel industry many firms who had previously viewed themselves as low cost found themselves undercut by new entrants. Many of the new entrants in the 1980s and 1990s were small companies offering low price, no frills flights with few extras, and operating out of regional airports. The prices of flights for these companies were far below those of the major airlines, resulting in many established firms going bust in the passenger sector.

  Looking forwards, the other major element of operator strategy is the choice between:

  – 'fragmentation' or 'point to point' models – offering a high frequency of non-stop flights to a wide range of destinations

- 'consolidation' or 'hub and spoke' models – using larger aircraft to fly into major hubs with passengers / freight then transferring to smaller aircraft for regional spokes.

3 Market growth

Most operators are predicting global passenger traffic growth of approximately 5% per annum until 2025 with the figure for cargo nearer 6% per annum.

Emerging markets are the major driver of overall growth. The 'BRIC' economies (Brazil, Russia, India and China) are the world's largest emerging markets. These nations have the potential to become the four most dominant economies in the world by 2050.

The propensity of people to travel in each country depends on their social, cultural and geographical characteristics, but is mainly linked to GDP per capita. The economic growth of the BRIC countries means that, together, they add around 80 million new consumers every year to the addressable market for air travel. As a result, demand for air travel in the BRIC countries has been growing at nearly 10% per annum for the last ten years.

Other emerging markets (in terms of air travel) include Indonesia, Malaysia, the Commonwealth of Independent States (CIS), Poland, Hungary, Turkey, Mexico, Argentina, Chile, South Africa, Morocco and Egypt.

4 Safety issues

Despite the high publicity plane crashes receive, studies suggest that air travel is still much safer than train or car. However the airline industry is affected by safety concerns:

- After the terrorist attacks on 9th September 2001 ('9/11') many potential passengers decided not to fly. The collapse of operators such as Sabena (Belgium), Swissair, Ansett Australia, and Vanguard Airlines (U.S.) was blamed partly on 9/11.
- Numbers of long-haul flights fell by between 5 and 10% in the months following the SARS outbreak in March 2003.
- There has been growing concern that air travel may increase the risk of deep vein thrombosis (DVT). The risk appears to be associated with long-haul flights, where passengers are seated and immobile for long periods of time.

5 Industry profitability

The International Air Transport Association (IATA) estimated that the global airline industry made losses of $4 billion during 2005. This fell to $0.5 billion in 2006 and a profit of $2.5 billion is forecast for 2007. The airline industry is a difficult one in which to make money!

The main reasons for these losses were:

- Intense competition (airlines have high operating gearing so are very sensitive to load factors)
- High oil prices (see section 7.11 below)
- IATA also blamed the presence of ongoing regulations restricting access to routes. For example, there are calls for less regulation in Europe (for a so-called 'Single European Sky').

Future profitability is linked to revenue growth, higher load factors and improving efficiency.

6 What passenger customers want

A survey by the US Department of Commerce found that the main determinants of passenger choice are the following (starting with the most important):

1. Price
2. Convenience of schedule
3. Frequent flyer schemes
4. Non-stop flights
5. Previous good experience
6. Other
7. Safety reputation
8. Loyalty
9. Employer policy
10. In-flight service
11. On-time reputation

7 Manufacturers' strategies

The two main commercial aircraft manufacturers in the world are Boeing and Airbus. (Note: It is probable that, in this case, 'F' is based loosely on Boeing and 'C' on Airbus.)

Boeing believes that airlines will accommodate future growth by adding new non-stop flights and by adding more frequency choices – not by an increase in airplane size. As a result it is only anticipating a 2% increase in average aircraft size. The new 787 'Dreamliner' typically has between 400 and 500 seats, but also has greater cargo capacity than comparable planes, offering greater flexibility.

Airbus on the other hand believes that more passengers will have to fly hub-to-hub using larger airplanes, connecting one or more times to complete their journey. Their expectation of a 20% increase in average aircraft sizes is reflected in the size of their new double-deck, 555-seater A380 airplanes.

8 Operator strategies 1: cost-based competition

Low-cost operators such as Ryanair in Europe, Hansung Airlines in Asia and Southwest in the USA have been very successful using a business model where profits are made on the basis of low costs and high utilisation.

- Low costs are achieved by cheap airport fees (e.g. by using 'secondary' airports or flying at less popular times), quick turnaround facilities, no free drinks or food in flight, and efficient booking and operating procedures.
- High utilisation is possible as a result of taking market share from other airlines, generating more business through low prices and restricting services to selected, popular routes.

While the 'no-frills' approach has been very successful for local and regional flights, it is less applicable to long-haul due to the following reasons:

- Customer expectations – the lack of free food and drinks would not be tolerated on an eight hour flight, for example.
- Whereas quick turnarounds enable extra flights to be fitted in on local routes, this more difficult with greater journey times.
- With long-haul flights fuel is a greater percentage of overall cost, so any savings made on food or booking processes are less significant.

However, increasing competition and the high price of oil are forcing all operators to reassess their cost base.

9 Operator strategies 2: quality-based competition

British Airways ('BA') is an example of a major airline that has had to deal with industry recessions and the threat from low cost operators. Strategies adopted include the following:

- Low price offers on certain routes to compete with no-frills operators.

- Despite claiming to offer high quality, many of BA's plans have focussed on ongoing cost cutting exercises. For example, plans to introduce automatic ticketing and check-in at its London Heathrow hub are expected to reduce annual costs by £200 million. However, BA has cut 14,000 jobs in the last three years and further redundancies may be deemed unacceptable by unions.
- Improving the quality for the business sector, including offering armchair style seats that can convert to beds.
- Plans for efficiency gains by moving to a new terminal 5 at London Heathrow.

10 Operator strategy 3: alliances

It is common for operators to form / join alliances. Benefits to customers include:

- More choice of flights and destinations
- Enhanced frequent flyer benefits
- Easier booking and check-in
- More lounges
- Easier connections.

Examples of such alliances include the following:

- The One-world alliance – includes British Airways, American Airlines, Cathay Pacific, Aer Lingus, Finnair, Iberia, Lan Airlines and Quantas.
- Skyteam – includes Aeroflot, AeroMexico, KLM, Air France, Korean Air, Delta, NWA, Continental Airlines, Alitalia and Delta.

11 Environmental issues

There has been much press focus on the carbon implications of air travel. For example, a one-way flight from London to Delhi produces an average of one tonne of CO2 per passenger.

Many consumers are questioning whether they should be flying as often and seek to reduce their 'carbon footprint' or make their trips 'carbon neutral' by funding projects such as renewable energy and reforestation. These either reduce emissions at source or absorb CO2 from the atmosphere.

However, according to the recent Stern report, worldwide aviation produces 1.6% of total greenhouse gas emissions - less than a sixth of the contribution from road transport, for example. Stern estimates that aviation's figure will reach 5% by 2050 if the industry takes no mitigating action.

British Airways supports carbon trading as the most environmentally effective method of limiting the impact of air travel on global warming. A trading system means you must either cut your own emissions, or bear the considerable (and increasing) cost of failing to do so by buying credits from other operators. However, the limited success of the Kyoto protocol on climate change has led some commentators to suggest that carbon trading is unlikely to be acceptable to many of the world's major operators, especially in the USA.

Other parties support higher taxation on aviation fuel as a way of ensuring that the polluter pays. However, if a tax on aviation fuel is to be introduced it must be on a worldwide scale and reflect the size and fuel efficiency of the aircraft.

Many airlines claim that greater efficiency is the solution. Certainly manufacturers are trying to ensure that newer aircraft are quieter and produce less pollution.

According to Michael O'Leary, Chief Executive, the last five years have seen Ryanair achieve a 50% reduction in carbon dioxide emissions and a 45% reduction in fuel burn and noise by investing over $10bn dollars in brand new aircraft.

12 Oil prices

High oil prices have had a major impact on airline profitability (or the lack of it).

- Global demand for oil is constantly increasing despite shifts to alternative fuels and improving efficiency. Increases are due mainly to developing countries (e.g. BRIC).
- Oil price fluctuations are thus due mainly due to supply issues (e.g. behaviour of the OPEC cartel members, impact of natural disasters such as Hurricane Katrina in 2005, ongoing unrest in Iraq, threat of military action involving Iran or North Korea, political instability in Nigeria, US views over Russia's relationship with Venezuela and a number of other political flashpoints).

Analysts' forecasts are mixed as to whether 2007 will see the same price volatility as 2005 or 2006. Some predict that prices will reach $100 a barrel but most economists anticipate a slight fall in average prices in 2007.

13 Simplifying the business

The industry is looking at how it can 'simplify the business' ('StB') by a combination of the following:

- E-ticketing (ET) - reduces ticket processing charges, eliminates the need for paper and allows greater flexibility to the passenger and the travel agent to make changes to itineraries
- Bar coded boarding passes (BCBP) - enables fast, convenient check-in by enabling the passenger to print the boarding pass on a home printer
- Paper-free e-freight services
- Common Use Self Service (CUSS) - shared kiosks offer convenient passenger check-in whilst allowing multiple airlines to maintain branding and functionality. As kiosks can be located throughout the airport, congestion is alleviated and passenger flow improved
- Radio frequency ID (RFID) – electronic tagging for baggage to improve tracking. Tags can be 'talked to' or 'written to', allowing the status of an item to be updated as it is processed.

All of these could enable FQA to reduce costs without compromising quality. On the contrary, many of the measures should improve passenger convenience.

chapter

8

FLYQUAL: FURTHER DETAILED ANALYSIS

Contents

1 Introduction

As well as a detailed paragraph by paragraph analysis, it is a good idea to perform more detailed analysis under the following headings:

- Business strategy
- Financial strategy
- Risk and control
- Ethics

This is a chance to use standard techniques, such as SWOT, along with more specific analyses.

Finally, you should précis the case study.

2 Business strategy analysis

2.1 Consolidate your understanding of the strategic position of Flyqual Airlines using a SWOT analysis

Strengths

- Successful strategy of differentiation
- Reputation for high quality customer service – especially punctuality and safety
- Good financials compared to competition, esp. high margins
- Improving financials, esp. growth in revenue, profit and ROCE.
- Asset utilisation
- High load factors
- Membership of N alliance
- Base in Asia is well placed to exploit future growth

Weaknesses

- Board lacks experience in some key areas (e.g. IT)
- Over aggressive negotiating style has resulted in low staff morale and problems with caterers
- Cost cutting exercises may be compromising quality

Opportunities

- Cost cutting exercises, e.g. online booking
- Expansion of BRIC economies
- Expansion into more short-haul flights
- Increase the quantity and mix of cargo transported from the current 5%
- Acquisition / merger of a competitor
- Expansion into car hire / hotels and other complementary products that passengers may require.
- New airport terminal in home country

Threats

- Oil price rises
- Intense competitive rivalry
- Fall in passenger confidence (e.g. due to health scares or terrorist threats)
- Misreading the direction that the market moves (fragmentation or consolidation) could leave FQA with aircraft that are not of the ideal size.
- Tax on aviation fuel
- Stricter regulation on emissions
- Stricter safety legislation

2.2 Assess the airline industry using Porter's 5 forces analysis

Competitive rivalry – very high

- Large number of competitors around the world – a global market
- High fixed costs, so firms compete to achieve break-even and to benefit from incremental revenue
- High exit costs (e.g. long leases for aircraft, low resale values of aircraft, long-term commitments for slots)
- Larger competitors can use their resources to compete selectively (e.g. lowering prices, offering upgrades, connections and other facilities which smaller companies would find difficulty in imitating).

Threat of new entrants – high due to low barriers to entry

Despite the existence of many barriers, the fact that many firms have entered the industry would suggest that barriers can be overcome. Barriers include:

- Gaining slots at major airports
- Government subsidies to some national airlines create cost barriers

- Capital investment
- Some economies of scale, though these can be countered by joining aviation alliances.

Threat from substitutes – low for international flights, higher for short-haul

- Shipping is a major substitute for heavier cargo where speed is not important
- Passenger shipping is not seen as a major threat to airlines due to cost/speed considerations
- Short-haul flights have a greater threat from high-speed trains and road.

Power of suppliers – high for airports, low for fuel and aircraft

- Aircraft manufacture is dominated by a few major suppliers but competition between then reduces supplier power
- Airports have high power by being able to control /allocate slots. This power is less for 'secondary' airports
- The price of a commodity like fuel is fairly consistent between suppliers.

Power of customers – low individually, high collectively

- Individual customers do not make up a large proportion of airline revenue
- However, availability of online information regarding prices enables customers to switch airlines easily if they are not competitive. The lack of product differentiation also contributes to high collective power, though airline frequent flyer schemes help offset this.

Summary: key issues are competitive rivalry and the power of airports.

2.3 Analyse the airline industry using a PESTEL/ PEST/SLEPT style analysis

Political / legal

- Political instability / war can affect oil prices
- Subsidies can give national firms an (unfair?) advantage
- Regulation / deregulation – lack of access to routes/slots can be an effective barrier to entry
- Legislation re safety
- Government policy on carbon emissions
- Tax on aviation fuel.

Economic

- Demand closely linked to disposable income / state of the economy
- Main opportunities in developing (esp. BRIC) economies
- High systematic risk
- Profits very dependent on oil prices.

Social

- Overseas holidays now seen as the norm in many (particularly Western) countries
- Increasing concerns over carbon emissions
- Increasing safety/health fears
- People are much more comfortable booking their own flights online
- At present 50% of the world's population lives in cities. This is expected to rise to 60% by 2030. This could imply that certain cities will become much larger, thus increasing the likelihood of the hub-hub scenario occurring, which in turn will influence which type of aircraft should be bought.

Technological

- New aircraft are more efficient and more environmentally friendly
- Internet - online booking
- Easier to implement frequent flyer schemes
- New high-tech products tend to be transported by air to reduce speed to market.

Environmental / ethical

- Growing concern over environmental implications of air travel (e.g. pollution, noise).

2.4 Industry life cycle

Question	Your response
At which stage of the life cycle model would you categorise the airline industry?	• Mature, possibly saturated • Global.

Question	Your response
What are the implications of your classification?	• According to Porter, the key danger in a mature market is becoming stuck in the middle • He also argues that in a mature market most innovations can be copied easily by competitors, so cost-leadership is likely to be the most viable long term strategy • FQA should thus analyse the sources of its competitive advantage to ensure that it can continue to be a differentiator (see below) • In particular the threat from low cost competitors needs to be assessed.

2.5 Competitive strategy

FQA is trying to compete on the basis of differentiation. Assess the sustainability of this option.

The key to a strategy of differentiation is to offer the customer something for which they are prepared to pay extra. This uniqueness or enhanced quality needs to be difficult for competitors to copy for the strategy to be sustainable long term.

FQA tries to differentiate by offering the following:

- Good reliability.
- Choice of routes and extra services provided by being part of the N Alliance
- High quality customer care.

All of these can be imitated, although to date FQA's results would suggest that the strategy is working. However, whether or not this continues could be key to this case.

The danger is that customers will not be willing to pay for FQA's fares if competitors' offerings are much cheaper with only a slight reduction in the perceived quality.

Certainly FQA's major shareholders are pressing for cost reductions. The danger is that this will erode FQA's perceived quality and undermine its competitive strategy. This is a particular concern as FQA is less exposed to 'no-frills' competitors anyway as it focuses mainly on long-haul routes.

2.6 Using Ansoff's matrix outline possible directions for growth for FQA

Ansoff's matrix – product / market mix

	Existing products	**New products**
Existing markets	*Market penetration* • Try to win new slots for passenger routes • Expand share of short-haul market • Expand share of cargo market • Use IT to 'simplify the business', e.g. to develop online bookings • Acquire a no-frills operator • Seek further alliances.	*Product development* • Offer complementary services such as car hire and hotels.
New markets	*Market development* • Gain new routes/slots in developing economies (esp BRIC – Brazil, Russia, India & China).	*Diversification* *Related diversification* • Vertically integrate backwards into catering provision • Expand into travel agency. *Unrelated diversification* • *Anything!*

2.7 McFarlan and McKenny's strategic grid

The case does not give much information concerning how FQA has utilized IT to date. The Director of Service Delivery has some experience of writing software but FQA does not have a dedicated IT director, suggesting that IT has been viewed more in a 'support' role.

IT is likely to become more significant in the future as more firms seek to implement the 'simplify the business' initiatives such as online booking, e-ticketing, barcode boarding cards, etc. Websites also make it easier to offer a range of different prices at different times to increase load factors.

IT should thus be viewed as being in the 'turnaround' quadrant of the strategic grid. Further investment is needed to avoid falling behind competitors who may have a head start in this respect.

3 Financial Strategy analysis

3.1 Analyse the financing arrangements used by FQA to date and comment on the options available for raising finance in the future

Arrangements to date

We are told very little about FQA's history so can only look at current funding arrangements.

- Equity – FQA is a listed company but we are not told on which stock market.
- Debt – FQA has a mixture of leases (for some aircraft) and bank loans. Current gearing levels appear high but are still below those of given competitors.
- The average cost of debt is 265□(0.5×(4,220+3,870)) = 6.55%
- Dividend and interest covers are both above 2, so are healthy (just!)

Future requirements

- Loan repayments – we are not told the composition of current liabilities to see if there are any loans that need repaying in 2007 but we do know that FQA will have to repay $1,000 million of debt in both 2008 and 2009.
- Aircraft replacement – we are not given details for aircraft replacement. All we are told is that 'a number' of leased aircraft need replacing in the next two years. Anticipated growth and high current load factors would suggest a need for further aircraft at a cost of between $150 and $250 million each. If revenue is expected to grow by 7% next year (6.9% growth in 2006), then this would equate to approxi-

mately 170×7% = 12 new aircraft assuming current load factors, without including normal replacement investment. These would cost at least 150 × 12 = $1,800 million.

- Given net profit of only $371 million and a dividend of $182 million in 2006, the combination of the above would suggest that FQA will need to raise significant further finance in the near future.
- (Alternatively this could be viewed as the loan repayments being cash flow constraints that FQA will have to incorporate when financing new aircraft.)

Future financing possibilities

Equity

- Retained earnings and dividend cuts are insufficient to meet financing needs.
- Growth prospects, improving margins and ROCE all suggest that markets would respond favourably to attempts to raise more equity.
- However, return to equity is still low so may not tempt people to invest in the highly risky airline industry.
- There is also a question mark over the two conglomerate shareholders mentioned as they may be unwilling to provide further funds unless they see the cost cuts that they have requested.

Debt

- Loans can be taken out to replace existing ones when they are repaid without altering company gearing. Also when loans are repaid, presumably the security is then freed up for new loans (depending on the assets concerned).
- To some extent loans may be secured on the aircraft that FQA needs to buy. However, the banks may be looking for better security in terms of land and buildings.
- We are not given sufficient detail on the non-current assets to assess the quality of security. However, the book value of non-current assets is $8,408 million compared to long term liabilities of $4,220 million, suggesting that adequate security exists.
- If FQA's gearing (based on market values) were increased from 0.9 to 1.0, say, to match competitors, then this would allow $480 million (4220×1/9) of debt to be raised. This would not buy many aircraft!

Leasing

- Despite being more expensive, leasing may be attractive in terms of cash flow and tax implications.

Other

- FQA could seek soft loans and subsidies from its domestic Government, subject to WTO rules.

3.2 Examine different ways of valuing FQA and comment on their suitability.

1 **Share price**

Share price = $9

Number of shares = 520 million

Market capitalisation = 9 × 520 = $4,680 million

2 **Assets**

Book value of equity = $3,948 million

- It is interesting that the book value of equity is only 16% lower than the market capitalisation. Given that new shares are normally issued at a larger discount on market value, this could suggest that shares were issued when FQA was worth more.
- No information on how assets could be revalued to give either a net realisable value and/or a replacement cost valuation.
- Key valuation issues could relate to aircraft, whether bought or held under finance leases.

3 **Dividends**

We only have FQA's dividend for this year and no dividend information for competitors, making the DVM difficult to use.

Predicting future dividend growth is particularly difficult. Profits attributable to shareholders have grown by 136% from 2005 to 2006 but this figure is unlikely to be sustainable for use in the model.

4 **Earnings**

Using market capitalisations FQA's P/E ratio is 12.6, whereas competitors' figures are 12.1 and 9.4.

This suggests that the market places a premium on FQA's earnings, usually due either to lower perceived risk and/or higher growth prospects.

FQA's P/E of 12.6 could be used to assess possible acquisitions.

5 **Discounted cash flows**

We are told that FQA has a money cost of capital of 10%. This likely to be a WACC type figure and could be used to value the business by discounting free cash flows.

However, there is insufficient detail to perform such a calculation.

Comments

- Valuation techniques are always difficult when high growth is involved – as is the case here.
- However, the fact that FQA is quoted allows us to derive figures (e.g. P/E ratios) to use when valuing potential acquisitions.

4 Risk and control analysis

4.1 Identify and assess the risks facing FQA under the following headings.

Risk areas	Flyqual
Business risks	• High competitive rivalry, especially from no-frills operators on regional short-haul routes. • High power of airports in allocating slots.
Financial risks	• There will be some exposure to movements in exchange rates, though to some extent these will net off for a global player. • Given the high levels of gearing most operators will face high interest rate risk.
Political and legal risks	• Regulation can still act as an effective barrier to entry in some markets. The US is highly deregulated for example, whereas Asia still faces further deregulation. • Political unrest often affects oil prices. • Main legal risks relate to Government action on pollution, e.g. tax on aviation fuel, carbon trading schemes.
Technology risk	• Risk that new technologies being used in aircraft have reliability issues. • The Global Distribution System (GDS) allows customers to search all airlines for routes/fares resulting in greater price transparency.

Risk areas	Flyqual
Economic risk	• Movements in oil prices can have a major impact on airline profitability.
Reputation risk	• FQA prides itself on its good reputation. Problems with suppliers and low staff morale could seriously undermine this image.

4.2 Suggest some KPIs that could be used to monitor operations, using the balanced score-card as a framework

Financial perspective

- Net income
- Cash surplus
- Average fares
- Margins
- Profitability by route and aircraft
- Cost control – especially price and usage variances for fuel.

Customer perspective

- % on time departures
- % repeat business
- % refunds
- % bags lost / delayed
- Success of frequent flyer schemes
- Satisfaction surveys / complaints
- Number of passengers carried
- Safety record.

Internal business perspective

- Growth in revenue passenger kilometers (RPK)
- Staffing issues – sickness days, staff turnover, days lost to strikes
- Efficiency issues – especially load factors and asset utiliza-tion
- Time lost due to aircraft being out of operations due to breakdown or routine maintenance
- Labour productivity.

Innovation and learning perspective

- Brand awareness
- Number of suggestions made for improvement by staff (including what % were adopted)
- % e-tickets issued compared with manual tickets
- % sales online.

4.3 Assess FQA's organisational structure

We are told very little about FQA's organisational structure.

- There are directors in charge of various functions, suggesting a functional structure. There is no evidence of anyone being in charge of cargo business as distinct from passengers.
- As stated elsewhere, there is no board emphasis on IT.

4.4 Assess FQA's information and reporting systems

There is very little information given concerning FQA's reporting system.

The nature of the industry would suggest that FQA needs to have an effective long-term strategic planning process that incorporates scenario planning (e.g. with respect to oil prices, health scares, terrorism, etc.) The 'unseen' may give further detail as to whether FQA has this.

Major shareholders will be sophisticated enough (and appear to take enough interest!) to insist that FQA adopts a system of targets and reporting based on increasing shareholder value. This could involve:

- Setting targets related to free cash flow rather than profitability
- SVA, EVA methodologies
- Using NPV to evaluate potential projects.

5 Précis of the case study

FQA is a quoted international airline based in Asia.

5.1 The industry

The airline industry is a truly global business characterised by the following:

- Underlying trend of high growth – especially due to economic expansion of China, India and other BRIC economies.

- High volatility – short term demand can be affected by health scares (e.g. SARS), fears over terrorism (e.g. after 9/11), political unrest and even the weather (e.g. hurricanes) as well as economic trade cycles.
- Highly dependent on oil prices, which in turn are also highly volatile.
- High risk – overall the airline industry made losses in 2005 and 2006. Profits are, however, forecast for 2007.
- High competitive rivalry is forcing most operators to examine their cost base, especially in response to 'no-frills' operators.
- Ongoing deregulation, though significant barriers to entry still exist in some areas.
- Increasing concerns over the environmental implications of aircraft emissions.

5.2 FQA's existing strategy

FQA offers services at the high quality end of the market only. This is based on the following:

- Strong reputation for customer service
- High levels of punctuality
- Membership of the N alliance

FQA offers mainly long-haul passenger flights, although it does also provide short-haul and cargo services.

5.3 Performance

In contrast to overall industry losses, FQA has performed well in 2006:

- Revenue has grown by 6.9% to $10,895 million
- Operating profit has grown by 70.8% to $760 million and net profit by 136.3% to $371 million
- ROCE has increased from 5.8% to 9.3%
- High load factors (80% compared to competitors' figures of 75% and 73%)
- High asset utilisation
- High P/E ratio (12.6 compared to competitors' figures of 12.1 and 9.4).

Areas of concern include:

- Low but improving margins (net margin only 3.4%)
- Low return to equity at 9.4%.
- Low current ratio.

5.4 Key issues facing the firm

The key issues facing FQA are as follows:

- Competitive advantage – FQA's strategy of differentiation has been successful to date. However pressure to cut costs threatens to undermine quality – e.g. current problems with caterers and low staff morale. FQA must decide how it wishes to compete in the future – can it reduce costs without compromising quality or should it switch to a low-cost strategy?
- Stakeholder conflicts between shareholders, suppliers and employees. Possible strike action could prove very damaging.
- Fleet strategy – the two main aircraft manufacturers are offering very different visions of the future. The F898 can land at existing airports and is more suited to a fragmented 'point-to-point' strategy. The C491 is bigger, will require investment in airport infrastructure and is more suited to 'hub and spoke' strategies. Lead times emphasise the need for FQA to examine future market trends.
- Future financing – purchase of new aircraft and loan repayments over the next few years will need careful planning.
- How best to exploit growth opportunities.

chapter

9

FLYQUAL: MARCH 2007 – TAKING THE EXAM

Contents

1 Introduction

On the day of the exam the material is presented in two parts:

- the question requirement
- further detailed information on the firm.

2 Exam question requirement

'You are the consultant appointed by the FQA Board.

Prepare a report that prioritises, analyses and evaluates the issues facing FQA, and makes appropriate recommendations.'

3 Unseen material

Flyqual Airlines – Unseen material provided on examination day

Read this information before you answer the question

Capital Investment Appraisal

Capital Investment Appraisal calculations for both the C 491 and the F 898 have been produced. Extracts from the calculations are shown at Appendix B. (Appendix A is shown in the pre-seen material.) The appraisals were based on the C 491 having 600 seats and the F 898 having 300 seats and the normal capacity of an 80% passenger load factor was assumed. That is to say that the passenger income values assume that on average 80% of the aircraft seats will be sold on each flight. Taxation depreciation allowances were calculated over a ten-year period on a straight line basis. The calculations are for one aircraft of each type.

A decision on aircraft replacement must be made by 30 June 2007. It has been decided that all replacement aircraft will be leased. The decision to lease has no effect on the risk adjusted money cost of capital rate applied by FQA, which is 10%. Therefore the decision to lease has no effect on the NPV calculation shown in Appendix B. The Finance Director is confident that the total cash commitment of additional leasing charges can be met from future cash flows.

After the calculation shown in Appendix B had been made, it became apparent that assumptions relating to insurance premiums payable by FQA were incorrect. Insurance premiums had previously been excluded by the management accounting team leader responsible for preparing the calculation. This was because he thought that they applied equally to all the aircraft in the FQA fleet. Therefore the team leader concluded they were a common cost and could be excluded.

However, research by a member of the team leader's staff revealed that there would be a differential charge for insuring the C 491 as compared with the F 898. This additional insurance premium would need to be covered by FQA irrespective of how the acquisition of the aircraft was financed. The annual additional differential insurance premium for each C 491 aircraft would be at the yearly rate of $10,000 for each seat in the 600 seat aircraft, rising by 5% compound per year. The premiums are payable in advance, meaning that the first payment would be made on 1 January 2008.

The member of staff brought this to the attention of the team leader. The team leader refused to change the calculations already submitted to the Finance Director because he said it was "insignificant" with regard to the overall decision and instructed the member of staff to ignore it. The member of the team leader's staff was unwilling to ignore it and raised the matter with the Finance Director.

Landing rights at the airport in the capital city of FQA's home country

In an attempt to encourage increased competition in the airline industry, the government has awarded landing rights at FQA's home airport (in the capital city) to one of FQA's competitor airlines. These rights relate to a long-haul route which is in direct competition with one which FQA already operates and which generates a large amount of passenger traffic. The government made sure that the airline which was awarded the landing rights provides a high quality service similar to that offered by FQA. The new service is due to begin on 1 July 2007. The Aviation Minister has indicated that this may be the first award of a series of landing rights which may or may not be awarded to FQA in the future.

Maintenance Issues

As a result of budget cuts at FQA, some procedures were not completed and this led to a number of aircraft not complying with safety checks. This, in turn, led to an adverse safety report following a series of incidents which called into question the maintenance procedures employed by FQA. The Engineering Director produced a report which stated that the safety procedures were being improperly applied by three technicians whom he dismissed. The Engineering Director went on to say in his report that the maintenance procedures were now perfectly safe.

The pilots' trades union sought re-assurance from the Chief Executive of FQA that the safety of aircraft was not being compromised. In order to provide that re-assurance the Chief Executive appointed an independent engineering consultant to carry out a review of the maintenance procedures employed by FQA. The report of the independent engineering consultant concluded that there were serious faults with the maintenance procedures and that the Engineering Director should have known about these. The independent engineering consultant's report went on to state that in his professional opinion, the budget for maintenance needs to be reviewed as it is inadequate to carry out the required maintenance procedures and it was down to sheer luck that no serious incidents had occurred.

The trade unions argued that engineering management rather than the three technicians were at fault and these staff, who had been dismissed, had been used by FQA management to cover up the failings at a more senior level.

Trade unions negotiations

The maintenance issues coupled with the earlier difficulties with staff, had further damaged relations between management and staff within FQA. Seizing the initiative, the trade unions, who act on behalf of FQA employees, including maintenance workers, entered into negotiations with FQA. This was in an attempt to improve the earlier agreement on pay for ground staff and working hours for the air crew and cabin staff. The trade unions did not rule out strike action at FQA. They threatened that the dispute might be extended to involve other people employed in the transport industry, which although illegal in the UK, is legal in FQA's home country.

Pressure on FQA was further increased when the Aviation Minister informed the Chairman of FQA that unless a general transport strike was avoided by FQA settling its internal disputes, there would be a withdrawal of government financial support for the airline.

Cost of strike action

The Board has received an evaluation from the Finance Director that the cost of strike action, in terms of lost revenue, if the whole airline were to be closed down is estimated at $30 million per day. (Variable costs of running FQA are estimated at about 40% of revenue). Added to this would be the cost incurred by the loss of goodwill. In addition, the Director of Sales and Marketing has explained that the potential cost of recovering lost business is likely to be substantial after a strike. She further expressed that she would strongly resist the Board's proposal to significantly reduce marketing expenditure in the event of strike action being taken by FQA's employees. The Finance Director had also calculated that the cost of settling the claims on the trade unions' terms would be about $220 million per year.

Emergency Board Meeting

The Chairman of FQA called an emergency meeting and the directors were inevitably concerned to ensure that FQA's flights schedule was maintained, but insisted that any renegotiation of pay and conditions of service must be coupled with further improvements in efficiency and increased productivity.

Catering services

There had also been disruption to the catering service due to the continued hard bargaining by FQA with its main outsourced catering supplier (CG) in its home country. In effect, the only way CG could continue to provide the service was to reduce its own staffing levels or renegotiate its employment contracts with its staff. A reduction in the staffing levels would mean that the catering service capacity would be reduced leading to a reduction in supplies to FQA. The approach CG adopted therefore was to attempt to re-negotiate contracts with its staff which resulted in strike action. This reduced supplies of catering to FQA which resulted in a suspension of its entire catering service on all short-haul routes. In its place, FQA provided passengers with a voucher which they could use to purchase food at the airport when they checked in.

TV and press interview

A television and press interview was given by the Director of Sales and Marketing. After the interview, the Director of Sales and Marketing made confidential comments that the trade unions had taken an unreasonable position and complained that they had been opportunist and were "blackmailing" FQA. She further went on to say that the staff employed by FQA enjoyed very satisfactory pay and conditions of service and that if any employee felt they could improve on these they should seek employment elsewhere because " there are plenty of unemployed people in the country who can replace them and would be happy to work for FQA".

These comments were given to the press by an FQA employee to whom the remarks were being made. He passed the comments to the press because he felt the attitude of the Director of Sales and Marketing was unreasonable. He did not know how to raise this matter internally within FQA. Subsequently the FQA employee, to whom the remarks were made, was dismissed, and this attracted negative press comment.

Meeting between Chairmen and the Chief Executive of FQA

A private meeting attended by both the Chairman and the Chief Executive of FQA and the Chairmen of the largest shareholding companies was held. Between them the two largest shareholding companies own 60% of FQA. At the meeting FQA's Chairman and Chief Executive re-affirmed their position of not giving in to unfair trade union pressure. The shareholders represented by the other Chairmen accepted this position but only in the short term. They felt a lengthy strike would be extremely damaging and instructed the FQA Board to restore a reasonable working relationship with the trade unions and insisted that the Director of Sales and Marketing should give no more press interviews. Further, they instructed the Chairman to dismiss her if the trade unions insisted that they would not negotiate with the company if she remained on the Board.

At the end of the meeting, one of the Chairmen of the two largest shareholding companies brought to the attention of the Chairman of FQA a matter relating to fuel purchases. It was apparent that despite holding down its fuel costs in the financial year ended 30th September 2006, FQA had since then purchased fuel at a price which was higher than that which would be charged by an alternative supplier. The Chairman of the shareholding company was aware of this as he is a member of the Board of the alternative fuel supplier. On investigation, he had been told confidentially that one of FQA's senior purchasing staff had received an inducement payment to obtain the fuel at the higher price from a specific supplier.

Reaction of the Chairman of C

C manufactures a major component of its own aircraft in FQA's home country. The Chairman and Board of C are becoming increasingly concerned that the dispute at FQA may begin to affect their own company's production. The national leaders of the trade unions had made it clear to the Chairman of C that they felt that he should try to bring some influence to bear on the FQA Board to settle the dispute quickly. The national trade union leaders did not rule out the possibility of industrial action taking place at C's manufacturing plants in FQA's home country if P10 18 March 2007 it continued to negotiate the sale of the C 491 to FQA while the industrial dispute was still taking place. They reminded the Chairman of C that this action would be legal in FQA's home country.

Staff Turnover

Staff turnover at FQA is increasing as cabin staff, in particular, are seeking alternative employment. Some of the FQA pilots sought employment with other airlines which were willing to accept them providing they had vacancies. FQA pilots are highly regarded among other airlines as their training programmes and procedures are considered to be world class.

Extraordinary General Meeting of shareholders

An Extraordinary General Meeting of shareholders was called. The meeting was attended by all 12 non-executive directors as well as the main Board members. After receiving major criticism at the meeting, the FQA Chairman and Chief Executive both resigned with immediate effect.

It was agreed by the non-executive directors that a consultant should be appointed immediately to review the issues facing FQA.

Appendix B – Extracts from the Capital Investment Appraisal calculations for each aircraft

All figures are at 31 December of each year.

	Years									
	1	2	3	4	5	6	7	8	9	10
	$m	*$m*	*$m*	*$m*	*$m*	*$m*	*$m*	*$m*	*$m*	*$m*
C 491 (per aircraft)										
	2008	2009	2010	2011	2012	2013	2014	2015	2016	2017
Total income	163.5	173.5	184.3	195.9	208.2	221.5	235.7	250.8	267.1	284.6
Total outflows (before tax)	103.1	110.9	119.7	129.4	140.3	152.6	166.2	181.6	199.0	218.5
Pre-tax cash flow	60.4	62.6	64.6	66.5	67.9	68.9	69.5	69.2	68.1	66.1

NPV of after tax cash flows: $97 million

F898 (per aircraft)

	2008	2009	2010	2011	2012	2013	2014	2015	2016	2017
Total income	95.4	101.2	107.3	113.9	120.9	128.4	136.4	145.0	154.1	164.0
Total outflows (before tax)	59.0	64.6	70.9	78.0	86.2	95.3	105.7	117.5	131.0	146.2
Pre-tax cash flow	36.4	36.6	36.4	35.9	34.7	33.1	30.7	27.5	23.1	17.8

NPV of after tax cash flows: $26 million

COST OF CAPITAL FOR NPV CALCULATIONS = 10%

4 Exam process

4.1 Reading time (20 minutes)

In the TOPCIMA exam you have 3 hours to answer the case plus 20 minutes' reading time. During the reading time you are not allowed to start writing your answer but you are allowed to annotate the question paper.

During the 20 minutes' reading time one approach would be to read through the (previously) unseen material and highlight the following:

- Matters to update your SWOT analysis, for example by highlighting and writing S, W, O or T in the margin.
- Possible issues to discuss to add to those you have brought forward from the pre-seen. In recent cases the headings used in the unseen material have generally been key issues.
- Possible ethical conflicts.

You could also be thinking about possible calculations highlighting key figures to use and which strategic tools you could incorporate.

Flyqual (FQA)

In FQA your 20 minutes could have derived the following:

New SWOT issues

- Landing rights given to a competitor (T)
- Poor control over safety checks (W or T)
- Possible strike action (T)
- Problems with catering firm have worsened (T)
- Bad publicity due to interview (W)
- Increased staff turnover (W)
- Resignation of chairman and CEO (W,T)
- Threat from Government to withdraw financial support (T)

- Increased pressure from shareholders (T)

Ethical issues

- Dismissal procedures
- Purchasing policy
- Complaints procedures
- Safety check
- Carbon footprint implications of aircraft decicion

Possible calculations (not all of them – be selective which you eventually do!)

- Financial cost of strike
- Revised NPVs for aircraft using correct insurance premium (Note: no need to redo lease v buy)
- Key ratios
- BEP between C491 and F898 in terms of capacity utilization.

Strategic tools

- SWOT (always!)
- Porter's generic strategies model to discuss competitive advantage
- PEST

4.2 Further planning time (20 minutes)

Once you are allowed to start writing your answer it is recommended that you spend a further 20 minutes planning and thinking (making 40 minutes in total).

Partly this will be spent finishing off the planning already started but, in addition, you should now focus on identifying the key issues to discuss and prioritising them. This will then allow you to structure your report and do detailed planning for each of the main issues.

A critical skill in TOPCIMA is identifying the key issues. These are usually signposted clearly in the unseen material by the use of headings.

One approach to doing this is to use a planning table with columns for

- key issues brought forward from the pre-seen material
- new issues from the unseen material
- key issues for the report.

FQA

For FQA this could look something like the following:

Key issues from pre-seen	New issues / facts	Key issues for report?
Competitive advantage		Use as a theme to link and discuss prioritised headings
Growth opportunity due to new terminal	Increased competition due to granting of landing fees to a competitor	
Pressure from shareholders to cut costs	Ongoing pressure	Use as a theme to link and discuss prioritised headings
Low staff morale	Worsened - Potential strike action Increased staff turnover	2. Strike has major potential to disrupt schedules and cause significant losses to FQA
Problems with caterers	Worsened – CG now have strikes and have suspended supply	5. Need for immediate action and has potential to damage FQA's reputation
Which new aircraft to buy and whether to lease or buy.	FQA have decided to lease but still need to make decision. C under pressure from unions if it continues to negotiate with FQA	3. Decision is central to future strategic direction and needs to be made urgently
Aggressive management style	Bad publicity due to interviews	
	Government may withdraw funding if a National Strike happens	
	Safety checks are not being carried out correctly	4. Significant safety implications with potential to damage FQA's reputation should an incident occur.
	CEO and Chairman have resigned	1. Shareholders will expect swift action to fill such key roles

When structuring the report you have a choice whether to use issues from the pre-seen or those from the unseen material. Continuing the above discussion the heading 'competitive advantage' would be very appropriate but it is better to let the unseen material drive the structure. Thus competitive advantage could be the basis of an argument when discussing bad publicity, say, to emphasis why the bad publicity is so potentially damaging.

For each of the major issues you could then plan key arguments, bringing in real-world factors and technical knowledge.

For example, for the problems with caterers you might identify the following as issues:

- Damage to reputation and hence competitive advantage
- Makes it easier for competitors to gain domestic market share at new terminal
- BA's experience with Gate Gourmet
- Switching costs.

4.3 Calculations (20 – 30 minutes)

Depending on the case you should allocate between 20 and 30 minutes to performing calculations. The examiner has indicated that a maximum of 10 marks will be available for these, thus suggesting spending around 20 minutes. However, the discussion implications of some calculations are so important that it may be worth spending longer to get an answer to discuss.

Note that feedback from examiners indicates that valuations and other key calculations are often done very badly.

Calculations should be labelled up as appendices.

4.4 Writing (100 – 110 minutes)

You should now start to write up your report. To start with you should complete the following:

- Title page
- Contents page
- Introduction
- Terms of reference, including disclaimers
- Appendix 1: SWOT – ensuring each of your key issues is in it! (if not completed already)

- Other appendices using other selected strategic planning tools (if not completed already).

You can then write up the section prioritising key issues and then the main analysis.

4.5 Finishing it off (30 minutes)

Allow 30 minutes to write up your recommendations, pulling together your main arguments and making it very clear what action the client should take. Weaker scripts are always let down by rushed recommendations and thus appear unfinished. In some respects the recommendations section should be the high point of the report, not half a page of scribbled lines at the end.

Then conclude.

chapter

10

FLYQUAL: MARCH 2007 – SAMPLE SOLUTION

Contents

1 Introduction

What follows is a sample script for the FQA March 2007 exam.

2 Sample script

REPORT (CONFIDENTIAL)

To: The Board of directors, Flyqual

From: A Consultant

Date: Today

Report to the board of Flyqual Airlines regarding the major issues and challenges facing it as of March 2007.

CONTENTS

Appendices

Prepared by a business consultant

24th April 2007

1 Introduction

Flyqual Airlines (FQA), an airline operating in the premium, quality end of the market, has reached a problem period. It has a major replacement decision to make, but it is under fire from a number of key stakeholders. The unions are threatening a strike, the shareholders are actively involved in the company's management and the government's previous un-stinting support appears to be waning. In addition, the maintenance department has some serious deficiencies in its procedures, calling in to question the safety of the fleet.

The airline industry is a difficult one in which to make profits due to high oil prices and intense competition, but with major growth opportunities in India and China. Despite the overall industry being loss making (according to IATA), FQA increased operating profit to $760 million and ROCE to 9.3% in 2006 (refer to Appendix D).

FQA needs to resolve its immediate difficulties in order to provide the right environment to work together with its stakeholders to secure a bright future.

2 Terms of reference

The purpose of this report is to provide the board of Directors of FQA with a clear picture of the company's current strategic position, in particular to identify and prioritise the main issues facing FQA, respond to the issues, assess the opportunities currently available, and make appropriate recommendations.

This report has been prepared by A. Consultant, and relies upon information and explanations provided by the board to date.

3 Prioritisation of issues

The following issues have been prioritised from the SWOT analysis in Appendix A:

3.1 Resignation of Chairman and Chief Executive

This issue is the most urgent issue facing FQA. The resignation of the Chairman and Chief Executive is often a very serious issue. However, with a large board and a wide range of experience in the other members, the business will function well for a time. On the other hand, the shareholders will expect a quick solution to their rudderless ship. Equally,

FQA face some important decisions in the coming weeks and so it must find at least a temporary solution quickly.

FQA should carefully consider its permanent replacement options in the coming months.

3.2 Threat of industrial action

It is clear that this is the most important issue facing FQA. The threat is real and imminent, the shareholders (and government) are heavily involved and the financial affect would be significant.

FQA must deal with this threat as a matter of urgency and restore proper industrial relations with its staff.

3.3 Capital investment decision

This is the second most important issue facing FQA. Part of the fleet needs replacing, which will be very expensive and an urgent decision is needed. A decision is needed as to which of the two main aircraft, C491 or F898, should be acquired.

FQA must decide on the mix of aircraft to buy. This is a crucial strategic choice as the two aircraft are very different sizes, have different NPVs and not all airports can or will cater for the larger of the two aircraft in question.

3.4 Maintenance Issues

This is the third most important issue facing FQA as an independent expert has found "serious faults" with maintenance procedures. One must not forget that FQA is carrying many passengers on each flight and their safety must rank as an important issue.

It could be argued that the expert may have found only "paper" procedure faults and that the airplanes themselves are perfectly safe. In this is the case, it would be justified to demote this issue down the priority order.

The Directors of FQA must respond immediately to the maintenance issue, as any subsequent incident would be viewed in the light of the expert's opinion leading to substantial adverse publicity.

3.5 Catering Services

This is the last priority facing FQA. This is perhaps more important than it first appears. FQA is a quality airline, providing flights at premium prices. The brand of FQA could easily be damaged if a lengthy disruption to catering services ensued. Customers pay a high price for key reasons; one of these could easily be the food and service on board the plane. This has been ranked behind the maintenance issue above, as there may be a real risk that the planes are unsafe.

FQA need to involve their suppliers as partners and seek to resolve the cost versus quality dilemma it is facing.

FQA needs to consider how to react to this new situation.

3.6 Other issues

There are a number of other issues which have not been prioritised as they are not considered to merit the strategic importance of the above priorities within the scope of this report. These are as follows:

- The granting of landing rights to a competitor is a concern in the longer run and it certainly represents an increased level of competition. FQA should consider investigating the reason for this change of heart by its government.
- The continuing problem with low staff morale and high turnover is a concern. FQA should seek ways to improve motivation and stop the damaging leak of its quality staff.
- Ethical issues are dealt with in section 9 below.

4 Replacement of Chairman and Chief Executive

4.1 The extent of the problem

The "heads" of organisations have an important role to play. The strategic direction of the company is often driven by these people. FQA faces challenges in their industry, which may change the strategic importance of many factors.

Shareholders will expect strong and experience leadership skills at the top of their organisation. A mistake made in replacement will be serious in these peoples' eyes.

The lack of leadership can have serious impacts on morale amongst others members of staff and it is best, therefore to have a quick solution in place.

4.2 Alternative solutions

FQA need experience and strength so internal promotion is probably not possible. FQA is a prominent airline and all the stakeholders will expect a "name" to take over.

Recruitment by advertising is also possible but this takes time. Many applications may be received and many from wholly inappropriate sources. Headhunting a new leadership would avoid these problems.

FQA should rush to make a permanent appointment. The decisions made hastily can be repented at leisure.

5 Possible industrial action

5.1 The extent of the problem

FQA have, to date, taken a very aggressive stance in the negotiations in respect of remuneration and working conditions with the trade union representatives, in spite of the threatened industrial action. The failure of the two sides, management and unions, to agree on pay and conditions and the sacking of seemingly innocent technicians has resulted in the threat of strike action, which will result in substantial financial loss.

An estimate of the financial loss is shown in appendix F. A two week strike would cost approximately $208m including an estimate for goodwill. This represents 27% of the total 2006 operating profit.

5.2 Alternative solutions

The main choice facing the board is whether to "tough it out" or to negotiate a compromise.

The estimated $208m cost of the strike should also be weighed against the annual cost of settling the dispute, estimated at $220m. The breakeven length of strike compared the cost of settling it is only 12 days (appendix F). Clearly some negotiation will still be possible and some productivity savings will reduce the ongoing cost. On these figures one might be tempted to fight the union. Many firms experience is that these problems do not simply go away and, unless a win-win scenario can be gained, further expensive disputes will result.

In 2005, BA had to cancel over 100 flights during the peak summer season owing to its ground staff going on unofficial strike in support of Gate Gourmet (outsourced supplier of BA's catering) staff who had been sacked. The disruption was estimated to have cost BA up to GBP40 million, with further damage to its reputation. More recently, a threatened strike by cabin crew on remuneration and working conditions, with similar expected adverse financial repercussions, was averted at the last minute by management being forced to concede.

Of equal concern is the involvement of many stakeholders in this dispute. The shareholders have given explicit instructions to avoid a costly strike. The management of FQA has a duty to follow the instructions of the majority of the shareholders, regardless of their preferred stance in the matter. The stakeholder power in this industry is interesting and in some cases a little unusual. Since flight safety is paramount, a plane cannot fly if ground crew have not done, or will not do, their job properly. The fact that the unions are so organised in this industry adds weight the employees' power. Appendix B shows an analysis of this power position. The unions and the shareholders are powerful players and cannot be brushed aside.

The government are also involved. This is perhaps a little unusual in other industries, but more common in an airline. A country is dependent on airline traffic for trade and tourism, equally an airline dispute will affect many other countries and pressure from these countries will be brought to bear on the local government. It is worth stressing that the government has the ability withdraw financial and other support from the company and so its wishes need to be heard. The government will have wider issues in mind when requesting a resolution (including the risk of a spread of the industrial action to C for example).

It is also worth pointing out that senior management time will be used up dealing with this dispute each time it occurs. This time does have a cost and should not be viewed as sunk or costless. New investment opportunities may go missed as management are pre-occupied by internal operational difficulties.

Options are available to FQA, but continuing to adopt an aggressive stance is unlikely to be successful. Equally, FQA does not want to become overly soft. Negotiations imply compromise from both sides.

6 Aircraft procurement

6.1 Introduction

The aircraft procurement decision is heavily linked to the decision about FQA's future strategic direction in terms of how it intends to compete and which products and markets it decides to remain in, enter or exit.

6.2 Arguments in favour of C491

The originally calculated NPV for each aircraft was:

F898 $26m per aircraft

C491 $97m per aircraft

This is before an adjustment for extra insurance on aircraft C491. Appendix E shows an insurance adjusted figure for the C491 as $59m, which is still way ahead of the smaller aircraft. This implies that the larger aircraft is the preferred choice, but there are concerns with this.

C491s are highly suitable for the long-haul market that FQA is keen to exploit, due to their ability to be able to transport more passengers in a single flight.

A useful feature of the C491 aircraft is an on-board medical facility, a product service enhancement that would appeal to many passengers on long-haul flights, and particularly older passengers who are becomingly increasingly important as the demographic profile of passengers' shifts more markedly to the older traveller.

6.3 Arguments against C491/in favour of F898

I have concerns about the capacity assumptions made in the original calculations. It is assumed that both the airplanes will operate at 80% capacity. This implies that if FQA buys the bigger plane it will suddenly have more passengers than it had before. This does not seem realistic. Demand for flights is dependent on customers travel plans and not on the size of the aircraft. The effect of this will be to further reduce the NPV of the C491 bringing it closer to the F898 see appendix G. As a result, the financial factor is likely to be much closer than the above numbers imply. Indeed if the capacity utilisation fell below 72% for the C491 then the NPV of that plane would fall below that of the F898. (See appendix G)

C491s will cost $250m each compared to the alternative F898s which cost $150m each. Accordingly the lease payments are higher, thus increasing the operational gearing further.

C491s could be considered to be the riskier option as they may result in a degree of inconvenience to passengers who will need to transfer to other flights from 'hubs' for onward travel. This may not be popular with them. FQA should consider research into this aspect.

The C491 will create a requirement for new infrastructures at airports, notably new runways and airport gates, which may be unacceptable to neighbours of the airports and the airport operators themselves. If these adjustments are not made to the infrastructure, then the larger planes will not be able to fly on the chosen routes. This would clearly be a disaster.

These 'super jets' have only just been introduced into the industry and may take time to become accepted by passengers and by the rest of the travel industry.

F898 aircraft have a smaller capacity but greater destination flexibility and passenger convenience. They could, therefore, become very useful in creating a highly flexible short-haul operation which makes less demand on airports in terms of the infrastructure that is required to accommodate the aircraft.

6.4 Additional factors to consider

FQA would also need to consider other factors such as expected demand, competition and additional costs, as well as its decision regarding the future direction of the business.

Of course, there is no need to make a stark decision between one type of aircraft or the other. It is possible to have a mixed fleet, as is currently the case. However, this can result in a loss of economies of scale. Indeed, FQA already has a mixed fleet and a like for like replacement may be sensible. FQA could also consider buying the C491 only for those routes where local airports had indicated a willingness to upgrade or on those routes where growth in passenger numbers would be more likely to support more business.

The competition is an important factor in all of this. It is sensible to stay with the majority in this case. If FQA is the only buyer of the large plane it is less likely that airports will support an upgrade. Most flight bookings are made by customers being unaware of the type of plane they will end up on. Hence, it is unlikely that any significant strategic advantage is to be gained.

7 Safety procedures

The poor level of safety checks is a potentially serious situation and one that needs action. An airline relies heavily on its safety record; it is doubtful that many passengers would travel on a plane where there were any doubts about safety. At the moment it appears that FQA has problems with its procedures rather than the quality of its maintenance work.

The directors are very exposed in this regard. The existence of a negative independent report will be very damaging should an accident occur. One could not rule out personal liability if negligence was shown. Regardless of the personnel situation, the directors would be well advised to act swiftly on the report and make appropriate changes to the control procedures.

Procedural gaps are important in that they break down the "audit" trail. It may not always be possible to prove that work was done or to show who carried out that work. These are important factors in any control system. Behavioural studies have repeatedly shown that people will work more diligently if they know checks are in place on them. These checks should be supportive, as opposed to aggressive, but nonetheless they should exist.

The lack of audit trail is likely to be a concern for any regulator in the industry. An airline not only needs to have safe planes, it needs to be able to prove it has safe planes.

New control procedures need not be expensive and a sensible assessment of the risks will be needed before new systems could be put in place. Proper documentation is the corner stone of any system

8 Catering partners

8.1 The extent of the problem

The problem that FQA has here is that a passenger will only pay higher than average prices if he is getting a higher than average service. The quality of the food is central to that service. The FQA brand is dependent on the catering service it provides and, as such, the directors should recognise the need for a change in position regarding how they see the relationship with the catering provider.

The second consideration is the extent to which a disruption to catering supply would prevent flights from operating altogether. The provision of water is essential to the health and safety aspects of a flight. On long-haul flights the provision of food could also be viewed as essential. In other words, the absence of a satisfactory and reliable catering supplier could in certain situations prevent a flight taking place. Appendix F shows the cost of a strike, but these figures could be used for any non-flight disruption.

8.2 Alternative solutions

Re-open negotiations with its existing supplier

The modern way to view the customer – supplier relationship is that it is one of partnership. Together a quality service is brought to the FQA customers. Adopting an adversarial approach rarely works in the long run. A quality provider such as FQA needs to be able to rely on the quality of food provided. Suppliers that are forced to work on very tight margins will often resort to reducing the quality or quantity of the inputs. This is counter-productive.

Put the entire catering business out to tender

This can be productive, producing higher quality at good prices. However, to maintain a sustainable situation, it is recommended that a change of stance with all suppliers be taken.

9 Ethical issues

9.1 Dismissal procedures

It is clear that FQA have had at least two issues with dismissal procedures. Dismissal is a very serious matter for all concerned, especially the one dismissed. The ethical point is that the dismissed person must be treated fairly and with no bias. They should feel that their treatment was just.

FQA may not have exercised total fairness in two cases. One could argue that the engineering technicians were simply following laid down procedures and the Director of Sales and Marketing was punished for a private conversation with another member of staff. Each case should be reviewed and the precise details discussed.

More generally, FQA should review its dismissal procedures and in particular:

- ensure all dismissals are approved by an independent board member
- ensure all employees have the right of appeal and independent review
- publish its dismissal procedure to all concerned.

9.2 Purchasing policies

There is evidence that a buyer has taken a personal incentive to encourage the purchase of fuel at a higher price than was available on the open market. This is clearly unethical in that an employee should not make personal gain at the expense of the company and hence its shareholders. An employee gets a wage for his work and that should be a fair reward for his efforts.

FQA should:

- ensure all purchase orders are authorised by a manager
- benchmark major cost lines to identify over payments
- publish purchase procedures, making it a disciplinary offence to accept gratuities from suppliers
- segregate duties within the purchase system
- require a minimum of two quotes for major purchases.

9.3 Complaint procedures

There is evidence that some of FQA's staff are unaware of how to address issues that are of concern to them. Complaint or other procedures should be clear to all. Staff should not feel they "must" tow the line regardless of their own moral or other stance on issues.

FQA should:

- establish adequate policies for complaints; staff should know who they can turn to in the first instance and have a fall back to a senior person who is not their line manager
- restate all policies to all staff.

10 Recommendations

Replacement of Chairman and Chief Executive

- Make a temporary appointment to steer the company through the important next few months, this cannot be delayed. Then in due course:
- Appoint a head hunting agent to produce a short list of potential candidates

Set up an interview board made of members drawn from both the executives and non-executives. In this way a balanced decision can be made

Set a pay and benefits package suitable for the position. This needs to generous enough to attract the right calibre of person but frugal enough to appease the shareholders

Possible industrial action

It is clear that avoiding the strike is necessary. In order to achieve this, FQA should:

- adopt a softer stance in relation to the union negotiation
- view the workers as a partner to work with for a common aim
- negotiate productivity gains to offset the full cost of settlement
- consider independent arbitration
- arrange an immediate meeting to avoid any imminent strike action
- increase communication with staff, to foster a partnership feel.

Aircraft procurement

A fleet decision is a vital one, fraught with risks. Therefore, FQA should:

- lease the smaller F898 planes in the main as this gives greater flexibility and reduces the risk of having aircraft with few airports they can operate out of.
- lease the larger C491 planes on routes where it has been confirmed that the airport infrastructure will be upgraded and the growth in passenger numbers is encouraging
- consult with competitors, whilst maintaining an ethical code, to ensure that FQA stay with the majority decision.

Safety procedures

FQA should:

- install a new control system to fully document all work done on each aircraft
- prepare and stick to a comprehensive repair and maintenance schedule
- train all staff in the use of the new system
- request a further independent review once the new system is in place to (hopefully) gain a clean bill of health.

Catering Partners

The catering situation is in need of a long term sustainable solution, therefore FQA should:

- put the supply of catering services out to tender
- produce a tender document that clearly sets out the importance of quality and the need to work in partnership with any new supplier

- honour in full the existing arrangement, to maintain existing supply
- negotiate an interim settlement with the existing supplier
- comply in full with all existing contractual obligations
- produce, in partnership with the new supplier, a binding contract with clear service level standards built in.

11 Conclusion

FQA can come through this problematic period if each of these issues is addressed properly. If the above recommendations are implemented, the airline should be on course to enjoy increased success and profitability in the future.

Appendix A – SWOT analysis

Strengths

- member of N alliance
- excellent reputation for quality and punctuality
- growth in revenue and profit
- good balance of skills and experience on Board
- good mixture of non-executive and executive directors

Weaknesses

- unhappy shareholders who are dominant
- poor HR record/management

Opportunities

- improve stakeholder management and market perceptions
- disposal of shares in subsidiary
- new aircraft decision
- short-haul operations
- expand Asian operations
- expand cargo operations

Threats

- strike action
- safety record damage
- loss of catering support
- environmental measures - air duty, fuel tax
- environmental pressures regarding new terminal
- economic recession affects premium market
- consolidation in the industry

Appendix B – Mendelow Stakeholder analysis

	Low interest – Minimal effort	High Interest - Inform
Low power		• Employees (Admin) • Customers*
	- Satisfy	- Key players
High power	• Government • Regulator	• Shareholders • Directors • Employees (Flight related)

* It could be argued that given the unionisation and the safety consciousness of the airlines that the employees have high levels of power. FQA should consider the implications of this and perhaps adopt a more involving and team working stance.

Appendix C – PEST analysis (extract)

Political instability / war can affect oil prices

- subsidies can give national firms an (unfair?) advantage
- regulation / deregulation – lack of access to routes/slots can be an effective barrier to entry
- legislation re safety
- government policy on carbon emissions
- tax on aviation fuel
- general political interest in industry

Conclusion

There is clearly a heavy amount of political influence exerted over this industry.

Appendix D - Key ratios for FQA

	2006	2005
Growth in revenue	6.9%	-
Growth in operating profit	70.8%	-
Growth in net profit	136.3%	-
ROCE	9.3%	5.8%
Return on Equity	9.4%	4.1%
Operating profit margin	7.0%	4.4%
Net profit margin	3.4%	1.5%

Appendix E – Capital investment decision calculations

NPV before insurance adjustment		$97.00m
PV of extra insurance		
First payment		($6.00m)
Yr 2 to 10 in advance ($6m x 7.172*)		($43.03m)
Tax savings	25% x 6 x 7.44**	$11.16m
Adjusted NPV		**$59.13m**

Discount factor given by

$$1 + e = \frac{1 + m}{1 + i}$$

$$1 + e = \frac{1.1}{1.05} = 1.048$$

* 9 year annuity at 4.8% is 7.172

** 10 year annuity running from years 2 to 11 = 7.797 x 0.954 = 7.44

Appendix F – Financial loss of a strike

A strike's duration is very variable. However, if I assume a week's strike, the cost of the action would be:

Lost revenue (7 days x $30m)	$210m
Saved Variable cost (7 days x $30m x 0.40)	$84m
Total loss (ignoring goodwill and future bookings)	$126m
After tax cost	$94.5m
A 2 week strike would therefore cost	$189m

The effect of goodwill and lost future bookings is hard to estimate. However, if I assume an extra 10% on the figures above then:

Cost of 1 week	$104m
Cost of 2 weeks	$208m

These are clearly very serious figures, with the larger figure above representing 27% of 2006 total operating profit.

Given the cost of settling the strike is estimated to be $220 million per year (after tax $165m) the breakeven length of a strike would be only 12.2 days.

Appendix G – Breakeven point between the C491 and the F898

There is doubt about the ability of FQA to maintain 80% capacity on the larger C491 aircraft. Buying a bigger plane does not mean more demand, although the future may be better with more passengers resulting.

If the C491 is bought what would be the required capacity utilization in order to realize the same NPV as the F898 as calculated?

If there is less passengers then revenue will fall (all other variables will not change or change only slightly)

PV of revenue flows = 115 x AF 1-10 years at 4.76%		= X
	115 x 7.812	= $898.4m
Less tax on revenue flows		$(224.6)m
PV of after tax revenue flows		$673.8m

At the point of indifference between the two planes the NPVs would be equal

The NPV of C491 would have to fall by $71.13m ($97.02m – $25.89m)

This is a change of $71.13m/$673.8m or 10.55%

The capacity utilization would therefore only have to fall by 10.55% to 72%

If the capacity utilization fell below 72% then the smaller F898 would be better than the C491

chapter

11

MERBATTY: PRE-SEEN MATERIAL

Scenario – Pre-seen material

This case study was the TOPCIMA case for the September and November 2007 examination papers. When analysing this material and answering the examination question for September 2007, you should assume that 'now' is late 2007.

1 Case– Merbatty

1.1 Market overview

The developing luxury boat building industry is one with a growing customer base of wealthy, successful individuals and corporate clients. The industry is mostly concentrated in Europe and the USA, although new boat building companies have recently entered the market in Australia and some areas of Asia. Classification of the market and its products can be done in different ways, but the most common are by boat length, engine performance or by hull type. In 2006, the luxury boat building industry generated approximately $5 billion in revenues and delivered nearly 3,500 engine-powered boats globally.

The material in this case is confined to boats powered by engines and does not include sailing yachts, which are a completely separate market segment.

There are a number of major international builders of luxury boats, which together produce a range of over 150 different models. Most luxury boats have living accommodation and crew quarters. The selling prices for these luxury boats range from around $0.4 million to over $9 million. Each boat type has a choice of different cost options, depending on customers' specifications and engine size.

Boat building companies typically appoint agents to secure sales from the end customer. The sales agent is the ongoing link with the customer from initial contact until delivery of the boat. Most boat building companies have agents in a wide variety of places globally in order to secure sales, even though they have boat building facilities in only one or two locations. Completed boats are tested, then inspected and then delivered to wherever customers want, with the sales agent fully involved.

The individuals and corporate customers who buy these luxury boats are successful, wealthy individuals who expect the highest standards of quality and customer care. As the market has become more competitive, the need to live up to 'what the customer wants, the customer gets' has become even more important. Boat building companies are facing the difficult task of balancing the need to deliver customer choice and a high specification at a price that is competitive. In addition, boat building companies need to generate sufficient profitability to invest in research for future designs in order to stay competitive and to give a return for their shareholders.

1.2 Merbatty

Merbatty was formed 33 years ago by its current Chairman and is based in a northern European country. Merbatty has enjoyed rapid growth in sales and profitability in recent years. Merbatty became listed on a European stock exchange in November 2006.

It currently has two boat building facilities, one at its Head Office base in Europe and a second on the West Coast of the USA. It has sales offices at the two boat building locations, staffed by Merbatty employees. The majority of Merbatty sales worldwide are secured through sales agents appointed by Merbatty.

Sales revenue is paid to Merbatty in three instalments. A deposit of 20% is paid by the customer on signing a binding contract for a boat as specified by the customer. A second instalment of 30% is paid when the boat's engines are delivered to the boat building facility. The final 50% is paid on completion of the boat, only after inspection by the customer. Delivery to the customer's choice of location is at an extra cost. Merbatty's price list is in Euros for European sales. Due to pressure from customers in the USA, sales there are priced in US Dollars. Sales to other parts of the world are in either Euros or US Dollars.

Merbatty currently has a range of 15 boats varying in price from between €0.4 million for a 5-metre boat to over €4 million for a 35-metre boat. The selling prices of Merbatty's range of boats are shown in Appendix 1 and relate to the basic model specification, as prices may vary depending on the customer's own selection of the specification for interior design and accommodation facilities.

Customers usually choose from a range of additional features, to enable them to make the boat very individual to personal requirements. To facilitate this choice, Merbatty offers a full interior design service. In 2006 these additional features generated €50 million of additional revenues. This represents a further 11% on top of basic selling prices.

The operating profit achieved for Merbatty's current range of boats in 2006 was as follows:

	Small boats (up to and including 24 metres)	Large boats (25 metres and over)	Additional features selected by customres	Total 2006 operating revenues and costs
Number of boats	223	57	-	280
	€ million	€ million	€ million	€ million
Revenue	256	196	50	502
Operating costs (including allocated overhead costs)	222	163	41	426
Operating profit	34	33	9	76
Operating profit %	13.3%	16.8%	18.0%	15.1%

During 2006, Merbatty commenced production on a record number of 280 boats, representing a global market share of around 8%. Merbatty's statistics for boat construction are based on the number of boats commenced in a year.

Depending on the model and the size of the boat, the time taken to build a boat varies from three months to around ten months. This time represents the period from the date of the customer signing the order contract to delivery of the completed boat. The boat is only delivered to a customer after successful completion of its sea trials and subsequent inspection by the customer.

The geographical analysis of sales according to the home base of the customer in 2006 and by the target markets for 2011 is shown in Appendix 2.

Merbatty currently has sales agents worldwide who generate sales. Most of Merbatty's agents worldwide work exclusively for Merbatty, except in a few locations where the agents also sell boats built by several other boat building companies. The agents receive a fixed percentage of the final revenues of around 4%, including any additional features that the customer orders for the boat. The agent's fee is paid in two instalments for each sale – 50% of the agent's fee at the point of signing a sales contract with the customer and the final balance on delivery of the boat to the customer. This split in the agent's fee creates an incentive for the agent to maintain close contact with both the customer and Merbatty's boat building facility in order to monitor progress and delivery details.

Market research has established that there is a growing market for luxury boats. Recent orders from both new and existing customers have supported this research. Indeed Merbatty has several customers who regularly replace their boats every few years. It also has other customers who have bought two or three boats to keep in different locations round the world.

1.3 Merbatty's personnel

The career histories of Merbatty's directors are shown in Appendix 3.

Merbatty employs almost 2,200 employees at the two boat building facilities which are currently operational. The total staff costs were €87 million in 2006. However, additional employees will need to be recruited later in 2007 when Merbatty opens its third boat building facility (see Section 1.7).

The table below shows an analysis by function of Merbatty's employees at the end of 2006:

	Number of emplyees at 31 December 2006
Skilled boat building technicians (including supervisory staff)	1,940
Office and administration staff	188
Senior management staff	22
Sales staff (excluding external sales agents)	17
Total employees	2,167

The employee numbers shown above exclude outsourced processes. In addition to using sales agents to secure the majority of sales, Merbatty chooses to outsource several elements of its boat construction process. These include the use of an interior design service, which Merbatty uses for all interior fittings.

1.4 Merbatty's recent history

Merbatty's sales have risen by over 10% each year for the last 12 years. The founding shareholder, Alberto Blanc, held the roles of Chairman and Chief Executive until September 2005, when the management team was strengthened in the lead up to the flotation of Merbatty in November 2006. The flotation issued 120 million new shares, each at a nominal value of €0.50 each. The flotation price was €2.80 a share and all shares were fully subscribed and generated a cash inflow to Merbatty of €336 million (before issue costs) in November 2006.

At the point of flotation Merbatty repaid its then existing bank loan of €120 million and its bank overdraft, which had reached over €120 million. Andreas Acosta also renegotiated a new loan at a more competitive interest rate. This new loan is for €200 million at an annual interest rate of 7%, and is secured on Merbatty's assets. This new loan, together with some of the equity raised in the listing will finance Merbatty's capital expenditure programme over the next few years, as well as finance the increase in working capital in order to achieve the growth targets planned.

To meet the growing demand, and due to capacity constraints at its boat building facility in Europe, Merbatty acquired some land in the USA in 2002 and developed a totally new purpose-built boat building facility. This has been operational since early 2004. There were some initial operational problems but Merbatty has been able to put in place experienced and committed employees who have the required skills to meet the exacting demands of Merbatty's growing customer base. The European and USA based boat building facilities both produce all 15 of the models currently offered by Merbatty, although the USA boat building facility rarely produces boats smaller than 20 metres.

Merbatty's profit, before dividends, was €40 million for 2006, a record profit level, as shown in the extract from the accounts in Appendix 4. The country in which Merbatty is based charges tax at 35% of operating profits less finance costs.

Merbatty's Chairman, Alberto Blanc, was awarded the 'Business Person of the Year' in a European awards ceremony in 2004 and this, together with Merbatty's listing, has raised the global profile of Merbatty.

1.5 Merbatty's current position

Merbatty had signed contracts, and received the required 20% deposits from customers, on future orders for 39 boats (building of which has not yet commenced) at the end of June 2007. The lead time from contract signing to start of construction usually averages six weeks. Sales are on target for Merbatty to meet the planned 300 boats commenced in 2007.

As soon as an order is contractually placed, Merbatty will order the required supplies, such as the hull, engines and other major bought-in components for the boat. Merbatty will also allocate a specific building space within the agreed boat building facility. However, until it has undertaken around 20% of the construction work, a proportion of customers' deposits will remain in the Balance Sheet (as a Current Liability) and not be recognised in the Income Statement.

The Financial Statements for 2006 (included in Appendix 4) include a revaluation reserve in Merbatty's Balance Sheet to reflect an increase in the value of the Non-current Assets, which had been valued in 2006 prior to Merbatty's flotation.

Merbatty was listed in November 2006 when a major change in the shareholdings took place. Most executive directors acquired shares in the company. In addition, all of the executive directors have share options in order to encourage them to achieve the planned results, which would lead to growth in Merbatty's share price. The share options allow all directors to purchase up to 5 million shares each, any time up to 30 November 2012, at a price of €5.00.

Alberto Blanc had previously held 90% of shares and chose to retain the same number of shares (54 million shares) but, after the flotation, his shareholding was reduced to 30%. The new issue of shares brought in external investors and much needed finance in order for the company to expand. Alberto Blanc believes in the huge potential of the Merbatty brand and aims to achieve the five-year plan. He then intends to retire.

Prior to flotation, Merbatty had 60 million shares at a nominal value of €0.50 each in issue and had a total of 500 million authorised shares. At flotation, in November 2006, Merbatty issued a further 120 million shares at a price of €2.80. At the end of 2006, Merbatty had 180 million shares in issue. The shareholdings at the end of 2006 were as follows:

	Shareholding at 31 December 2006
Directors:	
Alberto Blanc	30%
Jesper Blanc	8%
Henri Gaston	3%
Stfan Gil	3%
Andreas Acosta	3%
Tobias Houllier	2%
Lukas Dian	2%
Alain Mina	2%
Marie Lopp	1%
Bernie Ritzol	1%
Investors:	
JKL (has Board representative)	28%
Corporate fund investors	12%
Other shareholders:	
Small investors	3%
Employee-held shares	2%
Total shareholdings	100%

JKL is a listed company with a varied portfolio of investments in a range of international companies, mainly in the construction, engineering and maritime industries. At Merbatty's flotation, JKL purchased 50.4 million shares at a cost of over €140 million as it considers that Merbatty's growth to date and its range of products, together with its potential for the future, will lead to a substantial return on its investment. Following discussions prior to flotation, it was agreed that JKL's Investment Director, Simone Lellet would have a seat on the Board of Merbatty and would be involved in helping Merbatty to achieve its five-year plan. Simone Lellet has been involved in some operational planning meetings and she has proved to be a useful management resource.

Merbatty's shares initially traded at €3.48 shortly after flotation and Merbatty's directors are pleased with the market's confidence in the company. By 30 June 2007 the share price had risen to €3.65.

The market sector average P/E ratio at 30 June 2007 is 15.

1.7 Future plans for expansion

As a result of the company becoming listed in 2006, the Board of Merbatty was expanded with a number of new Board members. With the input of fresh ideas from the new members of the management team, a number of options have been put forward for expansion of the business. These include producing a much wider range of new models, which would enable Merbatty to offer customers a wider selection of boat sizes and engine capabilities than that currently produced.

Merbatty's five-year plan for the period up to and including 2011 is shown in Appendix 5. It is this five-year plan on which the prospectus forecast was based.

Currently, Merbatty produces 15 different models of boat (ranging from 15 metres to 35 metres in length). One new model is due to be introduced early in 2008 and there are possible enhancements to existing models by the middle of 2008. Lukas Dian, the Technical Director – Design, believes that there is a strong opportunity to build larger boats which would be in the range of 35 to 40 metres in length. The main market for these very large boats would be in the Middle East. The press launch of Merbatty's first 38-metre boat in May 2007 had a good response and this new model will go into full production shortly.

In the past, Merbatty has always been very cautious and produced boats when specific orders have been placed, except for a small number of boats built for demonstration purposes. However, after talking to some of Merbatty's agents in the Middle East, Jesper Blanc is confident that the demand in this region will be so great that Merbatty could sell any large boat that it builds. He has proposed that Merbatty should begin production of a range of large boats before any definite orders are placed, in order to capture sales from customers buying impulsively.

Stefan Gil is working on a proposal for Merbatty to open sales offices in over 20 locations worldwide. This would result in the termination of some sales agents' contracts. He considers that this will be needed to generate the additional sales required in order for the five-year plan to be achieved. Additionally, it would allow Merbatty to save costs, as it is anticipated that the costs of running Merbatty's own sales offices would be lower than that paid in agents' commissions.

Detailed operational plans were prepared in the form of Merbatty's current year budget for 2007, in order to ensure that the planned level of growth in sales and profitability is monitored and achieved. Merbatty is currently on target to achieve the budgeted number of 300 new boats to be commenced in 2007. This is the highest number of new boats Merbatty will ever have commenced building in one year.

The company currently has two boat building facilities, in Europe and on the West Coast of the USA. The maximum annual capacity for these two facilities will depend on the mix of boat models ordered, as several smaller boats can be built in less time than one larger boat. There is an increasing demand for larger boats. Based on Merbatty's current product mix during 2006, the existing two boat building facilities have a maximum capacity, in terms of space, of 320 boats in total each year.

The five-year plan includes forecast capital expenditure for the opening of Merbatty's third boat building facility in September 2007. Additionally, the five-year plan includes capital expenditure that would be required for a fourth boat building facility planned to be built during 2010 and 2011. Bernie Ritzol considers that this may be located in a new target market, perhaps in Asia.

1.9 Merbatty's development plans

Bernie Ritzol, the Global Market Development Director, would like to expand the range of models that Merbatty builds and considers that there is demand for a greater variation of designs within the range of hull sizes that are currently built. He is investigating the possibility of expanding the range of boats Merbatty builds, to have ten new models over the next two years, instead of the planned three new models per year. He has asked Lukas Dian, the Technical Director – Design, to prepare a proposal for investment in research and development needed for this expansion, for the Board meeting in September 2007.

Lukas Dian has identified the need for €10 million expenditure on the design of new IT systems, including state of the art boat building CAD and CAM systems, both of which would minimise man hours and thus increase net margins. A further €15 million of expenditure would be required on new boat design, particularly in the area of hull design and the building process for large boats and the new models proposed by Bernie Ritzol. This capital expenditure is included in the five-year plan which is shown in Appendix 5.

1.10 Current use of new technology

Merbatty currently uses the latest in modern marine production technology, including Computer Numerical Controlled (CNC) machining and robotic spray systems for automated precision spray painting for maximum hydrodynamic efficiency. Investment in technology in the last two years has increased by 10% and has cost the company a total of €10 million.

Merbatty has also spent over €4 million on technology to apply glass re-enforced plastic onto each hull to add an external enhanced performance gel coat to increase hull durability and strength. This process was introduced in the USA boat building facility earlier in 2007 and is proving successful in speeding up the time taken at this stage of production of the boats. The previous hull coating technology was very labour intensive, requiring a number of skilled operators using hand-held machines to apply the external gel coating. The old technology is still used in the European boat building facility and for smaller boats built in the USA facility.

1.11 Merbatty sponsorship contracts

Merbatty has signed two different sponsorship contracts which both generate a lot of positive public relations (PR) and have helped to increase Merbatty's brand recognition. The sponsorship contracts are as follows:

- €5 million per year for three years from July 2006 to June 2009 payable to a major global speedboat race organiser which generates significant publicity for Merbatty through advertising and TV coverage of the race events. The races are also sponsored by a number of other global brands, but Merbatty is the principal sponsor.
- €5 million per year for five years from January 2007 to December 2011 to a global travel and high quality hotel chain. This company promotes Merbatty boats in a variety of ways, including advertising on all of its websites world-wide and through promotional information at all of its hotels. Merbatty also works with this company to arrange travel for its customers to inspect their boats.

1.12 Merbatty's supplier relationships

Merbatty has a number of key suppliers. There has been a trend for more professional relationships with suppliers in Merbatty since Paul Lavie, Merbatty's new Procurement Director, joined the company earlier in 2007. Merbatty has introduced supplier rating systems and key performance indicators (KPIs) for all its suppliers. Paul Lavie would like to see Merbatty work more closely with a few key suppliers and to build long-standing supplier relationships.

Merbatty's ability to work closer with its key suppliers has also been facilitated by the recent development of an on-line order tracking and processing system between Merbatty and two of its key suppliers, which are MNE and Marinatron (see below). This system allows Merbatty to place specific orders for standard engines and satellite control panels to be delivered to Merbatty's boat building facilities and to track the orders right through from the early stages of the boat building process to delivery and installation.

Marinatron is Merbatty's key supplier of radar and satellite navigation systems. This USA based company supplies over 30% of the market for marine satellite navigation systems and they are used in all of Merbatty's boat models. It also supplies to a number of Merbatty's competitors in the USA.

Topcrest is a manufacturer of boat hulls and is based in the same European country as Merbatty's European boat building facility. Merbatty has been a long-standing customer of Topcrest and has built up a very strong relationship with

Topcrest's design and manufacturing team. Topcrest has a reputation as one of the top three hull manufacturers in the world and demand for its hulls (ranging from 12 metres to over 40 metres long) has been growing rapidly in the last five years. Merbatty is a key customer of Topcrest and both companies recognise the importance of working closely together on future designs. The lead time for hulls varies from two to six weeks depending on the size of the hull and the design specifications.

Sea Safety Equipment (SSE) is a European based company, which supplies most of the on-board safety equipment such as inflatable life boats and life jackets.

MNE Engines, based in Europe, is a large manufacturer of nautical engines for both commercial and military purposes and it supplies engines worldwide to a wide range of customers. MNE is one of only five specialised nautical engine manufacturers in Europe. MNE supplies all of the diesel engines for all models of Merbatty boats. The order value of engines in 2006 was approximately €38 million.

Aqua Designs is an internationally renowned firm of interior designers which specialises in the design and interior fittings for luxury boats. This includes all of the teak wood panelling to cabins and decks, air conditioning, interior furnishings, on-board entertainment systems, satellite telephone systems and underwater lighting facilities. All Merbatty boats have a standard specification for interior design, but customers can opt to add to this specification from a vast range of options provided by Aqua Designs. These additional internal specifications can add around 11% to the price of a boat, depending on customers' preferences. Aqua Designs operates throughout Europe and the USA, but it does not have operations in the Middle East. Aqua Designs has declined all requests from Merbatty to provide the same interior design service for Merbatty's new Suranian boat building facility. Merbatty is currently finalising alternative arrangements for its interior design service for boats built in Surania.

1.13 Charitable work

Alberto Blanc has been involved in charitable work for many years and feels strongly that Merbatty should continue to support a range of charities.

Merbatty financially supported a number of fund-raising events throughout the USA in 2006, which raised $4 million as a contribution towards a new hospital wing. Additionally, the company made donations totalling €0.5 million towards a European Child Poverty Prevention Charity.

Alberto Blanc spends much of his spare time advising and working for charitable organisations in Europe, as he strongly believes that those who are as fortunate as he is should do as much as possible to help those who are less fortunate. Merbatty receives much good publicity from Alberto Blanc's charitable work and every employee is encouraged to spend two to six months seconded from Merbatty, on full pay, to undertake a range of short assignments for charitable organisations. Every member of staff is eligible to participate in one charitable assignment every four years.

Appendix 1

Analysis of Merbatty's range of boats

Model	*Length (metres)*	*Maximum speed (knots)*	*2006 Standard selling price € million*	*Units sold in 2006*	*Units sold in 2005*
Performance motor boats: P series					
P-3000	35	40	4.4	10	-
P-2000	25	38	3.4	10	8
P-1000	20	38	2.9	11	10
P-Gold	19	35	2.8	12	19
P-Elite	18	31	2.3	16	21
Motor boats: C series					
C-34	34	31	3.4	11	-
C-31	31	31	3.2	10	10
C-28	28	31	3.0	16	13
C-23	23	30	2.5	20	29
Flybridge range					
F-1	22	30	1.0	25	22
F-2	20	30	0.8	24	24
F-3	16	32	0.6	27	27
Cruisers					
Z-1	18	34	0.6	30	24
Z-2	16	32	0.5	23	20
Z-3	15	30	0.4	35	26

Number of boats sold in 2006

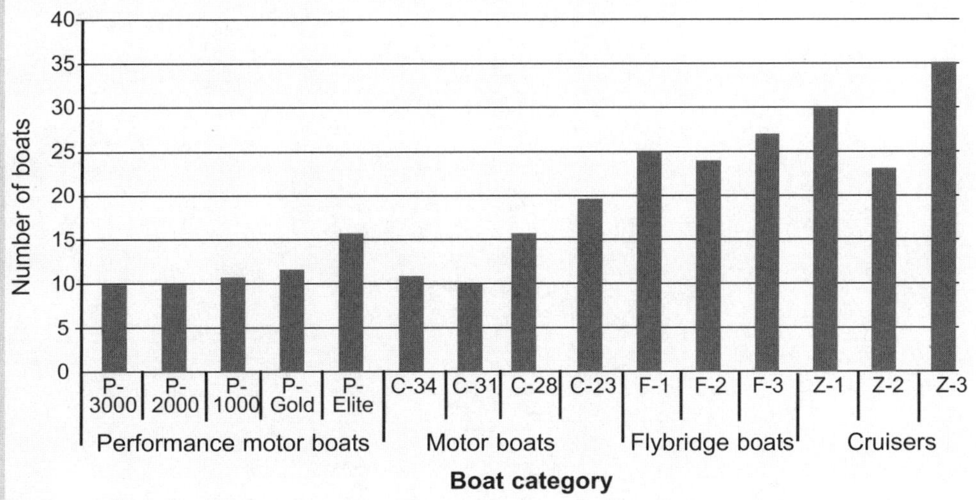

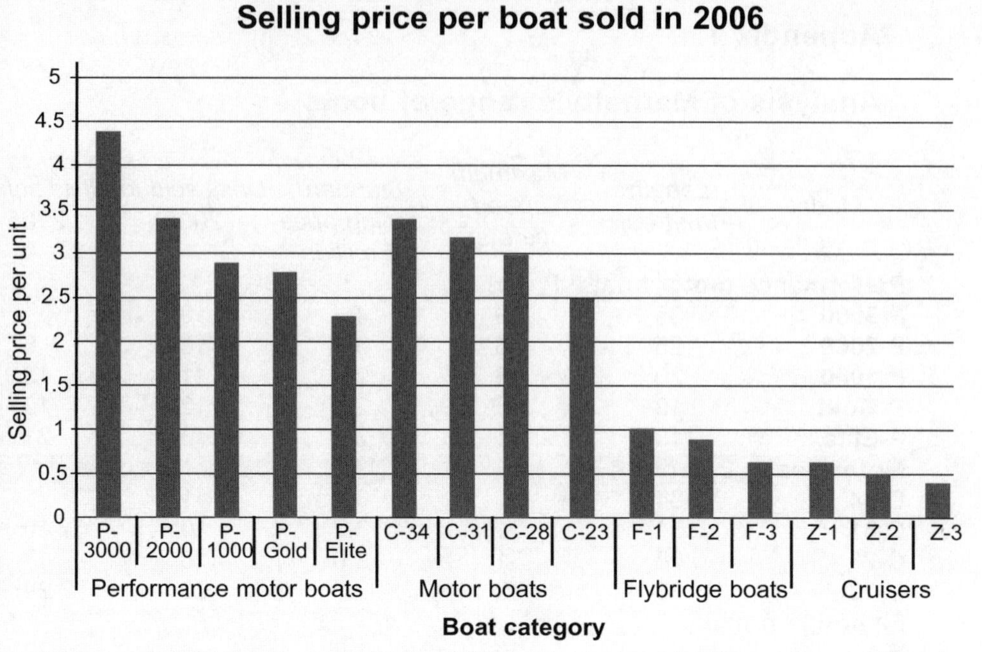
Selling price per boat sold in 2006
Selling price per unit
5
4.5
4
3.5
3
2.5
2
1.5
1
0.5
0
P-3000
P-2000
P-1000
P-Gold
P-Elite
C-34
C-31
C-28
C-23
F-1
F-2
F-3
Z-1
Z-2
Z-3
Performance motor boats
Motor boats
Flybridge boats
Cruisers
Boat category

Appendix 2

Sales revenue analysed by home base customers

	Sales revenue 2006 € million	Planned sales revenue 2011 € million Note: All figures shown are based on 2006 proices
Europe	219	420
USA	148	240
Middle East	40	180
Asia	45	65
Australia	30	60
South America	18	29
Africa	2	6
Total revenue	502	1,000

Appendix 3

Merbatty's key personnel

Alberto Blanc – Chairman

Alberto Blanc, now 62, had an interest in boats from an early age, when he used to spend his summer holidays at his uncle's boat building facility. Having a keen eye for design and a love of the ocean, he went to marine college in 1965 and became a marine engineer in 1968. He started Merbatty after his uncle gave up his business in 1974 and passed the boat building facility onto Alberto. He plays an active role in the business and is often seen in the European boat building facility, talking to and advising design and technical staff. He believes in a 'hands on' management style and that the best way to learn what is happening in the business is to see the boats actually being built. He is also a strong believer in the importance of charity work.

Henri Gaston – Chief Executive

Henri Gaston is a 35-year-old MBA graduate who joined Merbatty in September 2005. He has previously worked for one of Merbatty's major overseas rivals and has a number of contacts throughout the industry.

Stefan Gil – Sales Director

Stefan Gil, who is 52, has worked for Merbatty for 14 years and was previously a sales director of one of the main engine suppliers, where he worked for 10 years. He has a very strong technical knowledge and previously spent five years in the Middle East as an engineer. He is a keen sailor and has recently sailed single-handed across the Atlantic for charity. His main challenge since joining Merbatty has been to create a strong brand image for Merbatty in order to appeal to the wealthy European and American customer base. He is a great asset to Merbatty.

Andreas Acosta – Finance Director

Andreas Acosta, aged 45, joined Merbatty in 2000. He previously worked as a management consultant for a large international firm of auditors. It was during this time that he developed a keen interest in the boat building industry after being in charge of an international investigation of the industry. His main concern is the management of cash and the potential costs involved in overseas developments. Andreas leads a team of ten accountants in the European office and a further eight in the US office.

Jesper Blanc – Marketing Director

Jesper Blanc is the 30-year-old son of the Chairman. He graduated from university six years ago with a degree in Media Studies and has worked in the company since then. He has worked within the Engineering Department and in the Systems and IT Department for short periods but did not feel that his talents were in either area. His father initially appointed him as a Marketing Assistant, which he enjoyed immensely. His father promoted him to the role of Marketing Director 12 months ago. Since his appointment he has visited many different countries, talking to customers and agents and establishing contacts.

Tobias Houllier – Operations Director

Tobias Houllier, now aged 50, started as a junior carpenter and has now worked for Merbatty for the last 30 years. During his time he has worked in the Engineering Department, the Design Department and he has been the European boat building facility Manager. He has held the role of Operations Director for the last 10 years and is probably the most experienced person in the whole company. He is very keen on training and encourages all of the designers and engineers to become qualified.

Alain Mina – Technical Director – Systems and IT

Alain Mina, aged 35, has worked for Merbatty for the last eight months. Previous to this he was a senior IT project manager for an organisation specialising in building and distributing military radar equipment. This is his first role at director level and he is finding it difficult to take a less hands-on role than he has previously been used to.

Lukas Dian – Technical Director – Design

Lukas Dian aged 36, has worked for Merbatty for five years. He started as the Chief Designer but, owing to his leadership and his personnel management skills, he was promoted to director level within one year of joining. He leads a team of over 20 designers who meet on a regular basis and he encourages an open door policy in order to create a feeling of freedom of thought and creativity.

Marie Lopp – HR Director

Marie Lopp, now aged 40, has worked for Merbatty for three years. She is the first HR Director as previously Alberto Blanc did not believe in human resource departments. However, as the organisation expanded and staff issues and legislation became more complex, he finally agreed to appoint an HR

Director. Marie Lopp has a difficult job persuading Alberto Blanc of the importance of human resource issues and, in particular, she struggles to get him to invest in training for staff other than the engineers and designers.

Paul Lavie – Procurement Director

Paul Lavie, aged 38, joined Merbatty in March 2007. He has many years of experience working for a large supplier of components to the automotive industry. He is concerned that the Procurement Department has not established a close relationship with some of its major suppliers.

Bernie Ritzol – Global Market Development Director

Bernie Ritzol, now aged 46, joined Merbatty 12 years ago and has been responsible for a number of strategic developments including the acquisition of land in the USA and the opening of Merbatty's second boat building facility. He has also worked closely with Tobias Houllier in the development of new boat models and also with the Technical Director – Design, since Lukas Dian was appointed to this new position four years ago. Bernie Ritzol was one of the driving forces behind Merbatty's listing, to enable the company to raise additional finance in order to fund expansion of the company. Bernie Ritzol was also instrumental in the selection of the site in Surania for Merbatty's third boat building facility.

Simone Lellet – Investment Director, JKL

Simone Lellet, aged 42, is JKL's Investment Director and she was appointed to the Board of Merbatty in November 2006, when Merbatty became listed and JKL bought 50.4 million shares, resulting in a holding of 28% of Merbatty's issued shares. Simone Lellet is very enthusiastic about Merbatty's five-year plan and wants to participate in the decision-making process to help Merbatty achieve the goals set out when the company became listed. She has attended every Board meeting and has also been involved in some operational planning meetings, with the Board's permission.

Non-executive directors

Merbatty has six non-executive directors. The six non-executive directors hold various other directorships, in a variety of industries. Four of the non-executive directors are based in Europe and two hold directorships of USA listed companies and are based in the USA.

Appendix 4

Merbatty's Balance Sheet, Income Statement and Statement of Changes in Equity

Note: All data in this Appendix is presented in international financial reporting format.

	As at 31 December 2006		As at 31 Decemebr 2005	
	€ million	€ million	€ million	€ million
Non-current assets (net)		535		362
Current assets				
Inventory (including work-in-progress)	165		126	
Trade receivables and accures revenue	93		76	
Cash and short-term investments	171		7	
		429		209
Total assets		964		571
Equity and liabilities				
Equity	90		30	
Paid in share capital	318		42	
Share premium reserve	80		-	
Revaluation reserve	133		113	
Retained profits		621		185
Non-current liabilities				
Bank loan at 8% interest per year (repayable in 2010)	-		120	
Bank loan at 7% interest per year (repayable in 2014)	200		-	
Creditors: amounts falling due after more than one year	7		2	
		207		122
Current liabilities				
Bank overdraft	-		126	
Trade payables and accruals	101		112	
Customers' deposits	13		9	
Tax	22		17	
		136		264
Total equity and liabilities		964		571

Note: Paid in share capital represents 180 million shares of €0.50 each at 31 December 2006.

Income statement	Year ended 31 December 2006	Year ended 31 Decemebr 2005
	€ million	€ million
Revenue	502	445
Total operating costs	426	380
Operating profit	76	65
Finance costs	-14	-17
Tax expense (effective rate is 35%)	-22	-17
Profit for the preiod	40	31

Statement of Changes in Equity	Share capital € million	Share premium € million	Re-valuation reserve € million	Retained earnings € million	Total € million
Balance at 31 Decemeber 2005	30	42	-	113	185
New shares issued during 2006	60	276	-	-	336
Profit for the period	-	-	-	40	40
Revaluation reserve	-	-	80	-	80
Dividends paid	-	-	-	-20	-20
Balance at 31 Decemeber 2006	90	318	80	133	621

Appendix 5

Extracts from Merbatty's five-year plan

Note: All figures shown in the financial data below are based on 2006 prices

Financial data	**Actual**	**Plan**				
	2006 € million	2007 € million	2008 € million	2009 € million	2010 € million	2011 € million
Revenue (analysed by home base of customers):						
Europe	219	240	275	310	350	420
USA	148	160	170	190	210	240
Middle East	40	50	80	110	140	180
Other areas	95	105	120	130	145	160
Total revenue	502	555	645	740	845	1,000
Operating costs	426	471	552	634	725	863
Operating profit	76	84	93	106	120	137
Post tax profit for the period	40	45	51	60	69	80
Dividends	20	23	26	30	34	40
Capital expenditure						
New boat building facilities	90	30	0	0	60	100
Other capital expenditure	40	25	15	20	20	25
Total capital expenditure	130	55	15	20	80	125

Key business statistics	**Actual**	**Plan**				
	2006	2007	2008	2009	2010	2011
Number of boats commenced in the year	280	300	340	385	435	500
Number of new models introduced	2	3	3	3	3	3
Satisfied customers (as surveyed)	99.5%	100.0%	100.0%	100.0%	100.0%	100.0%
Staff turnover (calculated as a number of staff leaving as a percentage of total employees)	20%	18%	15%	12%	12%	12%
Charity - funds donated (€ million)	0.5	0.6	0.7	0.8	0.9	1.0
- man-years on secondmant for cahrity work	3.0	4.0	5.0	6.0	7.0	8.0

chapter

12

MERBATTY: ANALYSIS OF THE PRE-SEEN MATERIAL

Contents

1 Industry awareness

1.1 Introduction

The case involves the luxury boat building industry, excluding sailing yachts. Production is concentrated mainly in Europe and the USA, with Italian firms dominating the industry, having 38% of the global market.

1.2 Industry growth

As stated in the 'pre-seen' information, the developing luxury boat building industry is one with a growing customer base of wealthy, successful individuals and corporate clients.

The banking industry uses the term 'High Net Worth Individuals' or 'HNWIs' to describe such people:

- 'HNWIs' – Individuals with net assets of at least US$1 million, excluding their primary residence and consumables.
- 'Ultra HNWIs' – Individuals with net assets of at least US$30 million, excluding their primary residence and consumables.

In 2006, driven by a strong global economy, the wealth of HNWIs grew by 11.4% worldwide and the HNWI population by 8.3%. The number of ultra-HNWIs grew by 11.3%. The greatest growth in HNWIs has been in Singapore (21.2%), India (20.5%), China, Indonesia and Russia.

In the US demand is boosted by 'baby-boomers' who are now retired and wish to spend their accumulated wealth on luxurious living.

Demand is currently so high that some speculators are making millions by 'yacht flipping' – people who order boats and then sell them before they are finished for millions more than they have agreed to pay for them.

However, some analysts are concerned that future growth could be limited by:

- fears over the threat from terrorism
- economic downturns
- a shortage of suitably qualified staff to crew the boats.

1.3 Drivers of competitiveness

Despite the encouraging growth discussed above, many analysts believe that the market for luxury boats is becoming more competitive. It will no longer be enough to possess production capacity: on the contrary, there will be a need for companies to distinguish themselves from a strategic-competitive viewpoint with regard to ever more threatening international competitors.

Key drivers of competitiveness include the following:

- Innovation and R&D – both dealers and builders agree that innovation is one of the main reasons why some brands can achieve a clear premium. Typical reinvestment rates for R&D are around 3% of revenue.
- Skills and processes – most builders have reported problems obtaining suitably skilled staff.
- Investment – especially in new facilities and new technology. The Ferretti group typically spends around 8% of revenue on upgrading facilities. As part of its manufacturing process, Azimut uses robots to spray gel over moulds and employs advanced CNC tool-making equipment.
- Supply chain management – applying lean techniques to reduce costs and improve quality. The boat industry appears to be lagging behind the automobile industry where there are greater interdependencies between manufacturers and suppliers in areas such as development and integration.

1.4 Market trends

Luxury yachts are getting bigger, faster, more adventurous, and carrying an ever-increasing array of 'toys'.

Longer yachts

Particularly at the ultra-expensive end of the market, boats have been getting longer in response to customers' quests for greater comfort and luxury. Many of these yachts have celebrity status, regularly featuring in glossy magazines. For example:

- Excluding yachts owned by or on behalf of heads of state, the largest luxury yacht in the world is The Rising Sun, owned by Larry Ellison, founder of Oracle Software. It is 453 foot long complete with an aft-deck basketball court and eight staterooms.
- The second largest yacht at 413 foot is Octopus, owned by Paul Allen, co-founder of Microsoft.

It is also usually the case that the longer the boat, then the higher the price per tonne.

More toys

As the yachts grow larger and the owners more adventurous, there has been a corresponding growth in 'toys', including helipads, personal submarines and diving chambers.

In addition to toys, yacht designs are including features once reserved for homes firmly planted on land. These include Jacuzzi spas, lap pools with swim-in-place systems, fully equipped theatres with surround sound systems, steam rooms and saunas.

Even purchasers of smaller boats are expecting more luxury features than previously.

Expedition yachts

Another change has been a demand for yachts that actually 'do something'. Some owners are no longer content to just sit in a marina sipping cocktails but wish to explore.

A new breed of tough and capable yachts have thus been created that are just as comfortable rafting up to icebergs in the Arctic as they are pushing up a steamy jungle river.

1.5 Technological trends

Two main areas of boat design that have been heavily influenced by technological change are hulls and engines.

Hulls

As owners ask more of their yachts than just a place to spend long weekends, designers must look for ways to make them more seaworthy for offshore cruising.

For example:

- Making full use of the width provided by the catamaran design, the 70-foot Kingcat from France has a 31-foot wide salon.
- The SWATH is a twin-hulled design pioneered by the military. Unlike conventional catamarans, the SWATH has twin submerged hulls that resemble two huge torpedoes that support the yacht in the smooth water below wave level. The twin hulls can be ballasted to run smoothly in offshore waves or emptied to explore shallow waters inaccessible to similarly sized luxury yachts.
- The ARC 2000 also uses the twin hull form of a catamaran. A 65-footer is being built to show off the design and, with more than 2,400 square feet of living space, it will be roughly equivalent to a 130-foot monohull yacht.

Engines

Key issues with engines are speed, noise and vibration. Currently most boats use diesel engines. As future hull designs become more efficient, propulsion systems also come under scrutiny, with several major advances already in use:

- Combining conventional diesels with an aircraft-style turbine engine to increase top speeds.
- Diesel-electric propulsion, which uses diesel generators to produce power to run electric motors that actually turn the propellers. Since the generators can be completely isolated from the hull, a diesel-electric system is noiseless and vibration free.
- Water-jet drive systems.

1.6 Production strategies

Most boat manufacture involves a three-stage process:

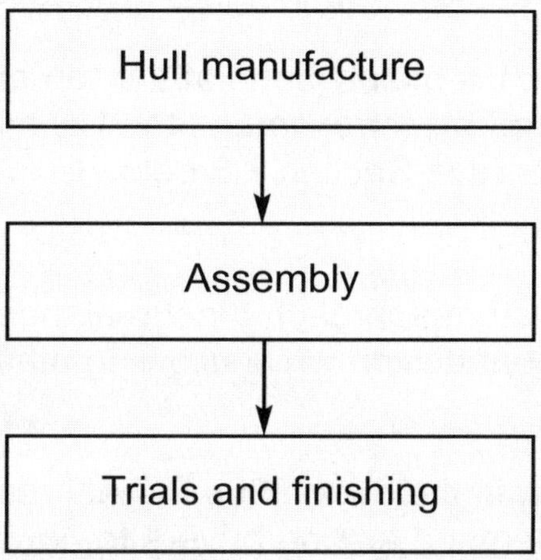

Within this there are a number of key questions to address:

- Should boats be built for inventory or only to order?
- To what extent should the above processes/stages be carried out in-house or out-sourced?
- To what extent should designs be standardised or have bespoke elements?

Outsourcing

Some manufacturers, such as Sealine, complete all activities in-house. Others may choose to outsource some of their production:

- Azimut outsources the production of larger hulls above 74 foot together with wooden furniture.
- Similarly, the Ferretti Group outsources a proportion of hulls and furniture to third parties, although the majority is manufactured by two group companies, Resin Sistem and Diesse Arredamenti who supply all the operating companies in the Group.

Customisation

There are three main customisation strategies pursued by boat builders:

- *Fully custom*

  With a fully custom approach each boat is viewed as a completely bespoke one-of-a-kind yacht. This allows customers to specify exactly what they want, but at a premium. The main problem for manufacturers is that it is very difficult to estimate the cost of such boats, especially when one owner wants a modified hull design, another makes repeated changes to the specification, and yet another wants materials the yard has never used before.

  This approach is mainly seen at the top-end of the market and is adopted by, for example, the US manufacturer Trinity Yachts (see Section 7.8 below).

- *Semi-custom*

  The semi-custom approach tries to standardise certain aspects of boat design while allowing other custom elements.

  For example, in the mid-1990s Benetti recognised an increasing demand among buyers for lower maintenance and lower priced yachts. It thus developed the Benetti Classic line of 35-metre fibreglass yachts. The yard built these in series to have more control over design and construction costs, yet offered owners a choice of three interior layouts for some customisation. The line was a success.

- *Full production*

  Particularly at the smaller end of the market, some manufacturers choose to offer a range of boats with no or few custom elements, in order to achieve production economies. This approach is adopted by Sealine Motor Yachts (see Section 7.8 below).

Building to order

While build-to-order is the preferred approach, there are examples of build-for-stock.

- One example is with new product launches where an initial boat is built for exhibition without a customer order.
- Sea Ray builds smaller boats for dealer inventory, but is targeting reducing this as electronic components become more integrated, thus reducing the scope for customer options to be added-on at dealerships post-manufacturing.

1.7 Marketing strategies

For most boat builders the key aspects of the promotional mix are as follows:

- Boat shows – for example, Azimut sold 60 yachts at the 2007 Miami boat show.
- Sales agents – for example, Ferretti has 41 dealers covering over 63 countries.
- Magazine exposure – firms are very keen for their boats to be featured in magazines such as Yachting Magazine, Power & Motoryacht, Boat International, Yachts International, Showboats and Sea Magazine. Ideally the articles will feature detailed reviews along with photographs emphasising the luxury lifestyle to which the boat owners aspire (or, indeed, have!).
- Websites featuring magazine reviews and articles, extensive high quality images, plans, etc.

1.8 Examples of strategies pursued by real-world players

(**Note:** Try to refer to some of these firms and their strategies in your TOPCIMA answer.)

Azimut-Benetti Group (Italy)

The Azimut-Benetti Group is the largest luxury boat building group in the world. Having started as a boat importer in 1969, the firm soon moved into boat design and production. Key acquisitions included the following:

- 1985 – Benetti Shipyards
- 1999 – the Moschini yards in Fano-Pesaro
- 2001 – the Gobby shipyard near Piacenza.

In 2004 Azimut-Benetti entered a joint venture with two other major players in the yachting and cruise industries to move beyond just boat manufacture:

- V.Ships Leisure – provider of ship management services, including crewing, leisure, financial, insurance, consulting, commercial and agency services.
- Fraser Yachts Worldwide – yacht sales, brokerage, yacht charters, management and crew placement.

Ferretti Group (Italy)

The second largest boat building group in the world, Ferretti has a wide range of famous brands in its portfolio. Acquisitions in the 1990s included Pershing, Bertram (the American shipyard producer of Fishermans), the prestigious CRN in Ancona, where the most famous luxury megayachts are made and the legendary shipyard Riva.

Have obtained a stock exchange listing during the 1990s, the Group was taken private again in 2002 after the launch of a takeover bid by the Permira Private Equity Fund.

The Group's stated growth strategy focuses on product evolution and on the technological innovation and design of the new yachts such as the anti-rolling gyro (ARG) system developed jointly with Mitsubishi.

The Ferretti name is represented by the worldwide sales network mentioned above, and by the after-sales services offered by more than 100 worldwide service points.

Trinity Yachts (USA)

Trinity Yachts is ranked by Showboats International magazine as the number one builder of custom yachts in the US. It is a good example of a boat builder that has developed its product range via acquisition.

In May 2007 Trinity Yachts announced its proposed acquisition of International Yacht Collection (IYC) This acquisition will expand Trinity's capabilities and enable it to offer its clients the entire range of yachting services: new construction, repairs, brokerage, charter management, retail charter, yacht management and crew placement.

Felix Sabates, Chairman of Trinity stated that 'due to the high level of satisfaction with their new Trinity yachts, a number of our clients have expressed an interest in Trinity providing additional services to these owners and we are simply responding to their requests. Our goal is to make it as easy and enjoyable as possible for an owner to purchase, operate and ultimately sell their Trinity yacht.'

Sealine Motor Yachts (UK)

The British builder Sealine is one of Europe's largest production luxury boat builders, producing over 300 boats a year. The range encompasses 15 models of sports cruisers and motor yachts, from entry level to full scale motor yachts, spanning 25 to 60 feet. (Note: Sealine has many similarities to Merbatty.)

Sealine is one of the few boat builders that runs an entirely in-house operation. From the drawing board through to the finished product, every stage of design and production is carried out within Sealine's own covered workshops.

With an international sales and dealer network comprising over 40 dealers, Sealine has representation across the globe and is continually seeking to expand into new areas.

Over the past three decades, Sealine has been recognised for its many, often unique innovations, which have revolutionised industry standards. Its stated aim is to create a product that captures adventure, relaxation and luxury.

Sealine also offers an official Sealine Sea School which offers everything from day cruising to yacht master training. This provides owners with a learning platform to develop key skills.

2 Financial analysis of appendices

2.1 Analyse the financial statements in appendix 4 using ratio analysis.

Your response

	2006	2005	2006 Working	2005 Working
Profitability				
Growth in revenue (%)	12.8	-	502/445	-
Growth in operating profit (%)	16.9	-	76/65	-
Growth in net profit (%)	29.0	-	40/31	-
Capital employed (€m)	828	307	621 + 207	185 + 122
ROCE (%)	9.2	21.2	76/828	65/307
Return on equity (%)	6.4	16.8	40/621	31/185
Operating profit margin (%)	15.1	14.6	76/502	65/445
Net profit margin (%)	8.0	7.0	40/502	31/445
Asset turnover	0.6x	1.4x	502/828	445/307
Liquidity				
Current ratio	3.2	0.8	429/136	209/264
Quick ratio	1.9	0.3	(93+171)/136	(76+7)/264
Receivables period (days)	68	62	(93/502) x 365	(76/445) x 365
Payables period (days)	87	108	(101/426) x 365	(112/380) x 365
Inventory holding period (days)	141	121	(165/426) x 365	(126/380) x 365
Investor ratios				
Gearing - D/E - using book values	0.3	0.7	207/621	122/185
Interest cover	5.4x	3.8x	76/14	65/17
Dividend cover	2x	-	40/20	-
EPS (€)	0.22	0.52	40/180	31/60

Your comments

Profitability

- Strong growth in revenue and profit.
- Extra funds raised have depressed ROCE, ROE and asset turnover. It will take time for the additional capital to result in sufficient extra profits to correct this
- Margins have improved, probably due to the growth.

Liquidity

- Cash injection has improved both current and quick ratios, both of which were low before the new finance.
- However, a longer receivables period, shorter payables period and longer inventory holding together have lengthened the operating cycle by 48 days, putting much more pressure on cash flow. The injected funds mean that cash flow is not an immediate problem but tighter controls are needed in the area of working capital.

Investor ratios

- Equity issue has improved gearing but reduced EPS. One would hope that shareholders are sophisticated enough for the fall in EPS not to be viewed in a negative light.
- However, a longer receivables period, shorter payables period and longer inventory holding together have lengthened the operating cycle by 48 days, putting much more pressure on cash flow. The injected funds mean that cash flow is not an immediate problem but tighter controls are needed in the area of working capital.
- Interest cover and dividend cover are adequate.

2.2 Prepare a cash flow statement from the information given and comment.

Your response

	Working	€m
Operating profit		76
Add back: depreciation	See working below	37
		113
Increase in inventories	165 - 126	(39)
Increase in trade receivables and accrued revenue	93 - 76	(17)
Decrease in trade payables, customer deposits and accruals	(101 + 13) - (112 + 9)	(7)
Increase in non-current creditors		5
Net cash flow from operating activities		55
Tax paid		(17)
Interest paid		(14)
Dividends paid		(20)
		4
Investment in non-current assets(Appendix 5)		(130)
Cash raised from share issue		336
Repayment of existing loan, originally due 2010		(120)
New loan raised		200
		290
Repayment of overdraft		(126)
Increase in cash and short-term investments	171 - 7	164

Working

		€m
NBV Bal b/f		362
Add: investment (appendix 5)	(90 + 40)	130
Add: revaluation		80
		572
Less: disposals	Assumption	0
Less: depreciation	Balancing figure	(37)
NBV Bal c/f		535

Your comments

- Extra money tied up in working capital = 39 + 17 + 7 = €63 million. Working capital management is often a key issue in growing businesses.
- Increase in working capital resulted in very little cash available from retained earnings for new investment.
- However, most of the funds required for new boats come from the deposit system.

2.3 Analyse growth, mix and margins assumptions in appendix 5 and assess whether the estimates made are reasonable.

Your response

(a) **Revenue mix**

	2006	**2007**	**2008**	**2009**	**2010**	**2011**
Revenue mix (%)	%	%	%	%	%	%
Europe	44	43	43	42	41	42
USA	29	29	26	26	25	24
Middle East	8	9	12	15	17	18
Other areas	19	19	19	17	17	16
Total revenue	100	100	100	100	100	100

(b) **Revenue growth**

	2006	**2007**	**2008**	**2009**	**2010**	**2011**
Revenue growth (%)	%	%	%	%	%	%
Europe	-	9.6	14.6	12.7	12.9	20.0
USA	-	8.1	6.3	11.8	10.5	14.3
Middle East	-	25.0	60.0	37.5	27.3	28.6
Other areas	-	10.5	14.3	8.3	11.5	10.3
Total revenue	12.8	10.6	16.2	14.7	14.2	18.3

(c) **Margins**

	2006	**2007**	**2008**	**2009**	**2010**	**2011**
	%	%	%	%	%	%
Operating margin (%)	15.1	15.1	14.4	14.3	14.2	13.7

Your comments

- As seen with Appendix 3, the main growth area is forecast to be the Middle East. The growth figures seem very high so could be interpreted as unrealistic/very ambitious. The new facility in the Middle East will facilitate growth but more information is needed to assess whether such growth is achievable.
- Historically revenue has grown at 10% per annum, so European figures (especially growth beyond 2007) also looks ambitious/unrealistic.
- Also, industry background information indicates that, even in 2006, a year with strong global economic growth, the global population of High Net Worth Individuals (HNWIs) rose by 8.3%.

2.4 Cash flow forecast

According to the pre-seen, 'This new loan, together with some of the equity raised in the listing will finance Merbatty's capital expenditure programme over the next few years, as well as finance the increase in working capital in order to achieve the growth targets planned'.

Given this, it would be useful to assess whether the cash raised is sufficient or whether further finance will need to be injected. We know that the However, forecasting cash flow can be done with a range of assumptions and corresponding levels of difficulty.

Step 1: Assume net profit = cash inflow from operating activities

Your response

	2007	**2008**	**2009**	**2010**	**2011**
	€m	€m	€m	€m	€m
Post tax profit for the period	45	51	60	69	80
Net cash from operating activities	45	51	60	69	80
Total capital expenditure	55	15	20	80	125
Dividends	23	26	30	34	40
Cash required	78	41	50	114	165
Net cash flow	(33)	10	10	(45)	(85)
Cash b/f	171	138	148	158	113
Cash c/f	138	148	158	113	28

Your comments

- Based on these figures, cash flow does not seem to be a problem.

Step 2: Try to incorporate depreciation using 10% of opening NBV

Your response

	2007	2008	2009	2010	2011
	€m	€m	€m	€m	€m
Post tax profit for the period	45	51	60	69	80
Add back: depreciation (W1)	54	54	50	47	50
Net cash from operating activities	99	105	110	116	130
Total capital expenditure	55	15	20	80	125
Dividends	23	26	30	34	40
Cash required	78	41	50	114	165
Net cash flow	21	64	60	2	(35)
Cash b/f	171	192	256	316	318
Cash c/f	192	256	316	318	283

W1: Depreciation	**2007**	**2008**	**2009**	**2010**	**2011**
	€m	€m	€m	€m	€m
NBV b/f	535	536	497	467	500
Additions (note)	55	15	20	80	125
Depreciation at 10%	(54)	(54)	(50)	(47)	(50)
NBV c/f	536	497	467	500	575

Note: e.g. 2007: charge = 10%×535 = 54

Your comments

- Net cash flow still positive each year, indicating no problem.

Step 3: Try to incorporate movements in working capital

Your response

The incremental investment in working capital is often calculated (e.g. as a part of SVA) as a fixed % times the increase in revenue from one period to another.

From 2005 to 2006, revenue increased by 502 – 445 = €57 million.

The net investment in working capital increased by €63 million.

This implies that the increase in working capital = 63/57 = 110.5% of the increase in revenue.

Use this figure to revise the cash flow forecast.

	2007	2008	2009	2010	2011
	€m	€m	€m	€m	€m
Post tax profit for the period	45	51	60	69	80
Add back: depreciation (see above)	54	54	50	47	50
Less: increase in working capital (W2)	(59)	(99)	(105)	(116)	(171)
Net cash from operating activities	40	6	5	0	(41)
Total capital expenditure	55	15	20	80	125
Dividends	23	26	30	34	40
Cash required	78	41	50	114	165
Net cash flow	(38)	(35)	(45)	(114)	(206)
Cash b/f	171	133	98	53	(61)
Cash c/f	133	98	53	(61)	(267)

(W2) Investment in working capital	2007	2008	2009	2010	2011
	€m	€m	€m	€m	€m
Increase in revenue	53	90	95	105	155
Increase in working capital (110.5%)	59	99	105	116	171

Your comments

- Incorporating working capital increases has changed the picture, indicating that cash reserves are insufficient for future growth.
- This shows how important the increase in working capital could be to the success of the five-year plan.
- The figures used indicate that refinancing is needed in 2010. This suggests that perhaps Merbatty is trying to grow too quickly.
- The possibility of building another facility in 2010 would require even more finance.

2.5 Capacity

Assess whether Merbatty has the capacity to make all of the boats in the plan.

Your response

	2006	2007	2008	2009	2010	2011
Number of boats commenced in the year	280	300	340	385	435	500
Capacity assuming smaller boats	320	320	500	500	500	500
Capacity assuming larger boats	320	320	460	460	460	460

Your comments

- If smaller boats are made, then there is sufficient capacity.
- If larger boats are made, then there will be a need for extra capacity in 2011. Industry trends are currently towards larger boats.

2.6 Key business statistics

Comment on the key business statistics data.

Your comments

- Why was customer satisfaction not 100% in 2006? Although 0.5% of customers is only one boat, is this indicative of a deeper underlying problem?
- Staff turnover seems very high given the importance of skilled production workers to Merbatty. This could indicate poor motivation which, in a quality focused business such as Merbatty's, could be a major problem. No indication is given as to how this figure will be reduced.
- Are other shareholders happy with the planned increases in charitable spending – especially JKL?
- A full balanced scorecard analysis would be more useful.

3 Business strategy perspective

3.1 Consolidate your understanding of the strategic position of Merbatty using a SWOT analysis.

Strengths

- Strong financial performance – growth in revenue, profit, margins and share price.
- Quoted following a successful flotation.
- Cash rich due to recent equity issue.
- Semi-custom approach to production should allow bespoke elements while keeping costs down.
- Alberto Blanc awarded the 'Business Person of the Year', raising Merbatty's profile.

- Uses latest marine production technology.
- Use of production management software.
- Experienced board (on the whole!).
- Good relationship with Topcrest.

Weaknesses

- May be trying to grow too quickly.
- Worsening working capital management.
- High staff turnover (20% in 2006).
- Poor training for non-production staff.
- Weak relationships with some key suppliers (implied by Paul Lavie).
- Ambiguity of role distinction between Chairman and CEO.
- Inexperienced Marketing Director.
- No evidence of FX hedging.

Opportunities

- Larger boats.
- Market development – Middle East, China.
- New production facility in Surania.
- New production facility in Asia.
- Acquire a supplier.
- Expedition-style boats.
- Improved supply chain efficiency.
- Improved labour efficiency.

Threats

- Opening of sales offices could compromise existing agent network.
- Competitive rivalry.
- Threat of new entrants.
- Raw material shortages (e.g. luxury hard woods).
- Competitors may buy key suppliers.
- Higher oil prices and tax on fuel.
- Economic recession.

3.2 Assess the luxury motor boat industry from Merbatty's perspective using Porter's five forces analysis.

Competitive rivalry – medium

- Large number of rivals.
- However, high market growth lessens rivalry.
- Reputation/name very important.

Threat of new entrants – high

- Barriers to entry include having a boat building facility, design expertise, experienced production craftsmen, brand name/reputation.
- Most of these can be bought (e.g. headhunt key designers), although the brand name could take some time to develop.
- The trend towards larger boats could allow commercial and military ship builders to enter the luxury yacht market.
- Overall would expect industry growth to attract new entrants so the threat should be considered high.

Threat from substitutes – low

- Substitutes would include customers buying other luxury goods instead of boats – cars, houses, helicopters, etc. Most wealthy individuals probably already have these if they want them.
- Threat of substitutes probably low.

Power of suppliers – high

- Over-reliant on key suppliers, e.g. Topcrest?

Power of customers – high

- Individual customer purchases are significant, especially for larger boats.
- Customers can easily switch to other suppliers for subsequent purchases if unhappy.
- Payment system is based on customers being completely happy before final payment (50%) is made.

3.3 Analyse the boat building industry using a PESTEL/PEST/SLEPT style analysis.

Political/legal

- State aid to support investment in technology.
- Health and safety – extensive rules re shipping, especially if boats are to be used for chartering.
- Government investment in infrastructure (e.g. waterfront development in Dubai) could boost demand.
- Greater risk of terrorism may dissuade people from buying and using yachts.

Economic

- Economic growth results in more wealthy individuals, especially in BRIC economies.
- While specific individuals' spending may not be very affected by economic conditions, the overall number of potential customers could fall if there is an economic downturn.

- Oil prices could affect demand for power boats.
- FX risk.

Social

- Increasingly viewed as ultra-luxury by HNWIs and hence desirable.

Technological

- CAD/CAM design, e.g. engine design, hull designs.
- Manufacturing technology – e.g. CNC machining, spraying, performance gel coating.
- Computer-based modelling for testing.

3.4 Competitive strategy: What type of competitive strategy is Merbatty trying to use? Assess the sustainability of this option.

Merbatty is pursuing a competitive strategy of differentiation based on the following:

- reputation (enhanced by Alberto and various sponsorship deals)
- use of IT (e.g. production management software)
- use of advanced production technology (e.g. CNC machining)
- skilled workforce
- world-class suppliers
- experienced agents.

The key threats to this are:

- high staff turnover
- loss of Alberto
- poor marketing.

3.5 Use Porter's value chain to analyse Merbatty.

Infrastructure	Simple organisational structure facilitating low costs and good control.				
HRM		• Skilled staff but high staff turnover may compromise quality.		• Mixture of agents and in-house sales teams.	
Technology	• Online order tracking and processing system.	• Production software system increases productivity and quality. • CNC machining/spray systems. • Performance gel coating.	• Production software system increases chances of delivery on time.		
Procurement	• Sole suppliers for main inputs. • Good relationship with Topcrest. • Few suppliers in both Europe and US, so cost issues.	• Purpose-built facilities.	• Arrangement with hotel and travel chain for customers to inspect boats.		
	• World-class suppliers.		• Retention of 50% of fees until customers are completely happy should motivate managers to ensure quality.	• Sponsorship deals. • Charitable work. • Alberto's reputation.	• Little information given about warranties.
	Inbound logistics	**Operations**	**Outbound logistics**	**Marketing and sales**	**Service**

3.6 Using Ansoff's matrix, outline possible directions for growth for Merbatty.

Ansoff's matrix – product/market mix

	Existing products	New products
Exisiting markets	*Cost efficiency* • Use new gel technology in European operation. *Market penetration* • Current plan = open new shipyards in Middle East and Asia. • Open more sales outlets. • Buy a rival.	*Product development* • Introduce longer yachts. • Greater range of boats. • New hull designs.
New markets	*Market development* • Middle East. • China.	*Diversification* • Broker – buy and sell yachts. • Crew placement service. • Skipper training schools. • Bring design in-house. • Buy a supplier – Topcrest, Marinatron, MNE, SSE or Aqua Designs.

4 Financial strategy perspective

4.1 Analyse the financing arrangements used by Merbatty to date and potential future financing requirements, and comment on the options available for raising finance in the future.

Prior to flotation

Prior to flotation Merbatty had used a mixture of equity, loans and a growing overdraft for financing. However:

- Current and quick ratios were very low, and gearing high, if 2005 figures are anything to go by.
- Operations were not generating sufficient cash flow to invest, though dividends could have been cut to help.
- An overdraft of €126 million exposed the firm to excessive financial risk and cost.

- In summary, refinancing was needed.

Flotation (November 2006)

The flotation appears to have been a success:

- Fully subscribed.
- Issue price (€2.80) was 20% below post-flotation market price (€3.48) – a reasonable discount.
- Working capital and gearing ratios restored to acceptable levels.
- Cash was made available for investment.

Future financing possibilities

Equity

- Dividend cut, although this could adversely affect the share price.
- Rights issue – Merbatty is quoted and has good growth prospects. However, shareholders may be unwilling to invest further so soon after flotation.

Debt

- Asset valuation of €535 million compared to debt of €200 million would suggest that further security exists for raising more debt if required.
- Similarly interest cover is very high at 5.4× and book gearing low at 0.3, both suggesting room for further debt.

4.2 Estimate Merbatty's WACC.

Approach 1: Using the five-year plan forecasts

Cost of equity

Using the five-year plan, projected dividend growth is given by $20(1+g)^5 = 40$, giving g = 14.9%.

$$k_e = \frac{d_1}{P_0} + g = \frac{23}{3.65 \times 180} + 0.149 = 0.184 \text{ or } 18.4\%$$

MV equity = 3.65 × 180 = €657 million

Cost of debt

$k_d = 7 \times (1 - 0.35) = 4.55\%$

MV debt = €200 million

WACC

WACC = (657 × 18.4 + 200 × 4.55)/(657 +200) = 15.17%

Approach 2: Using historic figures

When calculating the k_e we could have used historic data and ignored the plan:

Historic earnings growth = 10%. We can assume that the dividend growth was comparable.

$$k_e = \frac{d_1}{P_0} + g = \frac{20(1.10)}{3.65 \times 180} + 0.10 = 0.133 \text{ or } 13.3\%$$

This would then give a WACC of 11.3%.

4.3 Examine different ways of valuing Merbatty and comment on their suitability.

1. **Current market capitalisation**

   We have not been told details of the stock market on which Merbatty is listed. However, assuming the usual level of market efficiency, one would expect the share price to give a fair value for Merbatty, based on publicly available information.

   Share price = €3.65

   No. of shares = 180 million

   MV = 180 million × 3.65 = €657 million

2. **Net asset value**

   Merbatty operates in a very capital-intensive manufacturing industry, suggesting that an asset-based approach should be useful. However, there would be the normal problems in estimating the value of goodwill, brand names, etc. Given that Merbatty's assets were revalued at the end of 2006, the current balance sheet should give a reasonable valuation:

   Book value of equity = €621 million

3. **P/E ratio approach using industry average P/E**

   At present Merbatty has a P/E ratio that is higher than the industry average, due to higher growth and lower risk expectations. The industry P/E would thus tend to undervalue Merbatty at least in the short term. However, in the long run one would expect convergence.

   Earnings = €40 million

   MV = 15 × 40 = €600 million

4. **Discounted cash flow approach**

Theoretically a discounted cash flow approach should always be seen as useful, although practically it may be difficult to use.

In the case of Merbatty we saw in the analysis of Appendix 5 how assumptions had to be made concerning depreciation and working capital to derive cash flows. The assumptions made there resulted in cash outflows for each of the next five years, making it difficult to apply discounted cash flows without further information concerning years 2012 onwards.

5 Risk and control strategy perspective

5.1 Identify the risks facing Merbatty under the following headings.

Business risks

- Competitive rivalry.
- The proposed switch to sales offices could result in a reduced marketing impact compared to the current system of sales agents.

Financial risks

- Working capital management – is Merbatty trying to grow too quickly?
- Recent flotation has improved both gearing and interest cover.

Political and legal risks

- Higher income taxes for wealthy individuals could dampen demand.
- Higher taxes on luxury items could increase the prices of boats.
- Emissions legislation.
- Greater health and safety legislation could make boats more expensive to build.

Technology risk

- Most technological changes are likely to make boats easier and cheaper to make and will increase demand for luxury boats.

Economic risk

- Economic growth is resulting in more potential customers. Economic downturns could reverse this trend.

- Oil price increases will make boats more expensive to operate
- FOREX risk as costs don't always match revenue, e.g. a boat could be built in Europe (cost in €) for a US customer (revenue in $).

Reputation risk

- Quality issues because of staffing problems.
- Loss of Alberto.

5.2 Suggest some KPIs that could be used to monitor operations for Merbatty, using the balanced scorecard as a framework.

Financial perspective

- Share price.
- Investor ratios, e.g. EPS, dividend yield, dividend cover, etc.
- Sales versus target – overall, by region and by model.
- Operating margins – overall, by region and by model.
- Sales mix and quantity variances.

Customer perspective

- Customer satisfaction surveys – 99.5% in 2006.
- % boats delivered on time.
- % of customers who purchase further boats.
- Industry awards for quality.

Internal business perspective

- % boats built within budget.
- % boats finished on time.
- % boats sold via agents compared to sales offices.

Innovation and learning perspective

- % staff turnover – if staff leave then skills and experience are lost.
- Number of new models introduced each year.
- % of sales coming from new models.
- Industry awards for innovation.
- Product development lead-time.

6 Ethical considerations

6.1 Identify any ethical issues within the case under the following headings.

Corporate governance

- Merbatty has separated the roles of Chairman and CEO and has NEDs, all in accordance with Governance best practice.
- However, on a practical level, Alberto may still be exercising too much control and running the business as if his own possession.

Social responsibility

- Charitable donations and staff secondment scheme both point to Merbatty being socially responsible.
- However, it could be argued that the use of the earth's resources to make luxury yachts for the benefit of a tiny, wealthy minority is unethical.
- Also there is no indication that any materials used have been or could be recycled.
- Merbatty only makes power boats that use fuel. Sailing yachts would be more environmentally friendly.

Business ethics

- High staff turnover could be indicative of employees being mistreated.

Personal ethics

- No information given in the case so far to indicate anything here.

7 Précis of the case – Merbatty

Merbatty is a luxury motor yacht manufacturer with facilities in Europe and the US.

7.1 The industry

The luxury boat industry is a global business characterised by the following:

- Underlying trend of high growth due to a strong global economy and the economic expansion of China and India.
- Specific trend towards larger boats.
- Increasing competitiveness.

7.2 Merbatty's existing strategies

Merbatty is following a competitive strategy of differentiation based on the following:

- Strong brand name, reinforced by Alberto Blanc's reputation and sponsorship.
- Use of IT (e.g. production management software).
- Increasing use of advanced production technology (e.g. CNC machining, advanced gel coating).

Merbatty has adopted a semi-customised approach to production where customers can choose from 15 models and then specify the interiors they would like with Aqua Designs, an external interior design consultancy.

Merbatty uses a range of world-class suppliers including the following:

- Topcrest – hulls
- Marinatron – radar and satellite navigation equipment
- SSE – safety equipment such as life jackets
- MNE – engines
- Aqua Designs – interior design.

7.3 Financial performance to date

Merbatty's financial performance was strong in 2006:

- Revenue has grown by 12.8% to €502 million.
- Operating profit has grown by 16.9% to €76 million and net profit by 29.0% to €40 million.
- The operating profit margin improved from 14.6% to 15.1%.
- High P/E ratio (16.5 compared to industry average of 15).

The firm successfully floated in November 2006 raising €336 million.

- This enabled Merbatty to repay existing debt (loan and overdraft).
- Together with a new loan of €200 million, this improved Merbatty's quick and current ratios.
- However, the extra capital employed saw Merbatty's ROCE fall from 21.1% to 9.2%.

The main area of concern is that the operating cycle lengthened by 48 days, indicating that the high growth is not being controlled adequately.

7.4 Future plans

- Opening a new facility in Surania in the Middle East – due to be opened in September 2007.
- Expanding the range of models offered, especially focusing on larger boats. The five-year plan shows three new models a year, but Bernie Ritzol (the Global Market Development Director) has suggested as many as ten over two years.
- Jesper Blanc (the Marketing Director) has suggested building boats for inventory rather than just to order.
- Stefan Gil (the Sales Director) wants to open 20 sales offices rather than relying solely on existing agent relationships.

7.5 Key issues facing the firm

The key issues facing Merbatty are as follows:

- Product portfolio – whether and how quickly to increase its product range, whether to introduce longer boats and whether some models should be discontinued.
- Working capital management – a lengthening operating cycle is worrying given growth plans and may compromise the five-year plan.
- Managing growth – is Merbatty trying to grow too quickly?
- Sales and marketing – should Merbatty focus on the current system of sales agents or switch to sales offices? Should the current charitable giving continue?
- High staff turnover – is there a problem keeping skilled staff? If so, then why and could this compromise both quality and expansion plans?
- Supply chain strategy – should Merbatty continue with its emphasis on using sole suppliers or should it multi-source? How can better relationships with suppliers be developed?
- Corporate strategy – rather than building new facilities, should Merbatty consider acquisitions? Should it also be investigating joint developments with suppliers?

chapter

13

MERBATTY: SEPTEMBER 2007 – UNSEEN MATERIAL

Contents

1 Question requirement

'You are the consultant appointed by the Merbatty Board.

Prepare a report that prioritises, analyses and evaluates the issues facing Merbatty and makes appropriate recommendations.'

2 Rest of the unseen material

Proposal to enter the boat chartering market

The boat chartering market is defined as the renting of boats, which are owned and operated by a company, and rented on a weekly basis to private individuals or companies. A boat chartering company puts its own crew on board and pays all the fixed costs. The end customer who charters (rents) a boat typically pays the fixed weekly fee plus some additional charges. There are many boat chartering companies globally.

The prospectus forecast for Merbatty at the time of flotation included a number of new areas of revenue generation, one of which was a proposal to enter the boat charter market. Bernie Ritzol, Merbatty's Global Market Development Director, is very keen to see Merbatty generate revenues from new sources. He believes that the time is right for Merbatty to enter the highly competitive boat chartering market. Bernie Ritzol has prepared a proposal for Merbatty to initially build 10 large boats specifically for chartering, all 10 of which will be based in Europe. If this initial trial into the chartering market is successful, then Merbatty will build and operate additional charter boats to meet market demand worldwide.

If the Board approves this proposal, Merbatty would need to commence the building of all 10 boats by November 2007, so that they will be available for chartering during Summer 2008. Therefore a Board decision on this chartering proposal will need to be made by mid-October 2007.

The average capital cost of each boat is forecast to be €3.2 million, post-tax. The post-tax net cash inflows (excluding the capital cost and residual values of the 10 boats) are forecast to be:

Forecast post-tax net cash inflows (Total for all 10 charter boats)	2008 € million	2009 € million	2010 € million	2011 € million	2012 € million
Post-tax net cah inflows (nominal values)	10.5	13.9	16.9	17.9	26.6

These post-tax net cash inflows are based on the expected number of weeks that all 10 boats would be chartered each year and represent only about 40% of the year. Andreas Acosta, the Finance Director, recommends that a suitable risk adjusted discount rate is 14% post-tax and considers that this investment should be appraised over a five year period. The post-tax residual value at the end of year five is forecast to be €0.75 million for each boat.

Shortage of skilled employees

Marie Lopp has been actively recruiting skilled boat builders during 2007. Merbatty needs more employees at its existing facilities to build the increased number of boats and also to cover for employees who have been seconded to Merbatty's new boat building facility in Surania. However, there is a high demand for skilled boat builders in this sector and recruitment of new employees has been lower than required. Merbatty will need to recruit a total of over 100 skilled boat builders over the next two years to be ready to meet the forecast growth in the number of boats to be built.

Merbatty currently spends approximately €1 million per year on training, the majority of which is for designers and engineers. However, this is significantly less than its major competitors, two of whom spend in excess of €5 million per year. Alberto Blanc's philosophy is that too much time spent on training detracts from the actual boat building activity and that the best form of training is done whilst working on the job. A number of skilled employees and new apprentices have recently resigned from Merbatty. Some apprentices stated that they considered their future would be more secure if they worked for an employer who can support their studies.

Stock discrepancy

Andreas Acosta has received an internal audit report that states that there is a discrepancy of €0.2 million of electric power tools which Merbatty purchases for employees to use during boat construction work. This discrepancy was discovered at a stock take at the end of June 2007. On investigation, it has been established that many employees have taken these electric tools for personal use over the last few years. Recently, one long standing employee was dismissed for the theft of a €300 power drill when it was discovered in his possession on a random and unannounced check of employees when leaving the boat building facility.

Problem at Merbatty's boat building facility in the USA

A serious problem has been identified in Merbatty's boat building facility in the USA. This problem has arisen from the use of new technology, which was introduced only at the USA facility in February 2007. The new technology involves the application of glass re-enforced plastic onto the hull of each boat to improve its durability and strength. The glass re-enforced plastic technology has been used on a total of 32 boats.

However, in July 2007, sea trials were held for 4 boats whose hulls had been coated with this new technology. (Sea trials are defined as a rigorous series of "in-water" tests which are designed to test the boat under a variety of sea and weather conditions and are conducted as a final test before delivery to customers). The sea trials identified cracks in the hulls and significant water leakage on all 4 boats. During earlier tests on these 4 boats at the USA boat building facility, no faults had been identified at all and therefore these boats had been completed and prepared for sea trials prior to delivery to customers.

Following the discovery of these cracks, the problem was reported to Tobias Houllier. He immediately instructed a team of senior engineers be sent out to inspect the 24 boats built using this new technology which have already been delivered to customers. These inspection tests were conducted during August 2007. All 24 boats were comprehensively inspected and 6 of these boats were found to have similar cracks in their hulls.

Therefore at the end of August 2007, it had been identified that there are 10 completed boats with these serious cracks; 6 which have been delivered to customers and 4 which failed their sea trials. There are a further 4 boats that are still under construction where this technology has already been applied.

It is not yet known whether these serious cracks can be repaired, or whether the boats will have to be re-built. Andreas Acosta has estimated that if the 10 completed boats need to be re-built, then the additional cost to Merbatty, including penalty payments, would be around €11 million.

Fortunately, the previous technology is still available and is used within the USA boat building facility for some of Merbatty's other boat models. The boats built in the USA facility using the previous technology have shown no evidence whatsoever of leakages or cracking.

Delayed opening of Merbatty's new boat building facility in Surania

Merbatty was planning to open its third boat construction facility in Surania at the start of September 2007. This new facility was planned to cost a total of €120 million during 2006 and 2007.

However, there have been delays at the final stages of construction and also in the issue of import permits for specialised equipment. The Suranian facility was opened for trials and safety testing in August 2007 but it quickly became apparent that the air conditioning for this large building was not adequate. Therefore, the safety certificate was not issued by the relevant authorities.

Merbatty will not be able to install the remaining equipment, or install and test the more powerful air conditioning, required to ensure a safe working temperature in this hot country, until December 2007. The updated estimated date for the opening of this new facility has been put back to the end of January 2008, due to the time required for the authorities to test the working environment and to issue a safety certificate. It is also forecast that there will be cost over-runs of €20 million.

In the month of August 2007 alone sales in the Middle East region exceeded all sales targets. Sales of Merbatty's top of the range boats generated €25 million in August 2007. The total planned sales revenue for the whole of 2007 for the Middle East region was forecast to be €50 million.

At the end of August 2007, Merbatty had 13 signed contracts for large boats which were due to be built at the new facility in Surania, which was originally scheduled to open in September 2007. The latest forecast is that there will be further orders for 17 large boats in the Middle East region up to the end of 2007. Therefore there could be a forecast total of 30 large boats for the Middle East region that need to be built somewhere, as the Suranian facility has not opened on time. Tobias Houllier has stated that once construction on a boat has started in a boat building facility, it is not feasible to move the partially completed boat to another facility.

The boat building facilities in Europe and USA have the capacity to build all 30 large boats. However, if the location of the building of these boats were to be moved to Europe and the USA boat building facilities, neither of these boat building facilities would have any further spare space to commence any additional large boats until all 30 of these large boats are completed, which would be around the middle of 2008.

Therefore, there would not be any spare capacity to build the 10 large boats required for Merbatty's boat chartering proposal (detailed above).

If the location of the boat building for the orders from the Middle East were to be moved to Europe and the USA, this would necessitate additional costs. These additional costs include payments to compensate customers who would need to inspect their new boats at a different location and also to pay sub-contractors additional fees to relocate their employees to a different boat building facility. The additional direct cost of moving the building of these 30 boats to either of Merbatty's other two boat building facilities is forecast to be €4 million in total.

Alternatively, Merbatty could advise its Middle East customers of the five-month delay in commencement of construction of these boats. If the building of these 30 boats were to remain in Surania and the commencement of their construction is delayed for five months to the end of January 2008, the forecast effect on the company's operating profit for 2007 would be a reduction of €9 million, as the operating profits on these boats would be recognised in the 2008 accounting year. Additionally, Merbatty would be liable to pay an estimated €2 million as penalties for late delivery if all 13 boats currently contracted for, were to be delivered five months late.

Stock market analysts have advised Andreas Acosta that it is important that Merbatty achieves its planned profit target for 2007, as well as the target of 300 boats commenced in 2007.

It has come to the attention of Andreas Acosta that two new boat contracts for customers based in the Middle East have been given an immediate start date at Merbatty's boat building facility in Europe. Building of these two boats has commenced despite prior orders for other boats that should have commenced before these Middle East orders. On investigation, Andreas Acosta has established that the customers have made unofficial payments to several of Merbatty's employees and the sales agents involved, in order to speed up the delivery dates. Andreas Acosta has reported this to Alberto Blanc, who stated that payments are often made by established Merbatty customers in order to secure an earlier completion date.

Proposal to increase sales in Australia

Jesper Blanc, Merbatty's Marketing Director, has spent the last four months in Australia, reviewing the market position and meeting with boat builders and agents. He met with a very positive response to the possibility of Merbatty opening a sales office and renting space in a marina for the display of Merbatty boats in a key coastal city in Australia. This would enable Merbatty to service an ever growing market for luxury boats in this part of the world and its own sales office would replace Merbatty's current sales agent.

Jesper Blanc has proposed to the Merbatty Board that the full range of 15 Merbatty boat models should be on display within the sales marina. These boats could be sold if a customer wanted to buy a boat for immediate delivery. Usually, Merbatty only has 2 or 3 of its boats on display at any location, or at any of the international boat exhibitions. It had never before had such a large display of its range.

The total cost of the proposal is €31 million in 2008 and €10 million in 2009, including new boat models introduced. Jesper Blanc is confident that over the next few years this would increase boat sales in Australia from the 35 boats sold in 2006 to over 150 boats per year by 2011. The current agreed five-year plan only includes sales of 70 boats (generating sales revenue of €60 million) in 2011. The proposal also includes a marketing campaign, spread over two years.

If Merbatty were to be able to increase sales to 150 boats by 2011 by setting up its own sales office and undertaking the proposed marketing campaign, Andreas Acosta has calculated that this could generate a post-tax NPV of €30 million over four years. For this proposal to generate a break-even NPV, Merbatty would need to sell an average of at least 70 boats every year for four years.

Navigation control panels

One of Merbatty's major bought-in components for each boat is the navigation control panel. This is a highly sophisticated computerised system which guides a boat automatically and is linked to satellite navigation systems. At the end of July 2007, the manufacturer of this system, Marinatron, advised all of its customers, including Merbatty, that one particular model of its navigation control panels, supplied in the four-month period between March and June 2007 had a possible technical fault. As a precaution this panel was recalled by Marinatron.

During the period March to June 2007, Merbatty had installed this potentially faulty control panel into 100 boats. Marinatron supplied Merbatty with 100 replacement control panels (free of charge) in August 2007. Of the 100 boats fitted with this faulty component, 80 boats have been completed and delivered to customers. The other 20 boats, which are still under construction, have had the possibly faulty control panel removed and have been refitted with Marinatron's replacement control panel. Alain Mina, Merbatty's Technical Director - Systems and IT, is reluctant to send engineers to refit this control panel on boats already delivered to customers as he considers the risk of a fault to be negligible. He also does not want to inconvenience customers with the refit. Alain Mina does not consider that this operational problem should be referred to the Board.

Marinatron has asked Merbatty to return all of the faulty control panels to it for testing. Alain Mina's assistant, Joe Pickard, is very concerned that Merbatty has not yet changed these control panels. Joe Pickard has informed Tobias Houllier about his concerns.

Appointment of a consultant

At the Merbatty Board meeting held at the end of August 2007 it was agreed that a consultant would be appointed to advise the Board on the issues facing Merbatty.

chapter

14

MERBATTY: SEPTEMBER 2007 SAMPLE SOLUTION

Contents

1 Introduction

What follows is a possible answer for the Merbatty September 2007 exam. It is more complete (though still not perfect by any means!) than some of the other answers in this text book and gives a better idea of the potential scope of a solution rather that what could realistically be completed in the time available.

Given that, it is still just one possible solution and, as always, alternative interpretations may be valid.

2 Sample script

REPORT

To: The Board of Directors, Merbatty

From: A Consultant

Date: November 2007

Merbatty: Main issues facing the company and potential strategies for the future

CONTENTS

Appendices

1 Introduction

The luxury powered boat industry is currently experiencing high growth, due mainly to a strong global economy.

Merbatty had a strong financial performance in 2006, seeing revenue grow by 12.8% to €502 million, operating profit by 16.9% to €76 million and the operating profit margin improve from 14.6% to 15.1% (refer Appendix B).

The key challenge now facing Merbatty is how to achieve its ambitious five-year plan in the light of quality and production capacity problems.

2 Terms of reference

The purpose of this report is to provide the board of Directors of Merbatty with a clear picture of the company's position as at 4th September 2007, in particular to identify and prioritise the main issues facing Merbatty, respond to the issues, assess the opportunities currently available, and make appropriate recommendations.

This report has been prepared by A. Consultant, and relies upon information and explanations provided by the board to date.

3 Prioritisation of Main Issues facing Merbatty

The following issues have been prioritised from the SWOT analysis in Appendix A:

3.1 Quality problems at Merbatty's US facility

Coating technology used in the US facility has resulted in hull cracks in some boats.

This is the first and foremost priority because of its urgency, the safety implications for customers and the potential long-term strategic damage to Merbatty's reputation if not handled correctly. Management need to decide on how and which boats to repair.

3.2 Delayed opening of facility in Surania

Due to construction delays, the Suranian production capacity will not be available until 2008, instead of having opened in September 2007 as planned.

This is prioritised second on the grounds of urgency, its potential impact on other strategies and the implications for 2007 results. Management need to decide whether to delay or re-site production.

3.3 Proposal to enter the boat chartering market

Bernie Ritzol is keen that Merbatty enter the boat chartering market as soon as possible.

This is the third priority because of the strategic importance of market development in the five-year plan and because of the need for a decision by mid-October. However, there is not the same urgency as with the first two issues. Management must evaluate the proposal and formulate a plan of action.

3.4 Recall of navigation control panels by Marinatron

Marinotron has recalled one of its navigation control panels due to a potential technical fault and has supplied Merbatty with 100 replacement panels. However, Alain Mina is reluctant to refit panels as he considers the risk to be negligible.

This is prioritised fourth due to the potential safety issues for customers and the damage to Merbatty's reputation if an accident occurs that could have been avoided. Management need to develop an action plan to address the issue.

3.5 Shortages of skilled staff

Merbatty has a shortage of skilled production workers, a critical success factor for the firm.

This is the fifth priority because of its long-term strategic importance to Merbatty. High growth can only be maintained by having the resources to support it. Management need to review and develop an HR plan to close the resources gap.

3.6 Other issues

There are a number of other issues which have not been prioritised as they are not considered to merit the strategic importance of the above priorities within the scope of this report. These are as follows:

- The proposal to expand sales in Australia. While this proposal looks attractive, there is no need for immediate action and it can be explored further once more pressing issues have been addressed.

- The level of stock discrepancies is not material. However, ethical issues arising from these are discussed in section 9 below.

4 Quality problems in the US facility

4.1 The extent of the problem

Out of thirty-two boats constructed using new hull coating technology, cracks have been found in ten. It is not yet known whether cracks can be repaired or if boats should be rebuilt. The cost of rebuilding the ten boats is estimated to be €11 million.

Porter's generic strategies model is useful to identify the source of Merbatty's competitive advantage. Merbatty's competitive advantage of differentiation is based on a mixture of value drivers including world class suppliers, use of advanced production technology, skilled staff and reputation (Appendix E). The problems with the coating technology could thus seriously undermine Merbatty's competitive strategy, especially if an incident occurs affecting customer safety.

4.2 Possible courses of action

There are two key decisions that must be made in the short term:

(a) whether to repair or rebuild boats

(b) whether to address only boats with identified cracking or all boats where the technology has been used.

If feasible, then repairing cracks will be cheaper than rebuilding. However there is a risk that customers will view this as substandard and will expect a rebuild. There is also the risk that repairs will fail again in the future.

Similarly, only addressing boats with identified cracking is cheaper, but this must be weighed against the risk to Merbatty's reputation if other boats develop cracks in the future. Customers will be particularly aggrieved if they subsequently discover that Merbatty was aware of the potential problem and chose not to act.

For both decisions, saving costs in the short term could damage Merbatty's reputation in the longer term.

Merbatty must also decide whether to switch production back to older technologies or continue to roll out the new technology in Europe and Surania. The key issue here is to determine the cause of the failure – was it due to inadequate use of the technology, for example due to poor training, or is there a problem with the technology itself?

Failure to invest in new technologies could result in Merbatty falling behind competitors. The Ferretti Group, for example, typically spends around 8% of revenue on upgrading facilities and technology.

5 Delayed opening of the facility in Surania

5.1 The extent of the problem

Merbatty is experiencing high growth in demand in the Middle East, resulting in orders for an estimated 30 large boats that should be started by the end of 2007. In anticipation of this, the new Suranian facility was due to be operational by September 2007.

Problems with air-conditioning units and safety certificates have resulted in a revised forecast of January 2008, so the 30 boats concerned cannot be started in Surania as planned.

5.2 Possible courses of action

The key issue is whether to reschedule production of the boats to Europe and the US, or to wait and produce them in Surania with a five-month delay.

The main advantages of scheduling production to Europe and the US are as follows:

- Customers get their boats five months sooner, increasing customer satisfaction and goodwill. This is vital given the high growth plans for the Middle East.
- Operating profit estimated at €9 million would accrue to 2007 rather than 2008. This would allow Merbatty to achieve the 2007operating profit target in the five-year plan (appendix D).
- Furthermore, this plan would allow Merbatty to achieve its stated target of starting 300 boats in 2007, thus meeting Stock Market expectations and protecting the share price.
- As well as advancing profit, cash flows will be received five months sooner. This will improve working capital and, with a cost of capital of 14%, gives a benefit of €0.5 million (appendix D)
- Ongoing 2008 sales in the Middle East will be able to be built in Surania without "knock-on" delays.

The main advantages of building boats in Surania are as follows:

- Delaying construction would result in only €2 million additional costs rather than €4 million if made outside Surania, saving €2 million. Viewed in isolation it is thus cheaper to defer production. The Board of Merbatty thus needs to address the balance between meeting short-term stock exchange expectations and the interests of all shareholders in the longer term.
- Spare production capacity would exist in Europe and the US, facilitating the production of vessels for entering the charter market.

6 Proposal to enter the boat chartering market

6.1 Introduction

It has been proposed that Merbatty should build an extra ten large boats for the purpose of chartering them, a market development strategy according to Ansoff's product/market mix classification.

This strategy can be assessed using the "suitability, feasibility, acceptability" framework of Johnson, Scholes and Whittington.

6.2 Suitability

Market analysts have indicated that the chartering market is highly competitive, so the move may be a high risk one for Merbatty. However, the worldwide growth in the wealth and number of "high net wealth individuals" (HNWIs) would suggest that the chartering market should be high growth.

The chartering business would fit well into Merbatty's existing portfolio of boat building. For example, some customers who charter boats may then go on to purchase one, boosting boat sales.

6.3 Feasibility

Depending on how problems are resolved regarding cracked hulls in the USA and delays in the Surania facility, Merbatty may not have the capacity to make the ten additional boats required until 2008, delaying entry until summer 2009.

Staffing yachts may be problematic due to a current world shortage in experienced crews.

Chartering will require different expertise and core competences than boat building. It is unlikely that Merbatty currently has these skills, so they will have to be acquired through recruitment and training. On the other hand, Merbatty's brand name should transfer effectively to the chartering business.

As an alternative strategy, Merbatty could investigate acquiring a charter firm with the required expertise. For example, in May 2007 Trinity Yachts acquired IYC to diversify into yacht chartering and other areas.

6.4 Acceptability

Cash flow estimates give a positive net present value of €27.6 million, indicating that the proposal should increase shareholder wealth by this amount. Furthermore, sensitivity analysis indicates that the proposal is low risk as the proposed boat utilization of 40% could halve to 20% before a loss was made. (Refer to appendix C.)

JKL (the largest shareholder) will expect Merbatty to start boat chartering as this strategy was stated in the listing prospectus that was the basis for JKL's investment in Merbatty.

7 Recall of navigation control panels

7.1 The extent of the problem

Marinatron considers the potential problem with navigation panels serious enough to warrant supplying Merbatty with 100 replacement panels. To date panels have only been changed in 20 boats currently under construction. Alain Mina is unwilling to inconvenience customers for what he perceives to be a negligible risk in the 80 completed boats.

This difference of opinion is indicative of a deeper problem of a lack of partnership and collaboration between Merbatty and key suppliers. Such relationships are central to Merbatty's long-term innovation and competitive advantage.

7.2 Possible courses of action

Whether to replace panels on the 80 boats already built

As with the discussion of dealing with cracks in section 4.2 above, there is a trade-off between short-term cost and potential damage to long-term reputation and customer safety.

The cheaper option will be to ignore the boats already built. However, if a customer's navigation system is faulty, then they may get lost or stranded at sea and need rescuing. Such an incident would generate considerable bad publicity for Merbatty, especially if Marinatron disclose that they had supplied Merabatty with replacement panels.

Replacing all panels could be publicised as evidence of Merbatty's commitment to customer safety and quality and result in a higher profile for the company.

If panels are not replaced, then Merbatty will be unable to supply the old panels to Marinatron for testing, thus damaging Merbatty's relationship with its supplier.

Test the outstanding 80 boats

Merbatty could discuss the issue with Marinatron to see if it is possible for Merbatty and Marinatron engineers to work together and test the panels in situ without having to remove them. This would increase collaboration and would enable customer safety to be checked without the inconvenience of a recall.

Develop stronger relationships with key suppliers

Unlike car producers, boat manufacturers have been slow to take advantage of the gains that closer collaboration with suppliers can bring in areas such as innovation, design, scheduling and ordering. These could result in higher quality for Merbatty, shorter lead times and lower working capital investment, thus improving cash flow.

8 Staff shortages

8.1 The extent of the problem

Despite actively recruiting, Merbatty needs a further 100 skilled workers over the next two years to meet production plans. If the problem with coating technology results in a shift back to more labour-intensive methods, then this figure could be even higher.

Experienced staff are a key value driver supporting Merbatty's competitive strategy (appendix E), so it is vital that shortages are addressed. Also new strategies such as expansion into boat chartering and growth in Australia require extra staff resources to facilitate them.

A key factor here is the high turnover of both skilled staff and new apprentices. In 2006 staff turnover was 20%.The main reasons given are job security and a lack of formal support for studies

8.2 Possible courses of action

Do nothing

Alberto Blanc has always believed in on-the-job training and historically this approach has served the company well. However, high growth in the luxury boat market has resulted in fierce competition for skilled staff, so Merbatty needs to be more responsive to staff needs.

Increased emphasis on training

Production workers want to study and obtain qualifications as well as gain experience. Merbatty would have to increase its training budget from €1 million to €5 million each year simply to match major competitors' spending.

Extra investment in training will not only help retain staff, but will also increase quality, reduce mistakes and could prevent major problems such as with the hull coating technology discussed in section 4 above.

Improvements to pay and conditions

There is no evidence that pay is a problem, but a benchmarking exercise would be useful to confirm whether this is the case.

Reduce Merbatty's dependency on skilled staff

Despite the recent problems with cracked hulls, Merbatty could investigate the use of robotics to reduce the demand for labour.

Similarly, less critical aspects of the production process could be outsourced, provided quality standards can be guaranteed.

9 Ethical issues

The key ethical issues facing Merbatty are as follows.

9.1 Stock discrepancy

Given a stock discrepancy of €200,000, it may be that around 700 tools are unaccounted for, indicating a widespread culture of employees stealing or borrowing tools on a regular basis. Especially being a listed company, Merbatty should adopt corporate governance recommendations relating to the implementation of control systems to prevent, rather than simply detect, such problems.

However, the recent sacking of one long-term employee for taking tools home would probably constitute unfair dismissal as there appears to have been no formal clarification of company policy and no official warning given to the person concerned. It is vital that staff rights are not compromised in a knee-jerk reaction to the problem.

9.2 Dealing with quality problems

In respect of the issue with navigation panels addressed in section 7 above, it appears that Alain Mina was reluctant to inform the board of the problem. This is a concern on two counts:

- It appears that operational convenience is being prioritised before customer safety. This is clearly unethical and Merbatty needs to ensure that all staff are trained in the importance of customer safety.
- This may be indicative of an underlying culture of secrecy that could prevent Merbatty identifying and acting on potential problems soon enough.

9.3 Allegations of bribery and "queue jumping"

Some customers have made additional payments to agents and employees to jump the queue at the expense of longer delays for other customers. It is unethical for employees to benefit in this way at the expense of some customers.

Merbatty should eliminate this practice as soon as possible.

10 Recommendations

Quality issues at the US Facility

I recommend that cracked boats should be rebuilt, rather than simply repaired. This is necessary to both protect and enhance Merbatty's reputation for high quality and customer care.

As soon as possible an investigation should be carried out to determine the cause of the problems. If it is due to a lack of training resulting in incorrect use of the technology, then the solution is to implement better staff training and supervision (see below). This would also allow the continuing roll out of the technology to the European facility. If, however, the technology is flawed, then Merbatty should enter into discussions with the vendor to see if problems can be rectified.

In the longer term, I recommend that Merbatty look to increase the role of new production technologies to reduce production times and improve quality.

Delayed operations in Surania

I recommend that the thirty Middle East boats that should have been started in Surania be rescheduled for production in Europe and the USA. This will ensure that customer satisfaction is given a priority in this highly important growth market and that investor expectations for 2007 are met. To facilitate this, Tobias Houliier should contact the production facility managers concerned to discuss how production plans can be altered.

Once this has been scheduled, a working team should be set up to investigate why delays occurred in Surania. This is to reduce the chance of similar delays if a further facility is planned for 2011.

Expansion into boat chartering

I recommend that the proposal to diversify into boat chartering be accepted as a plan for expansion, as it should increase shareholder value without excessive risk.

However, as mentioned above, I recommend that boat orders for the Middle East market be prioritised, thus displacing capacity for the charter market. I thus recommend that the charter proposal be deferred to make boats for the summer 2009 season instead of 2008.

In the longer term I recommend that the plan be expanded to offering previous boat customers chartering services for their Merbatty boats when they will not be using them, thus offering customers a more comprehensive service.

Recall of navigation panels by Marinatron

I recommend that Marinatron be approached immediately to see if it is possible for Merbatty and Marinatron engineers to collaborate and investigate boats together.

Should this not be feasible, then I recommend that all boats concerned be recalled for the panels to be replaced. This is to ensure customer safety and to avoid the risk of bad publicity.

In the longer term a team should be set up to investigate forging stronger collaboration with suppliers in key areas such as logistics, innovation and quality assurance.

Staff shortages

In the short term management need to arrange meetings with production staff to communicate their commitment to them, especially given recent trouble over tool theft. As part of this, I recommend that Merbatty increase its training budget and initiate a structured training programme. These new plans should also be communicated to staff.

In the longer term Merbatty should investigate the use of robotics to reduce their dependency on skilled staff. For example, the Azimut-Benetti Group uses robots to spray gel over hull moulds.

11 Conclusion

Merbatty is facing many significant issues both internally and within the industry. Decisive action must be taken to ensure that ambitious plans are achieved.

In particular, the basis of Merbatty's competitive advantage must be consolidated through motivated employees, use of technology and improved relationships with suppliers.

APPENDIX A: SWOT analysis

Strengths

- Strong financial performance – growth in revenue, profit and margins
- Successfully floated, making equity finance easier to raise in the future if needed
- Good reputation in the industry, reinforced by Alberto Blanc's reputation

Weaknesses

- Quality problems - cracks have appeared in some US boats and some navigation panels have been recalled by the supplier
- Delays opening the Suranian facility
- Problems attracting / retaining skilled employees

Opportunities

- Boat chartering
- Increasing sales in Australia
- Refocus portfolio towards longer boats

Threats

- Economic downturn
- Quality problems could seriously damage Merbatty's reputation

APPENDIX B: Key financials / ratios for Merbatty

	2006	2005
Growth in revenue	12.8%	-
Growth in operating profit	16.9%	-
Growth in net profit	29.0%	-
ROCE	9.2%	21.1%
Operating profit margin	15.1%	14.6%
New profit margin	8.0%	7.0%
Inventory holding days	141	121

APPENDIX C: NPV calculation for chartering proposal

NPV

€ millions	2007 t = 0	2008 t = 1	2009 t = 2	2010 t = 3	2011 t = 4	2012 t = 5
Capital cost	(32.0)					
Net inflows		10.5	13.9	16.9	17.9	26.6
Residual value						7.5
Net cash flow	(32.0)	10.5	13.9	16.9	17.9	34.1
DF@14%	1	0.877	0.769	0.675	0.592	0.519
PV	(32.0)	9.2	10.7	11.4	10.6	17.7
NPV	+27.6					

Sensitivity analysis

(**Tutorial note:** with a paper-based exam the sensitivity analysis may be considered excessive. However, as part of the computer-based pilot the additional calculations would have taken very little extra time to do and so are included here).

PV of inflows:

€ millions	2007 t = 0	2008 t = 1	2009 t = 2	2010 t = 3	2011 t = 4	2012 t = 5
Net inflows		10.5	13.9	16.9	17.9	26.6
DF@14%	1	0.877	0.769	0.675	0.592	0.519
PV		9.2	10.7	11.4	10.6	13.8
NPV	+55.7					

Sensitivity to volume of business = NPV/PV of flows affected = 27.6/55.7 = 49.6%

Forecast utilisation could thus drop from 40% to 20% before the project becomes unacceptable.

APPENDIX D: Implications of Suranian decisions

(**Tutorial note:** there is a strong hint in the unseen that you should consider the overall impact on 2007 operating profit to address Stock Exchange concerns. However, due to the complexity of such a calculation, it is debatable whether it would have been a good use of time in the exam. It is included here for completeness).

(A) 2007 Operating Profit

	2007
	€m
Budget operating profit per 5-year plan	84
• Adjustment for stock discrepency	(0.2)
• Estimated cost of rebuilding cracked boats in US	(11.0)
• Impact of additional sales in Middle East (W1)	17.5
• Cost overruns in Surania of €20m will probably be capitalised	-
	90.3

Scenario A: additional Middle East orders built in US and Europe

	2007
	€m
Revised post-tax profit from above	90.3
• Additional costs	(4.0)
Revised profit forecast	86.3

Scenario B: additional Middle East orders delayed and built in Surania

	2007
	€m
Revised post-tax profit from above	90.3
• Additional costs	(2.0)
• Deferred profit	(9.0)
Revised profit forecast	79.3

W1:

- Budget 2007 sales for Middle East was €50m pa = €4.2m pcm, so sales in August of €25m were €20.8m higher than expected.
- Typical operating margin on large boats is 16.8%, so this would give extra operating profits of €20.8 x 16.8% = €3.5m
- Assuming sales are similarly higher for September to December 2007, the overall impact = 5 x 3.5 = €17.5m
- Note: issues of revenue recognition have been ignored here!

(B) Cost of delaying €9 million (net) receipts by 5 months

- Cost = 9 million x 14% x 5/12 = €525,000

APPENDIX E: Extracts from Porter's generic strategies analysis

Merbatty follows a competitive strategy of differentiation. Key value drivers include the following:

Inbound Logistics

- Use of world class suppliers of key inputs

Operations

- Skilled staff
- Production software system to increase productivity
- Use of technology (e.g. performance gel coating)

chapter

15

KADGEE: PRE-SEEN MATERIAL

Scenario – Pre-seen material

This case study was the TOPCIMA case for the September 2006 examination paper. When analysing this material and answering the examination question, you should assume that 'now' is early 2006.

1 Case and commentary – Kadgee

1.1 Clothing manufacturing in Europe

Since the 1960's there has been a decline in the number of UK and European clothing manufacturers due to competition from cheaper, and sometimes higher quality, imported clothes. The clothing industry generally has become much more fashion conscious and price sensitive. This has led to a reduced number of companies that are still in business in Europe. Some companies have moved all or part of their manufacturing processes to other countries to achieve a cheaper operating base, and up until recently this has allowed them to continue to compete on price.

Many companies have had contracts to supply High Street retailers for over four decades and are highly dependant on retaining these key customers who wield immense buying power over the small manufacturers. A number of family owned manufacturing companies, that had been highly profitable once, have ceased trading, or are operating at very low margins, as a direct result of the High Street retailers being able to dictate terms of business and prices.

An additional factor that has put the main High Street retailers under more price pressure has been the appearance and market growth of new High Street retailers and their new brands, who have procured their goods mainly from overseas sources.

The result is that the few companies that are based in the UK and Europe which are left in the business of clothing manufacturing are having to look very hard at their strategic plans in order for them to manage to maintain their business over the next few years.

1.2 Kadgee's personnel

The career histories of Kadgee's Directors and key employees are shown in Appendix 1.

1.3 History of Kadgee Fashions (Kadgee)

Kadgee was formed in post World War Two in a European country, and has remained as an unlisted company, although its shares are now held by others outside of the founding family. Kadgee quickly established itself as a high quality manufacturer of both mens and ladies clothes. It had no difficulty selling its products to retailers, as the demand for ready-to-wear clothing was very high during the 1950's and

1960's. Kadgee recruited several designers who based their designs on famous designer labels, but without causing any copyright breaches.

By the 1960's Kadgee had a turnover equivalent to €25 million, and had nine factories operating in two European countries. The founder of Kadgee, Bruno Burnak, wanted to expand the manufacturing base and introduce new machinery, but the then Sales Director had considered that the company should continue to establish a stronger customer base before Kadgee expanded and invested further. Each of Kadgee's factories then employed between 70 and 100 employees, who were mainly female employees, with many working part-time. Some of the employees had a range of specialised skills and were considered to be very experienced. Kadgee's Head Office was run by the then Managing Director, Anton Kramer.

During the late 1960's Kadgee suffered its first major fall in sales, and found that it had large stocks of men's clothes that had been manufactured without specific sales contracts. Kadgee managed to sell off some of the stocks, albeit at below cost price. However, the management decided that it should not manufacture clothes without a firm contract from a retailer in future. The company had been caught unaware and had believed that the previous high demand for its products would continue.

In the early 1970's the range and design of its men's clothing was changed several times, but it continued to make little profit. In 1973, Kadgee sold its men's clothing range and designs and some of its manufacturing equipment to a large listed company. Kadgee decided to concentrate on expanding its ranges of ladies clothing to meet the growing demands of its main customers (see below). The reduced range of clothing, following the termination of all manufacturing of men's clothing, necessitated closing three of its factories. This left Kadgee with six factories operational in 1973.

During the next few years, Kadgee consolidated its position and its profitability increased again. In the early 1980's its then Chief Designer persuaded the Managing Director to expand its clothing range to include a range of girls' clothes. This new limited range was launched in 1982 and was immediately sold out, as many of Kadgee's customers realised that there was a demand for well designed and well finished children's clothing. Kadgee has positioned itself at the upper price range of clothing, and has never tried to mass produce low cost clothing.

During the 1980's Kadgee continued to expand its ranges of ladies' and girls' clothes, but retained the same manufacturing base of six factories. New equipment had been installed and the overall manufacturing capacity at the six factories had been increased by over 20% due to new sewing and packaging machinery. A further change that occurred was that many of Kadgee's customers were starting to dictate the styles and types of clothing required and Kadgee's designers had to manufacture to customers' specifications.

However, during the 1990's Kadgee suffered a number of setbacks. It also saw many of its competitors suffer losses and some to cease trading. Kadgee had been able to stay profitable only because of its particular customer base and because it sold high quality clothes that commanded a premium price. However, Kadgee saw its margins on many product lines reduced greatly and also it started to lose many of its smaller customers, who choose to import, at much lower prices, clothing produced in Asia.

Bruno Burnak, the founder and then Chairmen of Kadgee retired in 1997 and his son Andrin Burnak took over as Chairman. Furthermore, the Managing Director, Anton Kramer left in 1998, and Andrin Burnak undertook this role in addition.

1.4 Kadgee Shareholders

Kadgee has remained an unlisted company and at the end of 2005 its shares were held as follows:

	Shareholding
Bruno Burnak	29%
Andrin Burnak	29%
Anton Kramer	10%
Dieter Stutt	8%
Frankie Bayane	2%
Andre Schnaffer	10%
Employee-held shares	12%
	100%

The company has 200,000 shares of €0.10 each in issue and has a total of 400,000 authorised shares.

The shares are not traded but the last time the shares were exchanged was in 1998, when Frankie Bayane purchased shares at €8.00 each.

1.5 Kadgee's customer base

Kadgee manufactures clothing for a number of European and international clothing retailers, including many well known High Street retailers. It manufactures clothing in the medium to higher price ranges and its customers require top quality designs and finishing to maintain their brand reputation. Kadgee has several contracts that were established over 40 years ago, although it has two contracts that have been secured within the last 10 years. Kadgee still manufactures ladies' and children's clothing for two retailers who had selected Kadgee in the 1980's, when the children's range had first been launched.

The majority of Kadgee's clothing is manufactured for its customers under the customers' own label, for example, clothing manufactured for one of its customers called Portrait is labelled as 'Portrait'.

In 2005, Kadgee's customer base, analysed by sales value, was as follows:

Customer	*2005 revenue € million*	*% of Kadgee's total sales*
Portrait	24.0	32.3%
Forum	16.8	22.6%
Diamond	13.5	18.1%
Zeeb	5.1	6.9%
Jay Jay	4.5	6.0%
Other retailers of ladies' clothes	7.3	9.8%
Haus (Children's clothes only)	3.2	4.3%
Total	74.4	100%

Most of Kadgee's contracts are renewed at the start of each fashion season. Kadgee is currently negotiating for clothing sales for the summer season of 2007.

1.6 Human Resources

In the clothing manufacturing business one of the most crucial aspects to achieve customer satisfaction is quality. Kadgee has been very fortunate in having a skilled, very dedicated workforce who have always adapted to new machinery and procedures and have been instrumental in suggesting ways in which quality could be improved. This has sometimes involved a very minor change in the design of a garment and the designers now work much more closely with the operational staff to ensure that the garments can be assembled as quickly and efficiently as possible.

The employees include a number of very talented people, whose skills are highly valued by the management team at Kadgee. There are five very highly skilled sewing machine operatives whose parents previously worked for Kadgee and they have passed their skills on. The machinery that is used to sew garments is very sophisticated but it is always the skills of the machine operatives which can make the difference to a finished garment. Additionally, Kadgee has always completed certain finishing touches by hand and this quality is appreciated by its customers. Kadgee is dependent on the skills of its employees to continue to deliver the same high quality on which it has established its reputation.

1.7 Losses made by Kadgee

Kadgee has suffered from falling operating profit margins due to the pressure exerted by its customers over the last ten years. For the first time in Kadgee's history, it experienced losses for five years starting in 1998 through to, and including, 2002. During this time Kadgee increased its loans and its overdraft to finance operations.

In 2000, Kadgee refinanced with a ten year loan, which was used to repay existing debt, and also to invest in the IT solutions discussed below, as well as to purchase some new machinery. Kadgee also invested in its design centre (see below), which was completed in 2001.

During 2001, the company invested in new IT solutions enabling its customers to be able to track all orders from the garment cutting process right through to completion of garments and through to the delivery to customers' premises.

The IT solutions also enabled Kadgee to monitor its production processes including machine usage, wastage at various stages of production and speed of production through the various stages. This has enabled Kadgee's management to reduce areas that did not add value to the finished garment. The use of TQM throughout the business has also increased Kadgee's efficiency and enabled it to eliminate some other areas which did not add value to the finished garments.

While margins are still low, Kadgee has been operating profitably again since 2003, albeit at lower margins to those achieved in the past.

Kadgee's employees have also taken an active role in increasing the throughput of garments and speeding up the manufacturing process. In fact, many of the changes made were at the instigation of key employees, who understood the actual processes and were able to identify where there were bottlenecks which caused delays. The reasons for the delays were reduced, leading to a faster manufacturing process. This enabled Kadgee to increase its annual number of garments manufactured from 8.25 million in 1998 to 10.9 million in 2005.

The consequences of some of the changes meant that some employees were made redundant at Kadgee's factories, and these were often part time workers, who worked fewer than 16 hours per week. The Kadgee management team fully understood that many of its skilled employees are female and that they do not wish to work full-time. However, Kadgee now do not employ anyone for fewer than 24 hours per week, and over half of the employees in the factories now work full-time. Many of these employees chose to work full-time rather than face redundancy. When employees are made redundant, Kadgee is legally bound to pay redundancy payments, which are payments made to employees as compensation for future salary payments, which are paid at the point when the employee's contract of employment ceases.

Many other European clothing manufacturers have ceased trading and Kadgee's employees have concerns that they would not find any other employment within their specialised field in the local area. Therefore, they chose to stay with Kadgee, but are working longer hours than perhaps they wish to.

1.8 Loss of sales contract with Forum

Forum is one of Kadgee's key customers and in 2005 generated revenues of €16.8 million, which is almost 23% of Kadgee's total revenue. The operating profit achieved on sales to Forum, in 2005, was €0.3 million. The operating profit on sales to Forum has been severely eroded over the last few years, with some product lines barely generating a positive margin at all.

Forum has over 50 retail stores throughout Europe and Kadgee has manufactured clothes for Forum since the early 1950's. The latest contract negotiations looked promising despite an expected price cut. Dieter Stutt, the Sales Director, felt that a price cut of 4% could be agreed. He had forecast that some of this lost operating profit could be recouped with cost savings that could be made in packaging and reduced material costs.

However, in the middle of April 2006, Forum's Managing Director contacted Andrin Burnak directly to state that Forum would no longer be purchasing clothes from Kadgee from the end of May 2006. Andrin Burnak was astounded that one of

Kadgee's oldest customers was giving a mere six weeks notice of the termination of the supply contract. Following various high level negotiations, Forum has since agreed to extend the current sales contract though to the end of August 2006. After this date Forum will no longer purchase any clothing from Kadgee.

The loss of the Forum contract was announced to Kadgee employees during May 2006, before it was announced in the national press. Employees were naturally concerned about their jobs. Staff morale is low and the quality of the clothing currently being produced is lower than normal. It is expected that initially there will be 34 redundancies in September 2006, affecting three of Kadgee's factories as a result of the loss of this major customer. Further job cuts are likely later in 2006 at the three factories which have manufactured the range of clothing for Forum.

Andrin Burnak has requested Peter Coletta, the Factory Operations Director, to take action to ensure that Kadgee's quality does not fall. Dieter Stutt is very concerned that two other major customers of Kadgee may try to use the excuse of falling quality to reduce their purchase price for further clothing contracts, following the discovery of a number of faults from recent production.

1.9 Changes in the supply chain

Many of Kadgee's customers have needed to speed up the process of supplying clothing to their shops, so as to meet the demands of the market and to remain competitive. Kadgee has worked closely with its customers in order to achieve shorter lead times from design to delivery of finished products.

In 2001, Kadgee introduced a new design centre, centralised at its Head Office. The design centre uses computer aided design techniques, which has helped Kadgee's customers to appreciate the finished appearance of new designs. Andrin Burnak is confident that this has helped Kadgee to win new business and to retain its current customers.

It has also contributed to Kadgee's ability to speed up the process from design board to finished article. Kadgee has also benefited from working closer with its customers and this has resulted in additional orders, which Kadgee's customers' would otherwise have procured from overseas sources.

1.10 Growing competition from China

During the 1990's and into the 21st century China has had a massive impact on the textile industry. China's manufacturing base is forecast to grow further and this will have a negative impact on many companies operating at a higher cost base elsewhere.

Many European companies have spent millions of Euros establishing manufacturing bases outside their home countries in the last 15 years. Many have opened factories in countries which have much lower operating costs. These include countries such as Turkey, Sri Lanka and Pakistan, as well as Eastern European countries.

The companies which have set up operations in these low cost countries did so in an effort to cut costs by taking advantage of low overheads and lower labour rates, but still managed to maintain quality. However, even the companies that have moved some, or all, of their manufacturing bases and have taken steps to reduce their costs, now have to reconsider their cost base again. This is because of the very low cost of Chinese imports, which they are having difficulty competing against.

Following the relaxation of trade barriers, there has recently been a deluge of Chinese clothing imports into Europe, the UK and the USA.

The quality of Chinese manufactured clothing is improving rapidly and it is now globally recognised that the 'Made in China' label represents clothing of a higher quality than many European manufactured garments. Furthermore, the Chinese manufactured garments are being produced at a substantially lower manufacturing cost.

Kadgee has so far been operating in a market that has not been significantly affected by imported goods, as it produces medium to higher priced clothing, rather than cheaper ranges of clothes. However, many of Kadgee's customers are now looking to reduce their costs by either buying more imported clothes or by negotiating substantial price cuts from their existing suppliers. The purchasing power of European retailers being exerted on its suppliers is immense and Kadgee is under much pressure to deliver high quality goods at reduced operating profit margins from all of its customers.

Appendix 1 - Kadgee personnel

Bruno Burnak – Founder and first Chairman

Bruno Burnak retired from Kadgee in 1997, aged 75, but has kept a close personal interest in the company that he founded in 1947 using family finances. His son Andrin Burnak is the current Chairman and Managing Director. The Burnak family is very entrepreneurial and Bruno Burnak's brother founded another company after the Second World War, which is also still trading profitably. Bruno Burnak has still retained his 29% shareholding in Kadgee.

Anton Kramer – First Managing Director

Anton Kramer retired from Kadgee in 1998, as he felt that he did not have the necessary skills to direct the company into the 21st century. However, he has retained his 10% shareholding in the company and has confidence that Andrin Burnak will manage to increase Kadgee's profitability to the levels previously attained.

Andrin Burnak – Current Chairman and Managing Director

Andrin Burnak, son of the founder Bruno Burnak had studied textiles and had worked in another European country for over 10 years for a large clothing manufacturer. He returned home in 1993 and joined the family company. He took over as Chairman and Managing Director when his father retired in 1997. Andrin Burnak was concerned that the clothing manufacturing industry was undergoing rapid changes, and he was confident that he could introduce the changes that would be required in order for Kadgee to remain successful.

Dieter Stutt – Sales Director

Dieter Stutt, now 39, had worked in sales for a number of clothing manufacturers before Andrin Burnak recruited him in 1999. He has had a challenging time since joining Kadgee, not only trying to secure new sales contracts and negotiate on prices, but has had to fight to retain Kadgee's current customers.

Dieter Stutt has established very good relationships with many of the key personnel in all of Kadgee's customers' companies. He has spent a lot of time personally dealing with several layers of management at all of Kadgee's customers, to ensure that Kadgee can deliver what they want when they require it. His excellent reputation has enabled Kadgee to be one step ahead of many of the customers' requests. In many instances Dieter Stutt would have already established what the customers wants, or fed back to his colleagues some comments on current deliveries. He has often found out about the demand level for a particular product line, or the need for a wider range of colours or perhaps fabric changes, from a manager within a customers' company, before Kadgee even receives the manufacturing order. This has enabled Kadgee to be seen to be meeting many of its customers' requests promptly and efficiently, due to Dieter Stutt's established connections.

Frankie Bayane – Chief Designer

Frankie Bayane, aged 35, joined Kadgee in 1998 from a rival manufacturing company. She has a degree in textiles and design and she first worked for a top couture house in France for three years and gained much experience. When she joined Kadgee, the two areas that she considered would have an impact on sales would be to increase the 'speed to the market' from design board to finished product at the retailer and to use the latest computer design technology to create designs. She considered that Kadgee had been too slow in the past reacting to changes in trends and latest fashions, and that there was a need to have a greater number of designs and smaller production runs, thereby giving customers a wider range of products to order. Frankie Bayane has trained and recruited a small team of designers over the last eight years who have worked closely with Kadgee's customers.

Andre Schnaffer – Finance Director

Andre Schnaffer, aged 48, has held the role of Finance Director for the last four years when the previous Finance Director retired early due to ill health. He has worked for Kadgee for over 18 years and prior to that had worked for several companies in a range of finance roles, all related to the clothing business. He has a good working relationship with Andrin Burnak, who trusts Andre Schnaffer's cautious judgement.

Andre Schnaffer has managed to renegotiate bank loans and has extended credit arrangements with many of Kadgee's material suppliers and this has helped Kadgee to manage its cash flow during several difficult trading periods.

Andre Schnaffer is very concerned over the number of rival manufacturing companies which have ceased trading, and he is very worried about the increasing pressure to reduce margins, which are very low already.

Sam Skala - Marketing Director

Until 2003, all marketing was undertaken by the Sales Director, but Dieter Stutt identified that all of his time was taken up in negotiating and securing sales and the important role of marketing was being neglected. Dieter Stutt pushed hard to get the Marketing Director role established, at a time when Andrin Burnak wanted to reduce management costs.

Sam Skala had established his reputation when he worked for a High Street retailer of ladies' clothing, which had expanded rapidly in the nine years he had held the role of Marketing Manager. Previous to that, he had worked in marketing for an international sportswear company. When he joined Kadgee he had hoped that the high quality of Kadgee's products and its ability to bring the latest products to the market quickly would enable him to establish its brand into many more high street retail chains. To date he has not been very successful in identifying new customers, but he has undertaken extensive, and much needed market research to try to establish gaps in the market for clothing manufacture.

Peter Coletta – Factory Operations Director

Peter Coletta, aged 52, has worked for several clothing manufacturers and joined Kadgee in 2001 when he was made redundant from his last company when it ceased trading following a severe downturn in business. He is very aware of the need to maintain quality and to reduce costs, having worked for his previous employer for over 15 years and seen the company decline due to competitive pressures. He has brought with him a wealth of operational experience and is well respected by all of the factories' employees, as well as by fellow directors. He has been instrumental in introducing improved working conditions and the use of TQM quality circles is as popular now as when it was first introduced in Kadgee by Peter Coletta's predecessor in 1990.The use of TQM has enabled Kadgee to be forever searching for new innovative ways to improve both the speed and quality of its output.

Lars Veel – Human Resource Director

Lars Veel, now 52, joined Kadgee in 1994, but he has not acquired any shares in the company. He has helped Kadgee to achieve increased employee efficiency and has seen the company's manufacturing capacity (in terms of the number of garments manufactured) rise by over 32% in the last seven years, still utilising the same six factories. This increase in Kadgee's manufacturing capacity has been achieved by changed work patterns, reduced wastage, changed factory layouts and much greater motivation by almost all of Kadgee's employees.

Lars Veel is very concerned for the future of Kadgee's employees, and understands the strains that have been put on them by high speed output and the need to maintain Kadgee's excellent quality reputation. He has had two employees, who are hard workers and have been with the company for many years, off work in the past 2 years with stress related illnesses, brought on by the constant pressure that all employees feel that they are under to achieve, or exceed, agreed targets.

Lars Veel introduced an employee share scheme 10 years ago, and many employees have been given free shares. However, none of the shares have been traded or sold yet. He has also encouraged the active involvement of all employees in the use of TQM techniques to reduce internal failures.

Jan Berzin – IT Director

Jan Berzin, now 35, joined Kadgee from the consultancy company that he had worked in for over ten years. Kadgee had appointed this consultancy company for advice on a range of IT solutions in 2000 and Jan Berzin was the consultant in charge of the Kadgee IT project. Jan Berzin quickly identified that there were several areas in which the use of IT could help Kadgee to compete with other manufacturing companies. Before Jan Berzin joined Kadgee, the Finance Director, Andre Schnaffer was responsible for IT. Andre Schnaffer agreed that Kadgee needed to embrace the use of IT in a far more comprehensive way than had been done and invited Jan Berzin to join the company. This additional expertise at Board level has enabled Kadgee to identify in which areas of the business the limited IT development budget could be best spent.

Appendix 2 – Extract from Kadgee's accounts for 2005 – Chairman's statement

The clothing industry in general has seen another difficult year and competition from all areas of the world has increased. However, against that backdrop, we are pleased to state that Kadgee has had another successful year and that we have managed to retain all of our customers and to increase the volume of sales.

Despite a very slow and difficult year's trading, I am pleased to report that Kadgee is still trading profitably, which is a significant achievement following the trading losses made only a few years ago.

I would like to record my thanks to all members of the Kadgee management team and to all of our loyal and hard working employees who have committed themselves to achieving these good results.

Trading in 2006 started well and orders placed for the Autumn season are slightly up on this time last year and I look forward to reporting a further growth in sales next year. We continue to work closely with all of our key customers, all of whom I am pleased to report are still showing their continued commitment to buying Kadgee's high quality ranges of clothes.

Andrin Burnak

Chairman

31 March 2006

Appendix 3 – financial statements

Kadgee's Balance Sheet, Income Statement and Statement of changes in equity

Note: All data in this Appendix is presented in international financial reporting format

Balance Sheet	As at 31 December 2005		As at 31 December 2004	
	€000	€000	€000	€000
Non-current assets (net)		9,830		11,514
Current assets				
Inventory	8,220		6,334	
Trade receivables and rent payments	19,404		18,978	
Cash and short term investments	119		131	
		27,743		25,443
Total assets		37,573		36,957
Equity and liabilities				
Equity				
Paid in share capital	20		20	
Share premium reserve	450		450	
Retained profits	21,787		20,863	
		22,257		21,333
Non-current liabilities				
Loans:				
Bank loan at 8% interest per year (repayable in 2010)		4,500		4,500
Current liabilities				
Trade payables	1,520		940	
Tax	8,900		9,667	
Accruals	396		517	
		10,816		11,124
Total equity and liabilities		37,573		36,957

Note: Paid in share capital represents 200,000 shares of €0.10 each at 31 December 2005.

Income statement	Year ended 31 December 2005	Year ended 31 December 2004
	€000	€000
Revenue	74,420	75,553
TOtal operating costs	72,580	73,320
Operating profit	1,840	2,233
Finance costs	520	509
Tax expense (effective tax rate is 24%)	396	517
Profit for the period	**924**	**1,207**

Statement of changes in equity	Share capital	Share premium	Retained earnings	Total
	€000	€000	€000	€000
Balance at 31 December 2004	20	450	20,863	21,333
Profit for the period	-	-	924	924
Dividends paid	-	-	-	-
Balance at 31 Decemeber 2005	20	450	21,787	22,257

Appendix 4: Kadgee's cash flow statement

	Year ended 31 December 2005		Year ended 31 December 2004	
	€000	€000	€000	€000
Net cash inflow from operations:				
Operating profit		1,840		2,233
Add back depreciation	1,965		1,949	
(Increase)/Decrease in inventory	(1,886)		(535)	
(Increase)/Decrease in trade receivables	(426)		(1,526)	
Increase/(Decrease) in trade payables and acccruals	(767)		(604)	
		(1,114)		(716)
Net cash flow from operations		726		1,517
Finance costs paid		(520)		(509)
Taxation paid		(517)		(390)
Purchase of tangible fixed assets		(281)		(350)
Dividends paid		0		0
Cash Inflow/(Outflow)before financiing		(592)		268
Increase/(Decrease) in bank overdraft		580		(194)
Increase/(Decrease) in cash and short term investments		(12)		74

chapter

16

KADGEE: ANALYSIS OF THE PRE-SEEN MATERIAL

Contents

1 Industry awareness

1.1 Market overview

The European clothing industry is a mature industry characterised to date by the following:

- Powerful retailers resulting in high pressure on manufacturers' margins
- Increasing globalisation resulting in many manufacturers switching production to cheaper locations outside Europe to reduce their cost base
- Increasing competition from Chinese manufacturers due to their lower costs, an improving reputation for quality and the relaxation of quotas. restrictions on the quantity of T&G imports from developing and emerging nations.

1.2 Globalisation and quotas

For over forty years the glodal trade in textiles and garments ('T&G') was governed by various quota systems. To protect their own locations, the industrialised nations had imposed restrictions on the quantity of T&G imports from developing and emerging nations.

To evade the restrictions of the quota system, many manufacturers thus internationalised their T&G production with the main recipients being Hong Kong, Turkey, China, Bangladesh and Sri Lanka. Today, about 160 producer countries compete for the three main markets in the US, the EU, and Japan, and global players such as Adidas receive supplies from about 60 countries.

The last of the major quota systems, the WTO Agreement on Textiles and Clothing (ATC), expired on December 31, 2004.

Clothing imports to EU countries from China rose fivefold within the following six months. After endless lobbying by retail groups, textile manufacturers and politicians who feared that cheap imports from China would destroy Europe's textile industry, trade officials with the European Commission (EC) sealed a voluntary deal with the Chinese to impose import quotas on 10 types of textile and apparel products, limiting growth in exports to Europe until 2008.

Just six weeks after the papers were signed, the first category—sweaters—reached its quota limit and no more sweaters were allowed into Europe. Within two months, there were some 48 million sweaters stranded on ships, at custom stations in Europe, and on docks in China. By mid-August, five more categories had reached quota—shirts, trousers, bras, blouses and flax yarn—all of which were piling up in warehouses and at ports across the EU. The so called 'bra wars' caused acute problems to many retailers within the EU, who found that they were running short of stock

Finally, on September 7, 2005, European Union governments backed a deal to unblock Chinese textiles held at EU borders, ending a trade dispute that saw some 77 million garments pile up after imports broke through 2005 limits.

After 2008 all quotas will be removed but until then the management of annual limits with China will be an ongoing problem for the EU.

Looking outside of Europe, the World Trade Organisation (WTO) is expecting China to increase its share of world textile manufacturing from 17% in 2003 to 50% by the end of 2006. This is not just affecting EU producers – Sri Lankan manufacturers, for example, are also finding themselves undercut on price.

1.3 Critical success factors

The main problem facing clothing retailers are as follows:

- There are few barriers to entry resulting in an intensely competitive industry with volatile profits.
- There is a trend for fashion tastes to change more rapidly, increasing the risk of 'fashion miss' (where stores do not stock the products customers want at the right time).

This has resulted in retailers focussing on the following:

- To minimise fashion miss, retailers want to have as much flexibility as possible with low operating gearing and low stock levels. They thus expect manufacturers to produce garments with shorter lead times and to be able to make and deliver smaller batches more frequently.
- To be competitive retailers are also looking to manufacturers to improve quality and/or reduce costs. Apart from the more high-end segments price/volume is a key driver for most products.

Manufacturers thus need to deliver on three counts:

- Design / quality
- Cost / price
- Speed to market / lead times

The relative importance of these three factors depends on the segment concerned – e.g. lead time is more important in more fashionable segments.

1.4 Quality issues

Quality, as always, is determined by meeting (even exceeding) customer expectations. For clothing manufacturers this will incorporate the following:

- Brand name - both of manufacturer and retailer (if different)
- Whether the garment is considered to be fashionable
- Styling / design features
- The choice of fabrics and materials used
- Garment integrity –e.g. the stitching is complete, buttons do not fall off soon after purchase, etc
- Close collaboration between retailer and manufacturer
- Hand finishing
- Ensuring garments comply with all relevant legislation
- Packaging – many manufacturers provide a garment that the retailer can put straight on a shelf in their stores
- Labelling – including putting retailers' own brand labels on garments.

1.5 Cost issues

It is a common misconception that labour is the biggest cost of any garment. While this may be true of haute couture creations that are completely hand-made, for most garments fabric is the biggest cost. Therefore firms have to make sure they are competitive on that before they look at other costs such as other raw materials, duties, freight and labour.

For example, a firm would not manufacture at a particular location unless it can get the fabric there cheaply and quickly. China has fabric and cheap labour so most analysts are expecting China to dominate the world market after 2008 when all quotas disappear (see below).

Target costing is becoming more commonplace in the industry.

1.6 Lead times

Lead times are becoming increasingly important within the industry. An interesting example of a company going against the conventional wisdom is Zara International, part of the Inditex group (Spain):

- Zara produces half of its garments in-house, whereas most retailers outsource all production. Although manufacturing in Spain and Portugal has a cost premium of 10 to 15 percent, the local production means the company can react to market changes faster than the competition.

- Instead of predicting months before a season starts what women will want to wear, Zara observes what's selling and what's not and continuously adjusts what it produces on that basis. This known as a 'design-on-demand' operating model.
- Rather than focussing on economies of scale, Zara manufactures and distributes products in small batches.
- Instead of using outside partners, Zara manages all design, warehousing, distribution, and logistics functions itself.
- The result is that Zara can design, produce, and deliver a new garment to its 600-plus stores worldwide in a mere 15 days.

By comparison a typical shirt manufacturer may take 30 days just to source fabric and then a further ten days to make the shirt. For some firms overall lead time could be between three and eight months from conception to shelf.

1.7 Brands

Brands are becoming increasingly important in many segments of the industry – e.g. jeans, sports and leisure wear and children's clothes.

The market can be segmented as follows:

- Exclusive 'haute couture' fashion houses (e.g. Calvin Klein, Ralph Lauren, Pierre Cardin, Yves St Laurent, Versace and Prada)
- Mid-market designer labels catering for the top end of the mass market (e.g. Moschino, Aquascutum, Hugo Boss, Dolce & Gabbana, DKNY, Diesel and Benetton). These are often sold through major department stores such as House of Fraser.
- Mass brands, usually focussing on particular segments of the market (e.g. Monsoon, Gap, French Connection, Adidas, Nike, Reebok). Some are sold in a number of different retailers' outlets whereas others are own-labels (e.g. the Per Una brand within Marks and Spencer)

With cheap and discounted products being so widely available, many younger consumers have switched their attention to formerly exclusive, internationally renowned brands, e.g. Prada (Italy), Chloe (France), Hugo Boss (Germany), Burberry (UK) and Donna Karan (US).

1.8 Market trends

The main changes in retailing are as follows:

- Supermarkets, such as Asda and Tesco in the UK, have teamed up with high-volume overseas suppliers to offer food shoppers a range of basic clothing items they might previously have accessed only through high street fashion shops.

- Increase in competition from discount specialists such as Primark and TK Maxx.
- Designer outlet villages (e.g. McArthur Glenn village near Chester in the North of England is the largest outlet village in Europe) account for 30% of US market and are seen as a growth area in Europe.
- Internet sales – this is currently a small segment of the market but is growing rapidly. Despite clothing being the third largest online market, the majority of clothing specialists have so far failed to develop online operations. (Note: one interesting feature of online sales is that men make up a much greater proportion of customers in contrast with clothing shops where most clothes – even those for men - are bought by women)

Other trends include:

- Increasing importance of brands – discussed above.
- The availability of cheaper imports has had the biggest impact on women's clothing with many women updating their wardrobes more frequently and discarding clothes once they go out of fashion (Note: linked to this there has been high growth in recycling clothing from Europe to be resold in African markets)
- Consumers have entered into an 'athleisure' generation that is very active, and in search of a cross-over look, sometimes described as 'casual urban' or 'urbaneering', 'mountain-sexual', and 'techni-cashz'. Such garments incorporate technical fabrics with casual styling. Modern technical fabrics are often soft, breathable, wind-proof, waterproof, abrasion resistant, washable, easy care and colourfast – or at least they have some of these characteristics.

1. 9 Strategy

Given the pressure from competitors outside Europe, most European clothing companies will have to position themselves into one of three categories in order to compete and survive in the world market:

- Purely sourcing operations, which will manage the design, production and distribution of products manufactured overseas.
- Niche manufacturers, supplying low-volume, high-value products.
- Balanced suppliers, having a European manufacturing base for sampling and small-batch, but sourcing larger orders to overseas manufacturers.

European companies will also need to play to their strengths – technical fabrics, dyeing and finishing, designer wear, capital intensive manufacturing and branded clothing.

Vertical integration is rare within the industry as retailers prefer to exercise buyer power and retain the flexibility to switch suppliers. One exception is provided by sportswear, which features three global manufacturers — Nike, Adidas and Reebok. Other exceptions include Zara, discussed above.

1.10 Real world players

European manufacturers include the following:

- LVMH (France) is the world's largest luxury goods conglomerate. Clothing brands include Christian Lacroix, Celine, Donna Karan, Kenzo and Thomas Pink (www.lvmh.com)
- Zara International (Spain) - part of the Inditex group – discussed above.(www.inditex.com)
- Triumph International (Germany) - Europe's largest manufacturer of women's underwear, lingerie, sports bras, swimwear and night clothes. (www.triumph.com)
- Jacques Vert plc (UK) – owns the ladies wear brands Jacques Vert, Windsmoor, Planet and Precis Petite. It also produces Melka (menswear) and Tenson (skiwear) clothing and has a large factory in Sri Lanka. (www.jacques-vert.co.uk)
- Slimma plc (UK) – has a portfolio of branded ladies wear. Global manufacturing base. (www.slimma.com)
- Adidas Clothing (Germany) – specialises in sportswear and owns Reebok and Rockport brands. (www.adidas-group.com)
- Benetton Clothing (Italy) – a global upmarket clothing brand. (www.benetton.com)

2 Financial analysis of appendices

Questions and comments on appendix 3 – Cash flow statement

Do a ratio analysis of the figures in appendix 3 and comment.

Your response

	2005	*2004*	*2005 Working*	*2004 Working*
Profitability				
Growth in turnover	(1.5%)	-	(74,420-75,553)/75,553	-
Growth in operating profit	(17.6%)	-	(1,840-2,233)/2,233	-
Growth in net profit	(23.4%)	-	(924-1,207)1,207	
Capital employed	26,757	25,833	22,257+4,500	21,333 + 4,500
ROCE	6.9%	8.6%	1,840/26,757	2,233/25,833
Returns On Equity	4.2%	5.7%	924/22,257	1,207/21,333
Operating profit margin	2.5%	3.0%	1,840/74,420	2,233/75,553
Net profit margin	1.2%	1.6%	924/74,420	1,207/75,553
Asset turnover	2.78x	2.92x	74,420/26,757	75,553/25,833

Liquidity				
Current ratio	2.56x	2.29x	27,743/10,816	25,433/11,124
Quick ratio	1.81x	1.72x	(19,404+119)/10,816	(18,978 + 131)/11,124
Total inventory days	41	32	(8,220/72,580)x365	(6,334/73,320)x365
Trade receivables days	95	92	(19,404/74,420)x365	(18,978/75,553)x365
Trade Payables days	45	48	(8,900/72,580)x365	(9,667/73,320)x365
Length of operating cycle	91	76	41 + 95 - 45	32 + 92 - 48
Investor ratio				
Gearing - Debt/Equity - using book values	0.20	0.21	4,500/22,257	4,500/21,333
Interest cover	3.54x	4.3x	1,840/250	2,233/509
Dividend cover	-	-	-	-
E.p.s	€4.62	€6.035	924/200	1,207/200

Your comments

- Worsening profitability – falling sales, profit and associated margins – some very quotable figures here! And these figures do not reflect loss of Forum yet!
- Operating and net margins are very low (e.g. Slimma plc had an operating profit margin of 4.7% in 2005), so profitability is very sensitivity to sales – e.g. Dieter offering more discounts!
- Working capital situation is deteriorating:
  - 41 days stock in a market where lead times are critical? Getting longer – why if sales are falling? Are Kadgee making speculative batches again or are customers insisting that Kagdee hold more stock to be able to deliver at short notice?
  - High debtors and lengthening credit period – is 95 days typical?
  - Falling trade payables days could indicate that suppliers are concerned over the prospects of firms in the industry, so are reinforcing payment terms more vigorously.
  - Worsening operating cycle, contributing to increasing overdraft.

Questions and comments on appendix 4 – Cash flow statement	Your response
Comment on the cash flow statement	• Cash outflow in 2005 – can this be turned around in 2006 or will the firm need to find additional finance? • Again - possible questions over Kadgee's future? • Main problem is the large increase in inventories – as mentioned with appendix 3. If this relates to WIP, then this could indicate worsening lead times. Difficult to see why Kadgee would increase stocks of fabric? • Decrease in creditors is also having a major impact on cash flow – why is Kadgee paying suppliers sooner than before?

3 Business strategy perspective: feedback

3.1 Assess Kadgee's current position using a SWOT analysis

Strengths

- Skilled, experienced, loyal workforce
- No obvious board conflicts.
- Deiter Stutt's reputation & strong customer relationships enable Kadgee to respond quickly to customer needs
- Innovation and survival in a very competitive market (IT systems, speed to market, TQM, design centre etc)
- Reputation and long relationship with customers at quality end of the market
- Family controlled therefore immune from takeover
- Geographical location should help delivery times
- Location in the EU? , therefore no import tariff barrier problem

Weaknesses

- Board have failed to embrace the challenges of globalisation
- Dependency on skilled workforce
- Morale problems affecting quality
- Stress related illness amongst staff
- Only 2 new customers in last 10 years
- 90% of sales to 6 customers in 2005, very high customer power
- Loss of second biggest customer (22.6% of sales)
- Own label operation has meant that many consumers are unaware of the Kadgee brand
- No separation of chair and MD role
- Move to full time workforce and hand finishing of garments hampers JIT approach
- European cost base, therefore difficult to compete on cost
- Exit cost of redundancy payments
- Financially poor profitability and cash flow. Falling sales and poor working capital management

Opportunities

- Improve differentiation – e.g. via better focus
- Set up factories overseas
- Source basic garments from overseas and finish them in European factories
- Some potential for cost savings on packaging and materials
- Other market segments (maternity/menswear etc)
- Move into more technical clothing
- Cost reduction by centralizing 6 factories
- Vertical integration?
- Outsourcing production
- New customers amongst new high street entrants (e.g. sell to supermarkets)
- Internet sales (Brand?)
- Exploit Skala's market research

Threats

- Liquidation!?
- Two other major customers may be looking for a reason to switch suppliers
- Short term quality problem may result in lost business

- Powerful customers may put more pressure on Kadgee to reduce prices
- Impact on reputation of Forum loss
- Increasing threat from overseas suppliers – especially China
- Danger that Kadgee could become 'stuck in the middle'
- Market trend towards cheaper clothes
- Low cost high quality overseas competition
- Increased rivalry amongst remaining European manufactures
- Recession hitting quality products

3.2 Assess the clothes industry using Porter's 5 forces analysis

Competitive rivalry – very high

- Large number of competitors around the world – a global market
- Improving productivity and quality in other countries make this an increasing threat
- Abolition of quota systems has increased level of competition, especially at the cost leader end of the market
- Difficult to differentiate the final product as made to customers' specifications and brand names of manufacturers are generally weak. As a result, products are treated more as a commodity.
- Technology has increased the level of competition by enabling easier price comparison (e.g. supplier e-auctions held by M&S)

Threat of new entrants – high

- Lifting of textile quota system enables rival exporting countries to compete for the first time.
- Textiles and clothing seems an automatic choice for many developing nations – mainly due to the industry being labour intensive (generally low skilled work) and them having low labour costs
- Political assistance to aid exports (e.g. China's aim to have 50% world market share of clothing)
- Strength of relationship with customer is a key factor within the industry helping to mitigate the risk
- As more technology is used in the industry this will increase entry costs and lower the overall risk

Threat from substitutes – low

- Trend towards 'business/casual' is reducing the demand for formal shirts
- In-house production and design by customers although many have moved away from this is an attempt to improve flexibility
- Home shopping (e.g. Internet) had 9% of sales in 2004 – growing. This could reduce demand by conventional retailers for Rayanka's products

Power of suppliers –low

- Relatively easy to find alternative sources of textiles
- Need to reduce lead times for end customer introduces an additional bargaining tool
- Skilled workers may be able to exercise some power but not significant

Power of customers – very high

- The retail market is dominated by major retailers (customers)
- Major retailers can threaten to switch suppliers
- Low switching costs (though can try to create some here via shared design)
- Many customers will have full knowledge of suppliers cost cards and will force prices down by threatening to move business elsewhere
- Arguably, some customers have taken this too far and have forced some of their suppliers out of business

3.3 Analyse the clothing industry using a PESTEL/PEST/SLEPT style analysis

Political / legal

- Relaxing of quotas for China in 2008 and interim measures
- Health and safety, employee rights

Economic

- Clothing is affected by the economic trade cycle, some segments more than others
- Prices have been falling in real terms
- Euro exchange rates could affect the competitiveness of European firms compared with Asian ones

Social

- Clothing styles tend to be more constant for older people
- For younger people products show much shorter lifecycles
- Brands are becoming more important.
- Most clothing is bought by women – even men's clothing!

Technological

- Greater use of IT (e.g. CAD, FMS) within clothing manufacture
- Development of new clothing materials – e.g. technical fabrics
- Rise of internet sales due to wider access to the Internet and broadband

Environmental / ethical

- Concern over ethical origins of materials (e.g. in 2004 People for the Ethical Treatment of Animals (PETA) called for a worldwide ban of Australian wool because of concerns over sheep welfare and in 2005 protested against Benetton in this respect)
- Employee welfare – e.g. are garments being produced in third world 'sweat shops' where workers are paid a pittance for their labour?
- Fair trade issues are well publicised for coffee but the situation with clothing is still murky – e.g. cotton producers are often paid a very low price for their crops. This could change as public awareness grows

3.4 Assess the clothing industry using the industry life cycle model

Question	Your response
At which stage of the life cycle model would you categorise the clothing industry?	• Mature, possibly saturated • Global
What are the implications of your classification?	• According to Porter, the key danger in a mature market is becoming stuck in the middle • He also argues that in a mature market most innovations can be copied easily by competitors, so cost-leadership is likely to be the most viable long term strategy • Kadgee should thus analyse the sources of its competitive advantage to ensure that it can continue to be a differentiator (see below) • In particular the threat from competitors in other countries needs to be assessed

3.5 Analyse Kadgee's competitive strategy and its future sustainability

Kadgee is trying to compete on the basis of differentiation. The key to any strategy of differentiation is to offer the customer something that they are prepared to pay extra for. This uniqueness or enhanced quality needs to be difficult for competitors to copy for the strategy to be sustainable long term.

Kadgee tries to differentiate by offering the following

- High quality designs similar to those of up-market designers (though not close enough to be a problem legally)
- Close collaboration with customers
- Highly skilled and motivated (!) workers to enhance the quality of stitching
- Finishing touches by hand
- Quicker speed to market made possible by new CAD techniques and the IT system introduced in 2001.

All of these can be imitated to some degree long term! Particularly as IT solutions (including CAD) become available to new entrants into the industry.

The danger is that customers will not be willing to pay for Kadgee's goods if competitors' offerings are much cheaper with only a slight reduction in the perceived quality.

In the long term Kadgee needs to improve the profile of its own brand name to enhance its differentiation and/or it needs to cut costs to reduce the price gap between itself and cheaper competitors.

In the short term the problems with low staff morale could seriously undermine Kadgee's reputation.

Quote: 'Kadgee is dependent on the skills of its employees to continue to deliver the same high quality on which it has established its reputation.'

3.6 Using Ansoff's matrix outline possible directions for growth for Kadgee

Ansoff's matrix – product / market mix

	Existing products	New products
Existing Markets	*Market penetration* • Reduce costs by setting up factories in cheaper countries • Outsource some clothing manufacture to, say, China • Buy a competitor	*Product development* • Start making men's clothing • Start making accessories to go with women's clothing
New Markets	*Market development* • Develop the Kadgee brand name to sell direct to ultimate consumers • Online sales	*Diversification* *Related diversification* • Integrate forwards and buy a high street retailer • Develop more technical garments aimed at younger consumers *Unrelated diversification (conglomerate diversification)*

Note that product development has been the main approach to date at the detriment of market development.

3.7 Assess the role of IT within Kadgee using McFarlan and McKenny's strategic grid

Current IT systems are making a major contribution to the management of cost, quality and lead times, so should be considered to have a high strategic impact.

Looking towards the medium term future IT systems will still be critical so the overall classification will be 'strategic'.

In the longer term most competitors will be using similar systems so IT will take the role of a threshold competence rather than a core competence and the classification will be downgraded to 'factory'.

Kadgee should thus continue to invest in enhancing its IT systems.

4 Financial strategy perspective: feedback

4.1 Analyse the financing arrangements used by Kadgee to date and comment on the options available for raising finance in the future

Arrangements to date

- Kadgee has remained unlisted to date, although some shares are held outside of the family
- Financed through retained earnings (little evidence of dividends having been paid), loans and overdrafts
- In 2000 the firm was refinanced with a ten year loan (repayable 2010) for €4.5 million @ 8% interest per annum.
- Current overdraft €1.52 million
- Current gearing (D/E using book values) = 0.2

Future possibilities

Equity

- Limited possibilities for rights issues due to the small base of shareholders.
- Flotation is the obvious solution to raising more equity but deteriorating performance makes this option less feasible.
- There would also be control implications as the Burnak family only control 58% at present. Any significant dilution would result in them losing control.
- In summary equity solutions look difficult.

Debt

- Current gearing is low, so further loans are possible without increasing the firm's gearing ratio to an unacceptably high level.
- Note: you could argue the opposite – given the high business risk in the market, Kadgee should keep its financial gearing risk as low as possible!
- Security – Non current assets are shown at €9.8 million NBV on the balance sheet. These are likely to comprise factories and machinery. While the machinery is unlikely to be viewed as high quality security, the building certainly will be. With the buildings, unless they have been revalued on the balance sheet, the market value is likely to be higher than the book value. However the existing loan of €4.5m will probably be secured on some of the existing buildings. Without further information it is difficult to determine how much security is available for new loans, but it should be feasible for Kadgee to raise an additional €4-5 million, say.
- The overdraft is likely to be a permanent feature of the balance sheet.

Other

- Debt factoring could result in a one-off receipt of 80% × 19m = €15m. This figure is higher than either of the debt or equity solutions discussed above!
- Large customers are unlikely to view factoring as a sign of financial distress but Kadgee will need to assess the cost v benefit of this method of finance. The ongoing cost (between 1 and 3% of the invoiced amount), could erode margins completely as Kadgee's existing net margin is only 1.2%.

4.2 Calculate the market value of Kadgee using earnings, assets and dividend approaches and comment on your results

1. **Assets**

Book value of equity = €22.2 million

- No information on how assets could be revalued.
- Machinery may be worth very little on a break-up basis (less than the book value?) but factory buildings are probably worth more than their holding value.
- Overall the asset value is likely to be higher than the €22.2 million given above.

2. **Dividends**

No evidence of any dividends having been paid or forecast so it is difficult to use this technique.

3. **Earnings**

We do not have any forecasts or plans (unlike most other cases!) so will have to work with 2005 earnings.

To obtain an indication of future sustainable earnings the 2005 figure should be adjusted for the loss of Forum. One approach could be as follows

	€000	€000
2005 profit after tax		924
Forum operating profit lost	300	
Tax saved @ 24%	(72)	
		(228)
Revised profit		696

The problem with this approach is that it fails to identify the incremental cash flows of losing Forum. A more detailed analysis is required to distinguish between

- variable costs, such as fabric and labour costs where these are paid on a piece rate or hourly basis
- avoided fixed costs, such as salaries of staff made redundant
- unavoidable fixed costs, such as factory overheads, where these have been absorbed into Forum costs when calculating the operating profit of €0.3 million.
- Possible knock-on effects – e.g. reduced staff morale could compromise quality, which in turn causes the loss of other customers.

The effect of all of these is that the loss of forum will cost Kadgee more than the €228,000 figure calculated above and so the earnings figure obtained is likely to be too high.

No P/E ratio is given in the pre-seen. If you need to value the firm, then a P/E ratio will probably be given in the un-seen material. To get an idea of the figures involved we shall use a figure of 10.

(**Note:** looking at real world companies reveals a large spread of P/E ratios, reflecting the high risks of the market. The figure of 10 is from smaller UK-listed companies that predominantly make ladies clothing. In contrast a typical P/E for retailers is 17),

MV = 696,000 × 10 = € 7 million

This figure is likely to be on the high side for the following reasons:

- The earnings figure could be much lower (see above)
- The P/E approach values the firm as if it were quoted. It is not so a discount of between 25 and 35% would normally be made to the final figure.

Comments

- The key observation for the above analysis is that the earnings value is significantly lower than the book value of the assets. This would suggest that Kadgee may be worth more on a break up basis.
- At the very least it would indicate poor asset utilisation, suggesting that the Board should consider closing less efficient factories.
- The company is big enough to consider a flotation on a smaller stock exchange, such as AIM in the UK, but may be too small for a successful listing on a larger market.

5 Risk and control perspective: feedback

5.1 Identify and assess the risks facing Kadgee under the following headings.

Business risks

- High customer power
- High competitive rivalry
- Loss of major customers (e.g. Forum)
- Increasing threat from new entrants – particularly from Chinese firms.

Financial risks

- How close to insolvency are they?
- Falling revenue and profit
- Cash outflow before financing activities in 2005
- Worsening working capital position
- Moving exchange rates – e.g. a strengthening Euro could make firms outside the EU even cheaper to EU retailers.

Political and legal risks

- Relaxation of quotas will increase threat of new entrants, though the EU may still implement quotas in the short-term
- Health and safety legislation, given that some employees have stress-related illnesses

Technology risk

- New technical fabrics create an opportunity
- Improved manufacturing processes could affect firms' cost base

Economic risk

- Clothing sales are linked to the state of the economy. Kadgee sells products at the medium/high end of the market

Reputation risk

- Falling quality
- Kadgee's brand name does not have a high profile

5.2 Suggest some KPIs that could be used to monitor operations, using the balanced score card as a framework

Financial perspective

- Revenue, both overall and by product line and customer
- Margins are particularly important
- Contribution , both overall and by product line
- Sales mix and quantity variances

Customer perspective

- Lead times – by customer
- Quality measures – e.g. % of garments returned by the customer
- % of products delivered on time – by customer
- Growth in orders by customer
- Satisfaction surveys

Internal business perspective

- Staff sickness days
- Staff turnover
- Quality measures – e.g. % of products rejected by internal QC procedures
- Throughput
- Machine usage
- Wastage
- Machine downtime
- Actual v target cost by garment

Innovation and learning perspective

- Brand awareness
- Staff turnover
- Number of suggestions made for improvement by staff (including what % were adopted)
- Design skills and innovation could be measured by the success of individual product lines – e.g. by comparing actual turnover v budget

5.3 Assess Kadgee organisational structure

We are told very little about Kadgee's organisational structure.

- There are directors in charge of various functions, suggesting a functional structure.
- They have six factories but Peter Coletta appears to manage all of them

- Dieter Stutt manages the relationships with all customers

There does not appear to be any distinctive product emphasis for ladies and children's clothing.

Clearly this structure would need changing if Kadgee decided to set up factories in other countries.

5.4 Assess Kadgee's information and reporting systems

There is very little information given concerning Kagdee's reporting system other than the IT system introduced in 2001. This gives the following information regarding production:

- orders can be tracked from garment cutting to completion to delivery
- machine usage
- wastage at various stages
- speed of production at various stages

This is all very good but is inadequate if, for example, contribution by product line is not measured.

6 Ethical considerations: feedback

6.1 Identify any ethical issues within the case under the following headings

Corporate governance

- No split between Chairman and Managing Director – both roles are currently performed by Andrin Burnak.
- Little evidence of structured risk assessments being carried out.

Social responsibility

- We are not given any information regarding whether the production process causes pollution (though fabric suppliers have probably already dyed the material used) or how energy efficient it is.

Business ethics

- To what extent are Kadgee's designers still 'borrowing' the ideas of other designers? They may be acting within the law but that does not necessarily mean that their behaviour is ethical.
- Kadgee mainly employ women to make clothing – they could be accused of sexual discrimination if they try to change working conditions to cut production costs further.

- Kadgee need to ensure employees are treated fairly and with dignity if further redundancies are envisaged. Communication and the adoption of best-practise guidelines regarding redundancy could be key issues here.
- Kadgee needs to ensure that other employees' health is not affected by high stress levels as many are working longer hours than they really want to.
- If Kadgee consider setting up factories in cheaper countries, then there are the ethical issues as to why those countries have lower wage rates – is it because working conditions and employee rights are inferior?
- It could be argued that Kadgee have acted unethically by forcing (mainly female) workers to accept longer contracts then they wanted or accept redundancy. Presumably the employees had good reasons why they wanted to work part time, including the provision of childcare.
- What is the ethical background of materials used? For example, are fair prices paid for raw material, such as cotton?

Personal ethics

- No indications of any personal conflicts of interest given in the case – yet!

7 Précis of the case – Kadgee

Kadgee is a clothing manufacturer based in Europe.

7.1 The industry

The European clothing industry is a mature industry characterised to date by the following:

- Powerful retailers resulting in high pressure on manufacturers' margins
- Increasing globalisation resulting in many manufacturers switching production to cheaper locations outside Europe to reduce their cost base
- Increasing competition from Chinese manufacturers due to their lower costs, an improving reputation for quality and the relaxation of quotas.

Retailers buy on three criteria and put pressure on manufacturers to improve each of the following:

- Design / quality
- Cost / price
- Speed to market / lead times

7.2 Kadgee's existing strategy

- Kadgee makes ladies and girls' clothing aimed at the medium/high price segments of the market. The majority are sold under retailers own labels.
- Kadgee's competitive strategy is to differentiate through good collaboration with clients, good designs and hand finishing of garments.
- Kadgee has resisted the pressure to source garments from cheaper countries outside of Europe.
- Instead the strategy has been to improve European factories by a mixture of
  - TQM
  - good use of IT
  - improved throughput
  - the reduction in the number of processes that do not add value and
  - high employee motivation and involvement.
- Whether this strategy will continue to be successful is debatable – see below

7.3 Financials

- Loss making between 1998 and 2002. Changes listed above returned the firm to profitability from 2003 to 2005 but with very low margins.
- Profit after tax fell from €1,207,000 in 2004 to €924,000 in 2005, a fall of 23.4%
- Net cash outflow of €592,000 in 2005
- Loss of Forum - contributed €16,800,000 to revenue and €300,000 to operating profit in 2005
- Worsening liquidity position – e.g. operating cycle up from 71 to 96 days

7.4 Key issues facing the firm

- How to manage high customer power in a very competitive industry. The Loss of a major customer (Forum) despite offering a 4% price cut and Kadgee's inability to win new customers would suggest that this is a major problem. The relationship with two other major customers is considered at risk.
- Increasing competition from overseas suppliers – especially China.
- Low staff motivation due to redundancies. This has resulted in falling quality and could seriously undermine Kadgee's reputation. (Note: the urgency of this issue should give it a high priority)
- Over-reliance on a small number of customers (Portrait and Diamond contributed over 50% of revenue in 2005)

7.5 Current plans / initiatives

- No major plans portrayed other than further cost cutting within existing factories
- Are the board failing to respond to the challenges of globalisation?

chapter

17

KADGEE: SEPTEMBER 2006 – UNSEEN MATERIAL

Contents

1 Exam question / requirement

You are the consultant appointed by the Kadgee Board.

Prepare a report that prioritises, analyses and evaluates the issues facing Kadgee, and makes appropriate recommendations.

2 Rest of unseen material

Meeting with Kadgee's bankers

Following the announcement of the loss of business from Forum, which was Kadgee's second largest customer, Kadgee's bankers, PGB, called a meeting in early July 2006. Both Andre Schnaffer and Andrin Burnak attended the meeting to reassure PGB that Kadgee had plenty of current orders and that business looked promising for the next 6 months. PGB has provided all of the loan finance to Kadgee which is due for repayment in 2010. Kadgee's existing loans of €4,500,000 are secured against the property owned by Kadgee. There is the capacity to borrow an additional €3,000,000 against Kadgee's assets.

PGB has also provided Kadgee with an overdraft facility. The overdraft is currently standing at €1,750,000 at the end of August 2006. This overdraft has increased from €1,520,000 at the end of December 2005. The agreed overdraft limit is €2,500,000. PGB stated that Kadgee will not be allowed to exceed the agreed limit, whatever the circumstances. PGB stated that if Kadgee were to exceed the limit, then the bank would call in the overdraft entirely.

PGB has requested Andre Schnaffer to supply a copy of Kadgee's cash flow forecast up to the end of 2006 together with a copy of Kadgee's latest financial plans, to reassure PGB. Andre Schnaffer agreed to these requests, and stated that they would be supplied after Kadgee had reviewed a number of strategic issues and possible contracts that it was currently considering.

Loss of another customer

In addition to the loss of one customer, Forum, another of Kadgee's customers, Zeeb, notified Kadgee in August 2006 that it would not be procuring any further clothing from Kadgee after its current contract for the 2006/07 winter season finishes. Sales to Zeeb amounted to 6.99% of Kadgee's sales revenue in 2005.

Some of Kadgee's other major customers are concerned about Kadgee's future ability to continue to manufacture and supply to them. Whilst Andrin Burnak has reassured all of Kadgee's remaining customers that Kadgee will continue to operate and manufacture to the same high standard that its reputation is based on, he considers that until a further large order is secured, Kadgee will see its profits substantially eroded. Andrin Burnak has communicated the loss of Zeeb to PGB (Kadgee's bankers) which has re-confirmed that the maximum overdraft that will be made available is €2,500,000.

Kadgee has six factories operational with a capacity to manufacture 10.9 9 million garments in 2005. The loss of both Forum and Zeeb results in an annual loss of around 3.3 3 million garments.

Forecast operating profit

The actual operating profit for 2005 was €1,840,000. Following Forum and Zeeb's decision not to place further orders with Kadgee, together with some deterioration in operating margins from other customers, Kadgee's latest forecast operating profit for 2006 is around €1,500,000. The forecast figures for 2006 include the 3 month trial for GREN (see below), but NOT the proposed one year contract with GREN.

The latest operating profit forecast for 2007, following the departure of both Forum and Zeeb, is €1,200,000. This does not include the proposed one-year contract with GREN.

August 2006 Kadgee Board meeting

At the Kadgee Board meeting held on 4 August 2006, the directors discussed how Kadgee could compete with the increasingly high quality output from China and the large volumes of imports into Europe.

The discussion included the following:

- Improve the quality or range of clothing, such as the proposed contract with GREN using recycled textiles, as outlined below;
- Move some, or all, of Kadgee's production to China. The Kadgee Board is agreed that the option of setting up in China on its own is not feasible, as it would face enormous obstacles which could delay production for several years. Therefore, a joint venture with a Chinese company should be considered. Alternatively, there is the possibility of subcontracting work to a Chinese manufacturer, as outlined below;

- Kadgee could aim to produce clothing for a selected market that is not currently being targeted by Chinese manufacturers, such as the proposed WintaWarm range of clothing, as outlined below.

New contract won by Kadgee

In May 2006, Kadgee recruited a new designer who has established a reputation for designing ranges of clothes using recycled textiles. The recycled textiles are procured at a very low cost from an international charity. Each new manufactured garment is different and requires a higher input from skilled manpower, especially cutters. Following discussions, a contract for a three month trial period was signed in late June 2006 between Kadgee and a new customer, GREN for deliveries in July, August and September 2006.

GREN launched a limited range in one of its flagship shops at the end of August. GREN has over 120 shops in several European countries. The average sales price per garment to GREN for the trial was €18.00 for an agreed volume of 60,000 garments for the three month trial period.

The trial has been a media success for GREN, and the garments using recycled materials were sold out in days. GREN is planning to expand the range and volume of clothes in this new recycled range and has offered Kadgee a 12 month contract, to commence after the three month trial period, ending in September 2007. However, the proposed one year contract will be at a lower sales price per garment, of €16.20. GREN believes that Kadgee should be able to achieve economies of scale and reduced manpower time spent due to the learning curve effect, as the contracted volume in the proposed one year contract is for 1 million garments.

The marginal cost per garment for manufacturing clothes using recycled textiles is €15.60.

If Kadgee accepts the GREN contract for the next year it would utilize over 9% of Kadgee's manufacturing capacity of 10.9 million garments. The proposed manufacture of 1 million garments using recycled textiles will be undertaken at two of its factories only. These two factories have spare capacity following the loss of the Forum and Zeeb contracts.

GREN has requested Kadgee to advise its intention to agree to the proposed one year contract by the end of September 2006, before the trial finishes. GREN has also used other companies for the trial, but has offered the one year contract to Kadgee only.

The Kadgee management team is very pleased with the success of the trial of recycled materials and the proposed one year contract to the end of September 2007. However, the reduced sales price, and therefore the reduced margin, is a great concern to Andre Schaffner, the Finance Director. Andre Schnaffer also has concerns about GREN's ability to meet Kadgee's usual payment terms. Whilst some payment delays are expected, at present Kadgee has not received any payments at all for any of the supplies to GREN for the 3 month trial. The first deliveries that were invoiced during July are now over 60 days old and have still not been paid. GREN has a poor reputation in dealings with its suppliers, including regular late payment of around 4 months after delivery.

Andre Schnaffer has forecast that the proposed one year contract will necessitate working capital financing of €1 million. The finance costs of the increase in working capital would be 13% per year, based on Kadgee's current overdraft rate. The cost of financing the working capital is not included in the above forecast cost figures.

Andrin Burnak was very pleased for Kadgee to be at the forefront of this new fashion trend. Additionally, Kadgee was receiving much positive PR associated with the high profile launch of the new recycled textiles.

Proposal to move some manufacturing to China

At the Board meeting in August 2006, there were some detailed discussions on the possibility of moving some of Kadgee's manufacturing to China. This could enable Kadgee to operate more profitably and would allow the company to be more confident in its ability to retain its existing customer base and also to allow it to compete much more effectively in order to win new business.

Andrin Burnak stated that Kadgee had been approached by a Chinese manufacturing company called LIN. It has proposed a joint venture with Kadgee. It proposes that Kadgee should concentrate on what it does best, which is designing and distributing to the European market. It proposes that Kadgee should continue to work with its current customers and agree designs, which could then be electronically transferred to a factory in China to manufacture. Kadgee would then continue to supply existing customers, but with clothes manufactured in China. This would necessitate closure of all six of Kadgee's European factories. The proposal is for the joint venture to be LIN 60% and Kadgee 40% for investment and all financial aspects of the proposed joint venture. The proposed joint venture with LIN would require the construction of a large purpose built factory with a manufacturing capacity of over 20 million garments per year. If Kadgee chose to invest in the joint venture, the investment cost is forecast to be €22.5 million, of which Kadgee's share at 40% would be €9 million.

However, both Sam Skala and Peter Coletta are very concerned whether the proposed joint venture could work well for the longer term and are worried about the security of Kadgee's intellectual property.

Andrin Burnak has also been consulting for the last few months with a Chinese businessman, Won Dong, who he has personally known for 30 years through business and family connections. Won Dong is based in China but travels extensively. Won Dong has advised Andrin Burnak of two different Chinese companies to which he considers Kadgee should subcontract work to, as an alternative to the proposed joint venture with LIN, which he knows little about. However, if Kadgee were to subcontract manufacturing work to either of the companies in China that Won Dong has suggested, it would necessitate closing most, or all, of its European factories.

Proposed new product line

Kadgee has, to date, only manufactured fashion clothing and has not made any outerwear such as jackets and coats. Following extensive market research by Sam Skala, he has identified that there is a substantial gap in the number of high quality coats manufactured for the North American market, including Canada.

Kadgee has purchased, on a trial basis, a small quantity of a new lightweight synthetic fabric called "WintaWarm" that is both warm and waterproof. The company manufacturing this new material is Ruzic, which is based in Europe. The new material is thin but hard wearing and has had favourable press coverage, following its launch in December 2005. All purchases of the material will be paid for in Euros.

Capital expenditure of €8 million will be required for the new product line.

Sales would be invoiced in US Dollars or Canadian Dollars. The NPV's in the table below include the forecast capital expenditure of €8 million. This proposal requires Kadgee Board approval in order to meet a launch date of January 2007.

NPVs for WintaWarm proposal	Probability	Number of garments manufactured per year	NPV's of post-tax cash flows for WintaWarm proposal assessed over 5 years
			€ million
High sales	10%	0.6 million	6.1
Medium sales	50%	0.5 million	3.6
Low sales	40%	0.4 million	0.9

However, Andre Schnaffer is concerned whether Kadgee can raise €8 million in loan finance to purchase the required new machinery. If the machinery is hired or leased instead of being purchased, the present value of the hire or leasing costs, post-tax, is forecast to be €10 million for the 5 year period over which the project is being assessed.

Legal case against Kadgee

Kadgee is facing a major legal case for allegedly copying designs by a major fashion designer, SM. Several of Kadgee's designs from its latest range bear a remarkable similarity to SM's designs, but Kadgee's designs were drawn up before the famous designer's clothes were launched. Kadgee has so far refused to back down and the publicity has boosted sales of Kadgee's designs to many of its customers.

Sam Skala has stated that all publicity is good publicity, and that Kadgee should not give into the pressure from SM, as the Kadgee management team is confident that it had not copied the designs. He stated that Kadgee should be flattered that it is being taken to court by such a famous fashion house. However, Kadgee's legal advisors are worried that if it is unsuccessful in the legal case, the damages could lead to major financial problems and that the costs of the case and legal damages, if Kadgee is unsuccessful, could exceed €3 million. If the case is settled out of court, Kadgee would have legal costs of €0.2 million and Kadgee would have to withdraw the designs.

The net effect on the operating profit of withdrawing these designs is forecast to be a reduction of €0.3 million in total for the lifetime of the designs. However, if Kadgee decides to defend the case, if it went to court, the chances of success are 50%.

Fire at one of Kadgee's factories

At the very end of August 2006, a fire broke out during the night at one of Kadgee's factories located in the town of Dem. The fire has destroyed the entire inventory of finished goods held there awaiting transportation to customers, as well as a large amount of work-in-progress and raw materials. The factory was one of Kadgee's larger factories, which manufactured 2.4 4 million garments each year.

In addition to the total loss of all inventories, there was several days loss of data from the computer systems at that factory. In accordance with usual routines, the IT systems had been backed up each night, but the back up files had not been stored in a fire-proof cabinet or off site, as required by Kadgee's IT instructions. Therefore, the factory manager has not been able to ascertain what deliveries have been made to customers over the preceding four days before the fire. Many of Kadgee's customers are still chasing Kadgee for deliveries in the confusion following the fire less than a week ago. Kadgee's management has been busy transferring orders to its other factories, and some orders may have been repeated. Also, as delivery data had not been transferred to the finance department, there was some confusion over what should, or should not, be invoiced, Several of Kadgee's customers have complained that they have been invoiced twice for goods that they never received.

The fire had also spread to neighbouring domestic houses and caused much damage. There has been much adverse press coverage of the fire and the damage caused. Local residents are seeking compensation from Kadgee for losses not covered by their own insurance policies. Kadgee is fully insured for the fire at its premises and there were no suspicious circumstances. The expected insurance payment, due in November 2006, will be for around €7.0 million. However, the forecast cost of rebuilding a similar factory with the same capacity, using the latest machinery, is €10.0 million.

The employees at the factory burnt down in the town of Dem are unwilling to relocate to any of Kadgee's other factories. The nearest of Kadgee's other five factories is over 200 kilometres away. The factory that burnt down employs 84 employees, all of whom have been put on half pay for 1 month. If the site is permanently closed, redundancy payments of €1.1 million as well as other closure costs of €0.3 million will be incurred.

Accidents at several Kadgee factories

Peter Coletta is under pressure from his fellow Board members to take action following a series of minor accidents during July and August at all six factories. Maintenance has been reduced and machine breakdown is common.

As a result of reduced maintenance and also due to much of the machinery reaching, or exceeding, the end of its useful life, there has been an increasing number of machine breakdowns. Most employees are under pressure to meet their daily targets of number of garments worked on, and choose to attend to the machine breakdowns themselves. They have had little direct training on machine maintenance. At one of the factories, when one of the main cutting machines broke down, many employees were unable to meet their daily targets and they lost a proportion of their wages that related to volumes produced. Therefore employees are keen to take action when machinery breaks down. In most cases the repairs are simple and straightforward and the machine is up and running again very quickly. However, there are a growing number of minor accidents that are happening on an almost daily basis and the employees are frustrated that management is ignoring these incidents.

The general feeling in the factories is that a major accident will occur before the management team either replaces the faulty and aged machinery, or improves the level of maintenance. The forecast costs of replacing just the machinery that has the worst breakdown records is €3.0 million or alternatively the increased maintenance costs to attempt to prevent many of the breakdowns is forecast to be €0.8 million per year.

Other Human Resource issues

Kadgee's employees are very concerned for their future employment, having seen many other clothing manufacturers in the same towns in which they work cease trading. Kadgee's manufacturing capacity has increased due to efficiencies in recent years. However, there is increasing unrest amongst employees that all of their efforts are not appreciated. There are a few employees that are trying to demand a better pay rate for their skills, but to date have been unsuccessful. The standard of quality is starting to fall. Furthermore, Kadgee employs a high proportion of skilled female employees and many are unhappy and have complained that they are paid a lower pay rate than their male colleagues who are doing the same work. However, Peter Coletta has explained to Lars Veel, the HR Director, that this is due to the extra responsibilities that many of the male employees undertake.

Appointment of a consultant

At the Kadgee Board meeting held on 1 September 2006, it was agreed that a consultant would be appointed to advise the Board on the issues facing Kadgee.

chapter

18

KADGEE: SEPTEMBER 2006 – SAMPLE SOLUTION

Contents

1 Introduction

What follows is a possible answer for Kadgee September 2006 exam. As always, it is one possible solution and alternative interpretations may be valid.

2 Sample script

REPORT (CONFIDENTIAL)

To: The Board of Directors

From: A Consultant

Date: Today

Report to the Board of Directors of Kadgee regarding the main issues facing the company and potential strategies for the future.

Contents

Appendices

Prepared by A Consultant
Date: 4th September 2006

1 Introduction

The clothing manufacturing industry is becoming increasingly competitive due to the combination of powerful customers who demand ever cheaper goods and low-cost, high-quality competition from China.

This has resulted in Kadgee's net margins falling from 1.6% in 2004 to 1.2% in 2005 (refer Appendix E).

The key challenges facing Kadgee are recovering its competitive advantage by re-examining its manufacturing strategy, finding new lower-risk directions for growth and ensuring that its overdraft does not exceed the limit set by PGB.

2 Terms of reference

The purpose of this report is to provide the board of Directors of Kadgee with a clear picture of the company's position as at 4th September 2006, in particular to identify and prioritise the main issues facing Kadgee, respond to the issues, assess the opportunities currently available, and make appropriate recommendations.

This report has been prepared by A Consultant and relies upon information and explanations provided by the board to date and financial information at 31st December 2006.

3 Prioritisation of main issues facing Kadgee

The following issues have been prioritised from the SWOT analysis that is attached as Appendix A:

3.1 Overdraft limit with PGB

In the light of the loss of the Forum contract, PGB have stated that they are unwilling to extend Kadgee's overdraft limit under any circumstances and will recall the overdraft in its entirety should the limit be exceeded. The lack of flexibility is the issue here, reflecting the bank's increased concerns over Kadgee's future.

This is the first and foremost priority because exceeding the limit could precipitate the liquidation of the company.

Thus management will need to develop a course of action to reassure the bank and to ensure that the overdraft limit is not exceeded in the immediate future.

3.2 Loss of customers

In addition to the loss of Forum, Zeeb has stated its intention not to buy Kadgee garments after the 2006/7 winter season. Furthermore, other customers have expressed concern over future trade with Kadgee.

Any further loss of customers could compromise Kadgee's future viability so this issue is prioritised second on the grounds of strategic impact.

Thus management will need to develop a course of action to reassure customer concerns and to win new business.

3.3 Proposal to move some manufacturing to China

Kadgee has been approached by LIN to set up a joint venture to manufacture garments in China. Being effectively an outsourcing of production, this represents a radical departure from Kadgee's existing production strategy.

Creating a low cost manufacturing base is vital for Kadgee's future success but only if the company can continue to operate in the short term and has business to manufacture for, hence it is third priority.

Thus management must decide whether to accept the proposal or not.

3.4 Proposal to extend GREN contract another year

The GREN trial to make garments from recycled materials ends in September 2006. This represents a departure from the types of garments traditionally made by Kadgee.

This is the fourth priority because Kadgee need to find new growth areas to compensate for high competition in traditional areas and because a decision needs to be made by the end of September 2006 whether or not to accept the contract for a further twelve months.

3.5 Proposed new product line using WintaWarm fabric

Kadgee is trialing the use of WintaWarm, a new technical fabric, to make coats for the North American market. As such, this represents a diversification opportunity for Kadgee.

This is the fifth priority because Kadgee need to find new growth areas to compensate for high competition in traditional areas and because a decision needs to be made before January 2007 whether to accept the proposal.

3.6 Other issues

There are a number of other issues which have not been prioritised as they are not considered to merit the strategic importance of the above priorities within the scope of this report. These are as follows:

- Factory fire - This has not been prioritised because spare capacity exists to remake the garments in other factories. However, management still need to act quickly to prevent any further loss of customer goodwill.

The following are dealt with under ethical issues in section 9:

- A potential legal case against Kadgee by SM for alleged copying of designs.
- Minor accidents at Kadgee factories.
- Machine breakdowns at several factories.

4 Overdraft limit with PGB

PGB have stated that they are unwilling to extend the current overdraft limit of €2,500,000 and will call in the full overdraft if this limit is exceeded. It is thus vital that this does not happen.

4.1 Short-term cash position at 31st December 2006

Including only current activities, the forecast overdraft at 31st December 2006 will be €1,032,000 (Appendix B), giving a margin of €1.5 million.

Additional demands on short-term cash flow include the following:

- Extending the GREN contract would result in a net cash outflow of €4.9 million (Appendix C) before 31st December 2006. This alone would exhaust the overdraft facility and leave over €3.4 million to be raised in the immediate future to avoid PGB calling in the facility.
- Accepting the WintaWarm proposal would require an immediate investment of €8 million if machinery were purchased, or around €2.3 million if leased (Appendix D). Given a proposed launch date of January 2007, presumably some, if not all, of this would be required in 2006.
- Redundancies and closure costs if the factory damaged by fire is not rebuilt will amount to €1.4 million. Much of this will have to be paid before 31st December 2006. This alone would exhaust the overdraft facility. If the factory is rebuilt, then these costs will be avoided but €10 million will be incurred in building costs with some in 2006.

4.2 Possible short term financing solutions

Debt

PGB have indicated that Kadgee have sufficient asset security to borrow a further €3 million. This can be used to reduce the overdraft and finance some of the above options, if accepted. If the overdraft is reduced, then PGB will view Kadgee as less risky as more of the debt will be secured. From Kadgee's perspective this will not increase gearing to unreasonable levels so should be considered.

Factoring

At present debtors typically take 95 days to pay (Appendix E). In the short term a one-off cash inflow could be generated by factoring trade receivables. A debt factoring arrangement usually gives an 80% advance with the balance, less commission and fees, payable when the customer pays or after an agreed period. Given sales of approximately €4 million a month for the last 3 months of 2006, a factoring arrangement could thus generate an additional inflow of approximately €3.2 million a month in 2006.

However, Kadgee will need to assess the cost of this method of finance. The ongoing cost (usually between 1 and 3% of the invoiced amount), could erode margins completely as Kadgee's existing net margin is only 1.2% (Appendix E).

4.3 Longer-term cash position

Even if Kadgee keep their overdraft to below the limit in 2006, there are still concerns over 2007 as cash demands could include the proposed joint venture with LIN (€9 million investment), the current legal case against Kadgee (possible damages of €3 million) and ongoing lease payments if the WintaWarm proposal is accepted.

In the longer term equity solutions should be considered. However, these are limited:

- There is limited scope for rights issues due to the small base of shareholders.
- Any significant placing to private investors would result in the Burnak family losing their control of the business.
- Flotation is the obvious solution to raising more equity but deteriorating performance makes this option less feasible.

5 Loss of customers

5.1 The extent of the problem

Porter's five forces analysis is useful to identify Kadgee's competitive threats and opportunities as well as assess the level of profitability in the clothing industry. The key threats to Kadgee are powerful customers, high competitive rivalry and high threat of entry from overseas firms. This has resulted in Kadgee's competitive advantage being eroded and the loss of customers.

To date Kadgee has lost business with Forum and Zeeb, who together accounted for 29.5% of Kadgee's revenue in 2005. Forum generated operating profit of €0.3 million in 2005, though the actual loss will be much higher due to unavoidable fixed costs. Other customers are known to be reviewing their positions.

5.2 Possible courses of action

If Kadgee continue with their current strategy, then it seems inevitable that more customers will be lost to cheaper competition and the future viability of the firm eroded.

Cutting prices could be considered but Forum was lost despite being offered a 4% discount and Kadgee's low net margin limits the scope for such discounts.

Kadgee has a long history of strong customer relations. This could be capitalised upon by having in-depth discussions with all customers to assess whether they are also considering moving and what their key concerns are – e.g. cost or deteriorating quality.

The main option that should be considered is changing the production strategy to reduce Kadgee's cost base. One approach would be to outsource production to China. This option is discussed in section 6 below.

Kadgee should also consider finding new product lines where competition from China is not so significant. Two such options are discussed in sections 7 and 8 below.

6 Proposal to switch some manufacturing to China

6.1 Introduction

Kadgee has been approached by LIN to set up a joint venture to manufacture garments in China. With joint ventures, control is normally split 50:50 but costs, profits, risks and rewards are typically shared between the two parties concerned, according to an agreed contract. In this case, Kadgee would contribute 40% of investment costs towards manufacturing but would still retain full control of product design.

6.2 Arguments for the proposal

The venture establishes a high-quality, low-cost manufacturing base, which would allow Kadgee to retain its customer base.

Kadgee may be able to win new business in the face of increasingly fierce competition as it will be able to take advantage of this new low cost facility and extra manufacturing capacity.

6.3 Arguments against the proposal

Kadgee's share of the investment cost is €9 million. Kadgee can only raise a further €3 million debt so this would necessitate a further €6 million equity, which is problematic at present, as discussed in section 4 above.

Lead times may be lengthened due to having to transport garments longer distances to European customers. This may be a critical concern for some customers.

Closure of existing factories would result in bad publicity, redundancy payments and a loss of key resources.

LIN will learn Kadgee's designs and production secrets – information that could be used by LIN to make other competing garments.

6.4 Alternative solutions

Rather than a joint venture, Kadgee could simply outsource production to Chinese manufacturers, as suggested by Won Dong. This would get the benefits of lower cost without the capital investment requirement.

Rather that making all garments in China, Kadgee could become a "balanced supplier", having a European manufacturing base for high quality small-batch production, but sourcing larger orders to overseas manufacturers. This would enable Kadgee to retain its most skilled workers.

7 Proposal to extend GREN contract for a further year

7.1 Introduction

Ansoff's matrix is a useful framework for analysing growth strategies. The GREN proposal to manufacture garments for the next year using recycled materials represents a product development strategy for Kadgee. The proposal is forecast to give a profit before tax of €470 million (Appendix C) suggesting it should be accepted. However, the following arguments should also be considered.

7.2 Arguments for the proposal

The main argument for renewal is that the move into recycled materials gives Kadgee a growth area that is not so exposed to competition from China, reducing the risk exposure of the firm and increasing its chances of survival.

The trial appears to have been a success with extensive publicity and demand exceeding supply.

The proposal will use up spare capacity generated by the loss of Forum and Zeeb, thus preserving jobs, particularly among skilled workers.

7.3 Arguments against the proposal

The main problem with extending the GREN contract is the likely adverse impact on short term cash flow, discussed in section 4 above. A contributing factor here is GREN's poor record on paying suppliers.

The forecast net margin of 2.9% (Appendix C), while higher than Kadgee's current margin of 1.2% (Appendix E), is still low by industry standards. This could be improved by learning effects and economies of scale.

7.4 Alternative solutions

Given the publicity generated by the trial, Kadgee could explore whether other customers (particularly those with better payment records) would be interested in similar garments.

8 Proposed new product line using WintaWarm fabric

8.1 Introduction

The use of WintaWarm to make coats for the North American market also represents a product development strategy according to Ansoff's matrix. This strategy can be assessed using the "suitability, feasibility, acceptability" framework developed by Johnson and Scholes.

8.2 Suitability

The move into "technical fabrics" such as WintaWarm gives Kadgee a growth area that is not so exposed to competition from China, reducing the risk exposure of the firm and increasing its chances of survival.

8.3 Feasibility

Kadgee would struggle to raise the €8 million investment required, as discussed in section 4 above.

Due to the factory fire, if the GREN proposal is accepted, then there will insufficient manufacturing capacity within the group to make the WintaWarm garments (Appendix D).

8.4 Acceptability

The proposal is forecast to give a positive net present value of €2.77 million (Appendix D) and thus should increase shareholder value by that amount.

Even if machinery is leased, the NPV is still positive but only by €0.77 million. However, this would increase the chance of failure to 40% (Appendix D).

8.5 Alternative solutions

Alternatives strategies are that Kadgee could continue with the WintaWarm project but outsource production and/or Kadgee could research possible demand for technical fabric garments within Europe.

9 Ethical issues

The key ethical issues facing Kadgee are as follows:

9.1 Claims of sexual discrimination

Many skilled female workers have complained that they are paid a lower wage rate than their male colleagues who are doing the same work. Peter Coletta has suggested that this reflects differing responsibility levels but that argument could result in female employees, particularly skilled ones, claiming that they have not been promoted on the grounds of gender.

Either way, there appears to be a case for Kadgee to answer. It is unethical for Kadgee to discriminate on the grounds of gender.

It is recommended that

- Kadgee introduce a system of job evaluation to ensure that employees get the same pay if they do jobs of equal value.
- Kadgee review responsibilities to ensure that there is no discrimination.

9.2 Accidents

In every factory, older machinery is not being maintained sufficiently to prevent minor accidents from occurring. It is unethical for Kadgee to boost shareholder profit by cutting costs at the expense of employee safety. It is also probably illegal under relevant health and safety legislation.

It is recommended that the maintenance budget be increased immediately. In addition suspect machinery should be replaced when financing constraints permit.

9.3 Copying other designers

Kadgee has always looked for inspiration from other designers' clothing without crossing copyright legislation. Copying other designers is unethical as it is effectively a form of theft. However, the distinction between being influenced by and copying is best left to the legislators and lawyers.

Given the pending legal case from SM, it is recommended that Kadgee review the garments in question and, if necessary, seek an out of court settlement.

10 Recommendations

Overdraft limit with PGB

To reassure bank concerns over Kadgee and to prevent the overdraft limit from being exceeded, I recommend the following:

Immediate action

1 The joint venture with LIN and the WintaWarm proposals should be rejected because of their demands on cash flow (see below).

2 Kadgee should seek a meeting with PGB to discuss taking out a further loan of €3 million. PGB will consider a secured loan less risky than a larger overdraft.

3 Kadgee should negotiate better payment terms with GREN to speed up payment.

4 Kadgee should prepare detailed cash flow forecasts and use debt factoring and invoice discounting to manage the overdraft whenever it approaches the limit. Factoring is commonplace within the clothing industry.

Longer term

5 In the longer term the company should be prepared for flotation to finance ongoing expansion into new areas.

Loss of customers

To prevent further loss of customers, I recommend the following courses of action:

Short term

1 As recommended below, Kadgee should switch at least some production to Chinese manufacturers in the immediate future.

2 While this is being implemented, Kadgee should arrange meetings with customers to identify their concerns, such as delays due to the fire, and reassure them that plans are in place to address them. In particular, Kadgee should communicate the plans to outsource production to reduce costs without compromising quality.

Medium term

3 With new customers Kadgee should negotiate clauses in contracts with longer notice periods, depending on the industry norm in this area.

Proposal to switch some manufacturing to China

I recommend the plan to switch manufacturing to China is pursued because it would give Kadgee the low cost base it needs to be competitive and help keep customers. With some notable exceptions, such as Zara, most high street retailers now source garments from outside Europe.

However, I recommend that the joint venture with LIN be rejected because of financing constraints and the implication that all European factories would be closed.

Instead, I recommend that some production be outsourced to other Chinese manufacturers to obtain the cost benefits without the capital investment cost. A project team should be set up to identify and investigate possible suppliers, starting with those recommended by Won Dong. Key priorities for the team should be quality, costs and lead times. Marks and Spencer, for example, have moved some production back nearer to the UK after concerns over lead times.

Proposal to extend GREN contract a further year

I recommend the proposal is accepted because it will increase long term profitability, use up spare capacity generated by the loss of Forum and provide a growth direction with less risk exposure to Chinese competition.

The key implementation issue with GREN is to negotiate how to speed up cash payments.

Proposal to develop new product lines using WintaWarm fabric

I recommend that the proposal to manufacture WintaWarm garments is not accepted because while it is expected to be profitable, it would be difficult for Kadgee to implement both the GREN and WintaWarm proposals due to financing and capacity constraints. If leasing is considered, then the risk of failure increases to 40% (Appendix D), which would be unacceptable.

Instead, I recommend that Kadgee pursue the strategy of using WintaWarm but investigate the possibility of outsourcing production.

11 Conclusions

Kadgee is facing many significant issues both internally and within the industry. Decisive action must be taken to avoid the company falling further which, ultimately, may threaten the very existence of the company.

Appendix A: SWOT ANALYSIS

Strengths

- Established and respected company with a history of producing a quality product
- Currently making profits despite very difficult trading conditions that has seen many competitors fail.
- Experienced board of Directors with industry knowledge.
- An innovative, highly skilled and committed work force but who are under immense pressure.

Weaknesses

- The loss of the Forum and Zeeb contracts (30% of sales in 2005) will be a significant blow to morale as well as financially.
- Working conditions are not what they used to be, resulting in stressed employees. This has led to some quality issues.
- The factory fire has reduced production capacity.
- Poor record on winning new customers.

Opportunities

- Establish manufacturing facilities in China – e.g. joint venture with LIN.
- Move into more technical clothing – e.g. using WintaWarm fabrics.
- Look for market segments that are less exposed to Chinese competition – e.g. the use of recycled materials in the GREN trial.
- Internet sales.

Threats

- The bank may call in the overdraft if the limit is exceeded.
- Other major customers may be looking for a reason to switch suppliers.
- Short term quality problem may result in lost business.
- Powerful customers may put more pressure on Kadgee to reduce prices.
- Impact on reputation of Forum and Zeeb losses.
- Increasing threat from overseas suppliers – especially China.

Appendix B: Cash flow forecast for the 4 months to 31st December 2006

	4 m to 31/12/06
	€000
Operating profit – excluding GREN trial (W1)	452
Add back depreciation (2005 figure pro-rated – 1,965 × 4/12)	655
Net cash flow for GREN trial (W2)	(216)
	891
Changes in working capital held (Note 1)	0
Finance costs paid – 2005 figure pro-rated – 520 × 4/12	(173)
Taxation paid – assume not due in the 4 months concerned	0
Purchase of tangible fixed assets – assume to be zero	0
Dividends paid – assume to be zero	0
Cash Inflow	718
Overdraft brought forward at 31st August 2006	(1,750)
Predicted balance at 31st December 2006	**(1,032)**

W1: Operating profit excluding GREN trial

	€000
Forecast operating profit including GREN trial	1,500
Deduct GREN profit: 60,000 × (18 – 15.60)	(144)
	1,356
Pro-rated profit for 4 months to December 2006 (1,356 × 4/12)	452

W2: Forecast cash flow re GREN trial

	€000
Receipts from GREN – 2 months – 60,000 × 18 × 2/3	720
Costs – 3 months - 60,000 × 15.60	(936)
Net cash outflow	(216)

Note 1: It has been assumed that any changes in working capital (i.e. receivables, payables and inventories) due to changing operating conditions, loss of customers, etc will already have taken place by the end of August 2006. In the four month period under review, no further changes in working capital are anticipated.

(**Tutorial note:** some major simplifying assumptions have to be made here to produce a cash flow forecast in the time available)

Appendix C Calculations to support GREN proposal

Profitability

	€000
Revenue (1m × €16.20)	16,200
Marginal production costs (1m × €15.60)	(15,600)
Contribution	600
Financing costs of working capital (13% × €1m)	(130)
Net profit	**470**
Net profit margin (470/16,200)	2.9%

Cash implications for 3 months to 31st December 2006

	€000
Working capital requirement – mainly upfront	(1,000)
Financing costs of working capital – 3/12 × 130	(33)
Production costs for 3 months – 3/12 × 15,600	(3,900)
Revenue – unlikely to receive any until 2007	0
	(4,933)

Appendix D Calculations to support WintaWarm proposal

W1. Expected Net Present Value (ENPV), assuming the machinery is purchased

	€m
ENPV = 0.10 × 6.1 + 0.50 × 3.6 + 0.40 × 0.9	2.77
100% chance of making a positive NPV	

W2. ENPV, assuming the machinery is leased

	€m
ENPV if buy (W1)	2.77
PV of extra costs if leased (10 – 8)	(2.00)
ENPV if lease	**0.77**

60% chance of making a positive NPV as low sales scenario would give a NPV of -€1.1million

W3. Production capacity (millions of garments)

	Sales	*Capacity*
6 factories in 2005 (100% utilisation)	10.9	10.9
Factory fire		(2.4)
Loss of Forum and Zeeb	(3.3)	
GREN proposal – production already allocated if proceed	1.0	
WintaWarm proposal (max)	0.6	
	9.2	**8.5**

There is thus insufficient capacity to manufacture WintaWarm garments in existing factories, if the GREN contract is extended.

W4. Annual lease payments, assuming the machinery is leased

	€m
Assuming a lease cost of 8%, say, and 5 annual payments in advance, the annual payment = 10million / (1 + 3.312) =	2.32

(**Tutorial Note:** Students could still have scored highly without all of the above calculations. While a cash flow forecast would be viewed as essential, the calculation of capacity, for example, is not)

Appendix E: Key ratios

	2005	*2004*
Operating profit margin	2.5%	3.0%
Net profit margin	1.2%	1.6%
ROCE (operating profit /capital employed)	6.9%	8.6%
Turnover growth	-1.5%	-
Operating profit growth	-17.6%	-
Trade receivables days	95	92